Diction&

political ideologies

Dictionary of modern political ideologies

M. A. RIFF editor

Manchester University Press

Published by Manchester University Press, Oxford Road,
Manchester, M13 9PL, UK

Reprinted in 1990

British Library cataloguing in publication data
Dictionary of modern ideologies.
   1. Political science. 2. Ideology — Dictionaries
   I. Riff, M. A.
   320.5'03'21   JA61

   ISBN 0-7190-1882-X *hardback*
        0-7190-3289-X *paperback*

Set in Eras and Bembo
by Koinonia Ltd, Manchester
Printed in Great Britain
by Billings Limited, Worcester

Contents

Notes on contributors

African Nationalism — David Killingray (Lecturer in History, Goldsmith's College, London)

Anarchism — Roger Briottet (Principal Lecturer at the Polytechnic of the South Bank, London, until 1985. Now fully involved in political and humanitarian work with liberation movements in the Horn of Africa)

Anti-Colonialism — Anthony Copley (Senior Lecturer in History, University of Kent at Canterbury)

Anti-Semitism — Michael Riff (Assistant Director, Leo Baeck Institute, New York)

Appeasement — Donald Watt (Stevenson Professor of International History, University of London)

Black Consciousness — Hugh Brogan (Lecturer in History, University of Essex)

Bonapartism — William Smith (former Head of History Department, Goldsmith's College, University of London, now Directeur d'Etudes (Associé Etranger), Ecole Pratique des Hautes Etudes, Sorbonne, Paris)

Christian Democracy — David Blackbourn (Reader in Modern History, Birkbeck College, University of London)

Coexistence — Donald Watt

The Cold War — Donald Watt

Collaboration and Resistance — Roderick Kedward (Reader in History, University of Sussex)

Communism since 1917 — Martin McCauley (Senior Lecturer in Soviet and East European Studies at the School of Slavonic and East European Studies, University of London)

Conservatism — Hugh Cecil (Lecturer in British History, University of Leeds)

Ecumenism — Peter Ludlow (Director of the Centre for European Policy Studies, Brussels)

The Enlightenment — Robert Wokler (Senior Lecturer in Government, University of Manchester)

European Integration — Peter Ludlow

Fascism — Antony Polonsky (Reader in International History, London School of Economics)

Federalism — Gordon Smith (Reader in Government, London School of Economics)

Feminism — Jill Stephenson (Senior Lecturer in History, University of Edinburgh)

Free Soil — Eric Foner (Professory of History, Columbia University, New York)

Gaullism — William Smith

Imperialism — Peter Hatton (Lecturer in History at Westfield College, University of London, 1965-75, now librarian in an east London college of further education)

Internationalism — Peter Hatton

Islamic Fundamentalism — Malise Ruthven (author of Islam in the World, Penguin Books)

Isolationism — Donald Watt

Keynesianism — Bernard Corry (Professor of Economics, Queen Mary College, University of London)

Kuomintang — Ellis Tinios (Lecturer in Asian History, University of Leeds)

Liberalism — E. D. Steele (Lecturer in History, University of Leeds)

McCarthyism — Oliver Carsten (Assistant Research Scientist in Social Science, University of Michigan)

Nationalism — *Michael Riff*

Non-violence — *Adam Roberts* (Montague Burton Professor of International Relations and Fellow of Balliol College, University of Oxford)

Pacifism — *Adam Roberts*

Popular sovereignty — *Roger Price* (Reader in History, University of East Anglia)

Populism — *Oliver Carsten*

Radicalism — Ernst Wangermann (Professor of Austrian History, University of Salzburg)

Romanticism — *Yehuda Safran* (Tutor at the Royal College of Art, London)

Socialism — *Richard Geary* (Head of Department of German Studies, University of Lancaster)

Syndicalism — *Roger Briottet*

Ultramontanism — *E. D. Steele*

Utilitarianism — *J. F. Liveley* (Professor of Politics, University of Warwick)

Whiggism — *E. D. Steele*

Zionism — *Robert Wistrich* (Associate Professor of Modern Jewish History, Department of Modern European and Jewish History, Hebrew University of Jerusalem)

Preface

This book had its origins, almost ten years ago, in the preparation of another project, *The Encyclopedia of Modern History*, conceived by Trewin Copplestone Publishing Ltd and published by Paul Hamlyn in 1978. I was commissioned to write a series of articles for that book on the various ideological movements emanating from the Enlightenment and the French Revolution.

In the end, not all that I had written appeared in the published version of the book. James Clark, the Editorial Director of Trewin Copplestone, however, felt that the groundwork for a separate publication for which he saw a concrete need had been laid. He envisaged a compact reference work outlining and explaining the ideologies and movements which helped shape the modern world. With the help of my friend and colleague James Joll, under whom I had taught 'The History of European Ideas since 1700' at the LSE in the late 1970s, a plan and outline were soon prepared.

As historians, it was natural that we should take a dialectical approach to the project. We took it for granted, moreover, that ideology and the flow of events in history are inexorably interrelated and intertwined. Each contributor to the *Dictionary* was, thus, asked to account for the origins of the movement he or she would be treating as well as track its political and societal context. Authors were also instructed to be mindful of the relationship of their own topics to the others in the book and always indicate where a cross-reference might be made.

In providing a basic outline of the ideological constellation of the age in which we live, the book should serve, in our view, as a companion to the study of the modern world. It has been conceived and written with the needs of the novice as well as the more experienced reader in mind, for students and interested members of the general public alike. Some readers will no doubt have questions raised or want to explore a particular topic in further depth. For this reason, whenever possible, we have included after each entry a list of further reading.

Although the *Dictionary*, in having the European Enlightenment as its starting point, has a Eurocentric bias, every effort has been made to take ideological development on other continents into account. There have no doubt been omissions and different approaches could have been taken. As editor, any resulting inadequacies are my responsibility.

This book almost did not see the light of day. Even though the staff of Trewin Copplestone, especially James Clark, in the wake of the demise of their firm did their best to find a publisher for this book, it was one of its authors, Robert Wokler of Manchester University, who managed to interest the Press of his institution in taking it on as one of their publications. The confidence and determination of Alec McAulay, Deputy Publisher of Manchester University Press, made its appearance in the end possible.

I owe special thanks to James Joll, whose counsel and encouragement were always available.

Michael A. Riff
March 1987

Introduction

This is not a dictionary or encyclopedia of political concepts or doctrines. Such introductions to political thought characteristically set out a collection of first principles of government and law, and, if successful, they shed light on the ideas of great thinkers as to how our political systems are or ought to be arranged. Much may be learnt from them about the nature of philosophical politics, but they have also been found to suffer from a fault frequently ascribed to political theory in general – in effect, that they do not offer any clear guide to the actual practice of politics. The marriage of kingship and philosophy, so long sought as a remedy to the mismanagement of government, remains largely unconsummated in the real world of public affairs, and students of political theory searching for some guidance through the labyrinthine operations of government have all too often come to the sad conclusion that political ideas, ideals and principles scarcely affect the practice of politics at all.

The authors of this dictionary have attempted to make clear how ideals and principles in fact lie at the heart of our political experience and aspirations. Some of the ideas at issue here did not in fact figure in the doctrines and writings of great thinkers, but our interest has not been in providing textual analysis or in tracing intellectual origins. Our concern, rather, has been with the ways in which certain ideas have been invoked and presented so as to win popular support, both by governments and by parties and groups in opposition. We have dealt with political ideas in their application rather than their first formulation, and with their influence upon collective behaviour rather than as the products of thought of their individual authors. We perceive them as widely shared beliefs which have been the springs of political action. We have tried to show how such ideas may shape public policy in the programmes of established governments, and how, equally, they may subvert those governments when they acquire support from outside. We wish to promote an understanding of political ideas that have come to matter in politics by treating them less as doctrines than as the inspiration for movements. It is, in short, this conjunction of the practice of politics with its theory, that we perceive here as the realm of ideology.

We believe that without the promptings and justification of ideology, political life neither has nor can have any direction or purpose apparent to those who take an active role in it. To politicians, ideologies provide reasons, both sincere and avowed, for promoting one political programme over another, and to individuals and parties which are not in power they offer grounds for allegiance to the state or, alternatively, for resistance against governments which have betrayed the trust enjoined by other beliefs. Because they define the relations between political parties and factions, rather then the different doctrines of individual thinkers, we concentrate upon their place in fixing the direction of collective action and behaviour. There, at that interface between principle and practice – where, indeed, our principles are embedded within the activities of our public life – we believe that political ideas have come to matter most.

In our description of ideologies here, we make no apology for their lack of such coherence or profundity as may be ascribed to the relatively purer doctrines of great thinkers; the interstices of political life are unavoidably obscure, mixed as they are with elements from several, including foreign, sources. Neither would we yield to those who, by contrast, prefer to describe politics as funda-mentally concerned with the pursuit of power, and not ideas. It is uncontenti-ously true that politicians and their adversaries seek power, and governments can scarcely survive without it. But political power can only be sustained over a long period when it commands assent, while the differences between great and minor powers throughout the world, or between political parties and factions within states, are at least as much due to ideological conflicts as to any other cause. In attempting to identify these differences and conflicts we have thought fit, in some instances, to examine the political histories of the move-ments through which particular ideologies were expressed in greater detail than might be warranted in other dictionaries of political terms of comparable length. This is so, above all, of the essays here on Communism and Fascism. But we have been drawn to that approach because we believe that the history of political movements imparts the real significance of the ideologies that inform them. Whereas political theories often come to diverge from their true meaning in the course of their development, political ideologies, on the other hand, take on the meaning which their histories impose. Indeed, the social movements and forces through which ideologies are enacted appear almost constitutive of those ideologies themselves, with the history of the one indispensable to uncovering the sense of the other.

We also have few qualms about selecting only modern ideologies, in effect since the French and Industrial Revolutions, while ignoring the great social forces, religious movements, and political struggles of previous epochs. For it was the dislocation caused largely by those two great modern revolutions, and by the reactions to them, which first shaped the ideological conflicts of the contemporary world. Both within and as a consequence of these upheavals, there arose many of the political perspectives and their terminologies – like liberalism, socialism, romanticism and utilitarianism – as well as new forms of older ideologies, such as anarchism and communism, that are at issue here. The world 'ideology' itself was invented in the course of the French Revolution.

Our concentration here upon ideologies within political movements, and as the practical expression of doctrines, of course cannot exclude other senses of the term. Its original meaning as 'the science of ideas' fell out of fashion with the demise of Destutt de Tracy and his associates at the Institut national who had thus defined it. But a good many of its subsequent meanings and implications, especially those invented and drawn by Marx or Engels since the mid-nineteenth century, have survived. If they regard the terms as possessing any meaning at all, most readers will not quarrel with the claim that an ideology is comprised of a set of beliefs, which largely reflect the interests of a particular social class or group, about the nature of man and the functions of government. Many will also allow that ideologies may sometimes conflict with the true interests of individuals who adhere to them, as, for instance, when a middle-class or bourgeois ideology is espoused by large sections of a proletarian working class, a condition Engels termed 'false consciousness'. Marxists and other sociologists of a later generation came to add utopian and revolutionary senses to the term, so that 'ideology' has come to mean a set of social, religious, or political beliefs which reflect either the true or false, progressive or reactionary, real or vain, hopes of any class of persons in the modern world. We may be inclined to accept, too, that at least with regard to the principal ideologies since the advent of the French and Industrial Revolutions, their quality of embracing claims about the whole nature of human life from a socially or intellectually circumscribed point of view lends each of them a bias which at once excites the enthusiasm of those who subscribe to it, and very frequently the contempt of those who do not. In the very partiality of ideological convictions can be found both their peculiar strength and the causes of conflict between them.

Our focus upon political ideologies in the historical context of political movements is not intended to imply criticism of these or any other alternative perspectives on the meaning of the term. But we take exception to one approach to the understanding of ideologies in the contemporary world – the judgment, that is, of those commentators who, in the light of recent history, have concluded that the age of ideologies is dead. At least in the West, it has been suggested, our mixed economies, political pluralism and general consensus around shared values have ensured that our old passions are spent and earlier forms of class conflict have been exhausted. A domestic observer of the Great American Achievement of the early 1960s could perhaps have believed this, but the end of ideology has never been apparent elsewhere, nor does its demise even in the United States now seem so obvious. Quite the contrary. Evangelical fundamentalism is a political force as powerful today as ever it was, and the ideologies of religious zealotry – Islamic, Christian, Jewish and Hindu – inspire some of the most intractable political conflicts of our time.

Some of the major ideological parties of the current day, moreover, have embarked upon crusades bearing weapons other than the armour of God. In the period since this work was commissioned and then its essays were completed, there has arisen in several Western countries a neo-Conservative movement which has seized the imagination of anti-Communists and critics of the Welfare State. Ideological parties of the Right have now garnered the enthusiasm of their adherents with no less vigorous conviction than was shown by parties of the Left before the Second World War, and when they have come to power they have sought, like their opponents before them, to put their own clear stamp upon the political course of history. If such events have occurred too recently to figure in this work, they are nonetheless a measure of the abiding and even enhanced importance of our subject, and certainly not of its decline. Ours *is* an ideological age, riven by radical and conservative, utopian and realist, parties alike. To ignore these tensions is to overlook one of the central features of the political landscape of the contemporary world, and, perhaps, the most prominent obstacle that will have to be scaled by our politicians to come. The authors of this dictionary have tried to light up some of the thickets of that dark terrain, in the hope that with illumination it may be traversed more safely.

Robert Wokler
University of Manchester

African Nationalism

In 1880 there were several thousand polities or states in Africa. By 1980 the continent was divided into nearly fifty independent states based on the territorial frontiers imposed on Africa during the period of European colonial rule (c. 1880-1975). In present day Africa, most states contain a variety of people who speak distinct languages and have different cultures. For example, Nigeria has over two hundred language groups within its boundaries and the northern area is predominantly Muslim. And yet Nigeria, like other African states, is referred to as a nation and many of its inhabitants increasingly think of themselves as Nigerians.

African nationalist aspirations have changed over time and varied from one territory to another. Although a sense of 'national' or ethnic identity existed in many parts of Africa before and during the colonial period, Nationalism is largely a modern idea borrowed from European political thought (see NATIONALISM). It first developed as a reformist response and reaction to the European presence in the late nineteenth century. However, the predominant forms of modern Nationalism have been expressed in anti-colonial political parties and movements which were established mainly after 1945. These parties sought to establish a popular following throughout the territory, to gain control of the central government of the colonial state by constitutional or revolutionary means, and to bring foreign rule to an end. The transfer of power, or decolonisation, was accomplished both constitutionally and by armed force between the late 1950s and 1980.

Although the new states of Africa are frequently referred to as nations within most of them there are ethnic (*tribal* is the word sometimes used) or regional groups which demand independence or automony. Seccessionist movements have led to rebellions and wars but not to the creation of permanent independent states. Only a few African states can be regarded as ethnic nations. (e.g. Somalia, Lesotho, Swaziland) but in many sub-Saharan states a sense of nationhood has been fostered by a common *lingua franca* (such as Swahili in Tanzania), established systems of law, education, and new institutions of government.

The earliest expressions of modern nationalism in Africa were in North Africa, where European ideas of liberalism mingled with those of Islamic militancy (see LIBERALISM). Egyptian national sentiment was stimulated in the mid and late nineteenth century by the Ottoman Empire's claims to suzerainty and European economic and political control, especially after 1882 when Britain began its long military occupation of the country. Nationalist ideas in Africa south of the Sahara were first articulated in West Africa by the small educated élite in the black republic of Liberia and the European colonial settlements on the coast. The élite, composed of Afro-American settlers, the descendants of freed slaves, African traders, lawyers and clergymen, held leading positions in the church and the colonial administration. Their ambition was to increase their role in colonial administration on equal terms with Europeans. The outstanding intellectual figure in early nineteenth century West African nationalism was Edward Wilmot Blyden (1832-1912), an Afro-American from the Caribbean, who believed that blacks could only achieve their full potential in Africa. Along with other Afro-Americans he encouraged blacks in America to return 'back to Africa', a movement which met with only a limited response. He also urged the creation of a unified pan-West African state.

The European 'scramble for Africa' and its partition among the colonial powers (c. 1875-1900) was associated with, and encouraged a belief in, white racial superiority. As a result educated Africans were progressively excluded from many social and political positions in colonial and church administration. At the same time the increase in Christian mission activity, especially in education, produced a growing number of literate Africans who challenged European control and sought to advance African rights and interests. The first African political organisations were formed in West and South Africa in the late nineteenth and the early twentieth centuries. They were led by the educated élite who protested at racial discrimination, threats to African rights over land and taxation, and demanded representation in the local colonial legislatures. In many ways these small groups were similar to the political parties that represented repressed nationalities in Central and Eastern Europe, or the anti-colonial movements in Asia such as the Indian National Congress.

Groups such as the *Aborigines Rights' Protection Society* in the Gold Coast (1897) and the *South African Native National Congress* founded in 1912 (later to be known as the African National Congress), were constitutionally-minded bodies which presented their demands through public meetings, the local press and the occasional delegation. They were invariably localised organisations with limited finances, support and influence. In Dakar in 1914, however, educated blacks, who were also French citizens, were successful in electing Blaise Diagne as the first African representative to the National Assembly in Paris.

Although some élite politicians did embrace a cultural nationalism which advocated adherence to African names, dress and customs, this was more characteristic of the politics of anti-colonial protest in East and Central Africa. There the leadership came from men of humbler position such as clerks, teachers and catechists, who attempted to articulate the grievances of ordinary peasants and labourers. This was done through small 'native welfare associations' but more importantly by numerous independent 'Ethiopian' churches which attracted popular followings. Varying in size, religious belief and practice, these black-run churches enabled Africans to assert their own identity free of foreign mission control. They also often provided a vehicle for the expression of economic, political and social protest against white colonial rule. Independent churches were involved in a number of anti-colonial rebellions, for example, in Natal

(1906) and Nyasaland (1915), while some millenial sects in Central Africa in the 1920s and 1930s (e.g. the Watchtower movement) preached the imminent end of white rule.

The economic and political consequences of the First World War fuelled anti-colonial discontent over a large part of Africa. Egyptian Nationalism became more militant and the country gained a limited independence in 1922. In West Africa the National Congress of British West Africa, founded in 1920, advocated self-government for a pan-West-African state and measures to protect and advance African economic and social interests. In Kenya there were protests by the Kikuyu against white settler control, especially over land. The various Kikuyu political groups formed in the immediate post-war period, such as the Young Kikuyu Association led by Harry Thuku, were suppressed by the settler dominated government. With few exceptions the sub-Saharan nationalist groups of the inter-war years did not advocate the end of European rule but rather reform of colonial government, greater equality and representation for Africans, and in East and Central Africa, limits both on the power of white settlers and to further alienation of land.

In certain territories, notably in West Africa, nationalists were permitted a limited political role in municipal and territorial affairs. But over most of the continent, especially in the Belgian and Portuguese colonies and in those territories dominated by white settlers, Africans were excluded from any participation in government. As a result some nationalist parties abandoned attempts at negotiation with colonial regimes and turned instead to more militant anti-colonial policies. Throughout the 1920s and 1930s there were all kinds of protest against alien rule – revolts, strikes, and opposition to European demands for taxes and labour. Many of these movements and activities cannot strictly be called nationalist although many modern political parties in East and Central Africa claim a continuing link, both human and symbolic, not only with the political protests of the inter-war years but back to the earlier movements of primary and secondary resistance to colonial rule.

From the 1920s onwards African nationalism was influenced by socialist and pan-African ideas. Algerian workers in France formed militant nationalist organisationss while French-speaking West Africans established a socialist party in Senegal. The most successful movement was the *Industrial and Commercial Union* founded in South Africa by Clements Kadalie in 1919. The ICU assumed a political as well as a industrial role and claimed 100,000 members. After a few years, weakened by internal strife and government opposition, it collapsed. A small number of Africans studied abroad in Europe and North America and on their return home they helped encourage a new and more outspoken nationalist challenge to colonial rule. For example, in British West Africa the *Youth Movements* of the 1930s criticised not only the political and economic policies of the colonial governments but also the more passive attitudes of older nationalist leaders.

Pan-African ideas also had a significant influence on African politics. The

3

first pan-African congress was held in London in 1900 and others followed after 1919 but the membership was predominantly Afro-American until the fifth congress at Manchester in 1945. At each of these congresses representatives demanded an end to racial discrimination and reforms to the colonial system. Pan-African sentiment was encouraged in the early 1920s by the short-lived *United Negro Improvement Association* formed in Jamaica but transferred to New York by Marcus Garvey (1887-1940). Garvey said that Africa was the true home of the black people to which they must return if they were to be truly free and happy. He started a shipping line to take blacks back 'home' and also prophesied that a black prince would be crowned in Africa as a sign of deliverance. Garvey's populist racial politics and his message of a united 'Africa for the Africans' received little sympathy from the more intellectual pan-Africanists in America represented by the dominant figure of W. E. B. Du Bois (1868-1963) (see BLACK CONSCIOUSNESS). Nevertheless, Garvey's ideas had a considerable influence and many blacks in America, and a few in Africa, were given a new sense of racial pride. When Ras Tafari was crowned Emperor Haile Selassie of Ethiopia in 1930 some poor landless blacks in Jamaica saw this as a sign to return to Africa. The Rastafarian cult, a religious nationalist movement which regarded white culture as evil, made several unsuccessful attempts to repatriate blacks to Ethiopia. Rastafarian ideas have been taken to North America and Britain by Jamaican migrants.

During the 1930s Leopold Senghor (b. 1906) and Aimé Césaire (b. 1913) and other French-speaking intellectuals from Africa and the Caribbean formulated the cultural idea of *négritude* (see BLACK CONSCIOUSNESS). Négritude is the French word meaning 'blackness'. Its proponents rejected the idea that African culture was inferior to European. They emphasised the value of African art, literature and experience, and challenged the cultural assimilation implicit in French colonial policy. Négritude proclaimed a pride in the heritage of Africa but it was primarily a movement among intellectuals and had little impact on ordinary Africans. The Italian invasion of Ethiopia in 1935-36 was a more effective means of mobilising pan-African sentiment among blacks in Africa and the Americas.

The Second World War weakened the global economic and political position of the colonial powers. European imperialism was on the retreat in Asia and the British and French decided on the need for changes in their colonial policies in Africa. Neither power thought in terms of decolonisation but the British gradually abandoned the system of indirect rule through traditional rulers and sought accommodation with educated Africans, while the French extended civil rights to Africans and attempted to tie their colonies into a closer union with the metropolis. In the years immediately after 1945 inflation, post-war unemployment and colonial economic policies led to unrest among the expanded urban population and peasant producers who provided support for newly established nationalist political parties. Over the next ten years dynamic and often charismatic leaders organised political movements which secured a

4

popular following and demanded the transfer of power to African hands.

Nationalist organisations varied greatly in size and ideology. Some were well-organised parties based on modern ideas. They had party branches throughout the territory and sought to mobilise the electorate in order to secure control of the central government of the colonial state. Typical of these new parties was the Convention People's Party in the Gold Coast, formed in 1949 by Kwame Nkrumah (1909–72). Within three years the CPP won an electoral majority and Nkrumah was appointed prime minister of a self-governing colony which became the independent state of Ghana in 1957. Another modern party was the Rassemblement Démocratique Africain in French West Africa. The RDA was an inter-territorial grouping which had the initial aim of securing greater equality for Africans within an integrated Franco-African community. By the late 1950s, however, most nationalist politicians in French Africa were steadily abandoning the pan-African ideal and opting for territorial autonomy. Guinea was the first black French colony to become independent in 1958.

These nationalist parties have often been described as 'mass' parties. Many did have wide and popular support but also they were often opposed by, or coexisted uneasily with, other parties representing provincial, religious, traditional and ethnic interests. Much of the rivalry within and between nationalist parties was over which groups should control the levers of economic power in the post-colonial state. In certain states there were strong regional parties (e.g. Nigeria, Belgian Congo, Kenya) which demanded federal systems of government. Besides the 'modern' nationalist parties there were movements and organisations which represented traditional and peasant interests. Some were led by educated men but overwhelmingly their support came from peasants within a specific region. For example, the *Mau Mau* movement in Kenya which fought a guerilla war against the settler government in the 1950s drew its support mainly from the Kikuyu in both the rural areas and from migrants and traders in Nairobi.

Over a large part of Africa by the mid-1950s many colonial authorities, especially the British and increasingly the French, were prepared to collaborate with the nationalist parties in order to bring about a peaceful transfer of power. But in colonies or states dominated by white minorities (Kenya, Rhodesia, Algeria and South Africa) or ruled by authoritarian governments (the three Portuguese colonies), the transfer of political power was accompanied by violence. Frantz Fanon (1925-1961), a black doctor from Martinique and one of the chief ideologues of the Algerian rebellion, argued that colonisation was in itself a violent act and could only be ended by violence. Serious revolts occurred in Madagascar (1947) and Kenya (1952-62), and nationalist-led guerilla wars were fought in Algeria (1954-62), Angola, Mozambique and Guinea (1960-74), and Rhodesia/Zimbabwe (1972-80).

In South Africa, white Afrikaner nationalism took control of the state in 1948 and with little difficulty crushed African nationalist organisations. Since then the South African government has coerced black political organisations and

5

trade unions and under the policies of apartheid attempted to encourage the development of separate 'independent' black homelands or 'bantustans'. By 1965 most of Africa north of the Zambezi river was independent of colonial rule, as was the whole continent, apart from South Africa, Namibia and Western Sahara.

Pan-African unity has been largely an ideal. Many African states have serious problems in maintaining a sense of national unity let alone inter-territorial unity. Cultural, economic and religious differences and rivalries exist in many states and major seccessionist wars have been fought in the Sudan, Nigeria and Ethiopia in the cause of 'sub-nationalism'.

After independence some ruling nationalist parties banned rival parties and established one party states. Opposition to the ruling party was frequently equated with disloyalty to the nation state. In a number of countries, for example Ghana under Nkrumah, the ruling CPP virtually ceased to exist, becoming little more than part of the bureaucratic framework of the state. Some nationalist leaders in power became tyrants and profiteers and changes in government could only be brought about by a political revolt or military *coup d'état*. In a good number of states the party in power adopted populist economic policies which often drew heavily on Socialist ideas and practices. Some African governments claimed to be Marxist, an ideological position also adopted by several of the nationalist parties involved in the continuing guerilla wars against white dominance in South Africa and Namibia.

Further reading

R. Oliver & A. Atmore, *Africa since 1800*
Basil Davidson, *Africa in modern history*
Immanuel Wallerstein, *Africa: the politics of independence*
Thomas Hodgkin, *Nationalism in colonial Africa*
James S. Coleman, *Nigeria: background to nationalism*
Richard Rathbone, *African nationalism*
Robert W. July, *The origins of modern African thought*
E. Roux, *Time longer than rope*
Peter Walshe, *The rise of nationalism in South Africa. The African National Congress 1912-52*
T. O. Ranger, *The African voice in Southern Rhodesia (1898-1930)*
Imanuel Geiss, *The Pan-African movement*
J. A. Langley, *Pan-Africanism and nationalism in West Africa 1900-1945*
David Kimble, *The political history of Ghana. The rise of Gold Coast nationalism*
Henry S. Wilson (ed.), *Origins of West African nationalism*
R. S. Morgenthau, *Political parties in French speaking West Africa*
Robert I. Rotberg, *The rise of nationalism in Central Africa*

Anarchism

The term *anarchism* describes related doctrines, attitudes and movements whose common and uniting feature is the belief that government is by nature oppressive. As a consequence of this belief, anarchists urge that men should rid themselves of all form of governmental authority prior to building a new society based on justice, love, and a spirit of co-operation. It would be vain to attempt to define anarchism more precisely at this stage since such a doctrine profoundly influenced as it has been by varied – and often contradictory – philosophical, historical and emotional factors, was bound to give rise to differing interpretations. The detractors of anarchism have condemned it as a negative, almost suicidal, doctrine which threatens to rend the very fabric of society. By contrast, most anarchists have stressed that the destruction of an oppressive social order was but the first, inevitable, step towards the realisation of a new society in which men would at last be free to develop their abilities for the benefit of all.

A long and rich tradition paved the way for modern anarchism: Zeno and the Stoic School, religious sects such as the Cathari (whose gnosic doctrine threatened the Christian faith in the thirteenth century), the political theorists of the Reformation, Winstanley and the Digger Movement, the so-called *philosophes* of the Enlightenment (see ENLIGHTENMENT) – all these and many others, despite the variety of their creeds and ideals, shared the belief in the need to free the individual from the oppression of authority, be it religious or secular, and to vindicate the right and duty of responsible men to co-operate in order to establish a purer and more humane society. It is above all from the Englightenment that anarchists have inherited not only their rationalist, 'scientific' approach to society and their insistence on the primacy of individual rights, but also their deep, almost religious belief in the goodness of human nature and man's innate faculty to better himself and his fellow men, through love, education and co-operation.

The first systematic exponent of anarchism, and the first to carry it through to its logical conclusions, was Godwin. His chief work *The Inquiry Concerning Political Justice* was published in 1793, when the Terror had already all but ruined the hopes that radicals in England and elsewhere had placed in the French Revolution. The fundamental principle of Godwin's philosophy is that man's unhappiness is essentially caused by injustice. By birth, man is neither good nor bad. Remove injustice, show men the path of virtuous life, and they will avoid error and find true happiness. The authority of the State – which prevents the individual from acting in accordance with reason and virtue – must be abolished. Property which leads to exploitation must disappear. Because any complex social organisation requires a central government using coercion at all

7

levels of authority, Godwin proposed that the future, ideal society should consist of small units in which no man will be allowed to impose his will on his fellow men. Carrying the logic of anarchist thinking to its ultimate consequences, Godwin views common exploitation of property with disfavour in contrast to later 'communistic' anarchists. His condemnation of partnership extends to the family based on marriage since such a legalised union always implies or results in the subordination of one 'partner' to the other and necessarily rests on the common usage of property. Godwin, who was celebrated in his time, influenced Shelley and Robert Owen. But he was virtually ignored by the anarchist theorists of the nineteeth century.

By constrast, Pierre Joseph Proudhon exerted a profound and durable influence on radical ideologists and movements not only in France, his native, country, but all over Europe and America. Proudhon's work is complex and abundant and the fact that his various statements on anarchism cannot be easily reconciled explains why his doctrine led to differing interpretations. In his early work *Qu'est-ce que la Propriété?*, published in 1840, Proudhon clearly sets himself as an anarchist rejecting the laws of the present society which prevent man from following the true laws of nature. The economic system must be reformed so that the distance between rich and poor may be reduced. Private property is not bad: it is the misuse of property which leads to the exploitation of man by man. Proudhon therefore advocates a 'mutualist' system in which peasants and workers of all trades would run small enterprises in common, with the help of credit provided by mutual banks (see SOCIALISM). These small units could in turn organise themselves on a federal basis, thus dispensing with any form of central and authoritarian government. Despite his vehement attacks upon authority, Proudhon does not advocate violence as a means to achieve the desired political and economic change. Towards the end of this life he recognisd in *Le Principe Fédératif* that for a long time to come anarchists should be content to limit themselves to reducing the most oppressive powers of the state and to encourage mutualist groups. In France and other Latin countries the success of Proudhon's ideas hindered the progress of Marxist Socialism. His writings inspired many anarchist propagandists such as Landauer and Moses Hess (see ZIONISM) in Germany and, above all, that professional European revolutionary, M. Bakunin. Proudhon's belief in the revolutionary role of the working class, which he developed in his last book *De la Capacité de la Classe Ouvrière*, prompted large sections of the trade union movement, notably in France, to reject parliamentary democracy and to rely on industrial action in their struggle against capitalism.

With Bakunin, anarchism took a more collectivist form. In his early life Bakunin was associated with revolutionary movements in Eastern Europe. He supported Polish independence from Tsarist Russia and took part in an aborted revolution in Dresden. As a result he spent many years in Russian prisons. In 1861, having escaped from Siberia, he made his way to Europe where he had already established himself as a leading revolutionist. He joined the International

Workingmen Association in 1864 and became the most influential leader of libertarian revolutionism and the chief opponent of Marx's socialism. Bakunin approved Proudhon's federalism but rejected his conception of individual property rights. How his ideal, collectivist society would come into existence after the collapse of the state, Bakunin did not venture to explain. His was the vision of a man of action who passionately – and paradoxically – believed in the goodness of man and the necessity of violence. Revolution would be the outcome of a spontaneous rising of the poor, rural classes of Eastern and Southern Europe rather than the inevitable result of the conscious struggle led by the authoritarian party leadership of the urban and industrial working class, as advocated by Marx. Bakunin set up his own organisation, the *International Democratic Alliance*, whose influence swiftly spread to French speaking Switzerland, Southern France and, above all, Spain, where anarchism found a fertile ground and soon developed into a powerful movement.

The bitter opposition between Bakunin and Marx resulted in the destruction of the first International in 1872 (see SOCIALISM). Long after his death in 1876 Bakinin's doctrine, and above all his aura and messianism, continued to influence the anarchist movement.

Prince M. Kropotkin stands as the most influential leader of the most extreme collectivist form of anarchism known as *anarchist communism*, which became the mainstream of the doctrine in the 1880s. For his ideal society, reminiscent of Thomas More's *Utopia*, Kropotkin advocates complete 'communism' in terms of distribution as well as production. Once the state had been eliminated by violent and spontaneous revolution, men would organise themselves in village communities in which all goods and activities would be shared. Total individual freedom and the observance of moral law would render the evil division of labour, and even any system of representation, unnecessary. Freedom would be so complete that 'free agreements would not be enforced.'

Kropotkin's patient efforts to persuade and educate inspired many followers in the West, while it is above all Bakinin's apocalyptic appeal to emotions and violence which attracted revolutionists in the oppressive political climate of Tsarist Russia. There already, in the 1860s, young men in revolt against the social and political order had adopted an uncompromising, agnostic and materialistic view of society. Some of them were encouraged, however unwittingly, by the writings of radical essayists like Chernishesky and Debrolubov whose main concern was the emancipation of the serfs. Those were the Nihilists: and it was Pisarew who gave an ideological form to the sombre yearning of those young intellectuals in revolt. Pisarew saw the only hope of progress in the violent and resolute action of an enlightened minority to overthrow the state. Some writers were indeed tempted to draw a parallel between nihilism and the most extreme forms of Bakunian anarchism. In such a climate, Bakunin's appeal to emotions fell on fertile ground, especially as Netchayev, one of Bakunin's disciples, together with other anarchists, preached that not only mass uprisings but also individual terroristic deeds were to be encouraged as they shake the mass out of their apathy and hasten the coming of the revolution. But the two doctines differ in their ultimate aim. Even in its most violent form, anarchism is never entirely negative for its powerful motivating impulse is the vivid and constructive dream of a society founded upon the brotherhood of man.

Despite Bakunin's attempts to infiltrate and conquer the first International Workingmen Association, the anarchists never managed to control it. Later, their efforts to combat 'German Communism' in the second International were unsuccessful since they ended with the exclusion of all anarchist factions at the London Congress of 1896 (see SOCIALISM). Although anarchist international congresses were held subsequently, notably in Amsterdam in 1907, anarchism never really developed into a mass movement except in a few countries such as France, Italy and Spain, where it attracted enough followers to cause concern in the public opinion and government circles. In Italy, agitation inspired by Malatesta first took the form of rural insurrections, then, as these failed, some anarchists chose to resort to individual acts of terrorism. This limited but impressive movement spread to France and Spain. In all, between 1890 and 1901, half a dozen heads of state or government were assassinated, and countless other 'acts of propaganda by the deed' were committed, especially in Spain where the unstable political climate was conducive to violence. Everywhere, the authorities reacted by bringing in anti-terrorist legislation which, at least in France, swiftly brought to an end the violent phase of individual terrorism. Many leading anarchists disapproved of terrorism and remained committed to education and political propaganda. Between 1870 and 1910 anarchism influenced *avant-garde* painters like Courbet, Seurat and Picasso, and writers like Mallarmé and Oscar Wilde.

More important still was the adoption of the main tenets of anarchism by large sections of the labour movement, notably in France, Italy and Spain, where the new working class gospel crystallised under the name of Syndicalism. The Syndicalists advocated 'direct', that is industrial, action against the capitalist ruling classes, and totally rejected any compromising alliance with political parties (see SYNDICALISM). Despite the anarchist origin of some of its most influential leaders, Syndicalism developed into an independent movement which leading anarchists like Malatesta regarded as too organised and too exclusive to be equated with anarchism. By the end of the First World War it had lost its momentum except in Spain where the *Confederación Nacional del Trabajo* (CNT) combined with the most powerful anarchist movement in the world. In 1927 Spanish anarchists set up their own *Federación Anarquista Ibéria* (FAI). Both organisations, which remained clandestine until 1931, wielded a considerable influence on the Andalusian peasantry and Catalonian industrial working class. Until the end of the Civil War in 1939 the CNT remained the best example of anarchist de-centralised movement.

By that time anarchism as a movement had virtually disappeared outside Spain. In Russia, anarchist groups had been eliminated by the Bolsheviks in, or shortly after, 1917. In Italy, the strong anarchist movement which had developed in the 1920s was destroyed by Mussolini's fascist dictatorship. In most other countries anarchist groups fell victims to autocratic régimes, or greatly suffered from the competition of communism which in many cases, as in France, absorbed them.

After the Second World War, and notably in the 1960s and 1970s, anarchism as a doctrine, if not as a movement, attracted much interest among the New Left. A profound distrust for state authority and bureaucracy, mutual help, federalism, the protection of the natural environment, the rejection of traditional left-wing politics, and the reliance on direct action – all were seminal anarchist beliefs which combined in the West with Marxist criticism, nuclear disarmament, ecological preoccupations and even Eastern religions and philosophies to inspire the student revolt of the late 1960s in Europe and the USA. To a degree, recent phenomena as diverse as the demand for workers' control of industry or the wave of terrorism can be said to owe some of their motivation to the anarchist tradition. For many of those who watch with apprehension the evolution of modern society, anarchism remains an attractive ideal, and its apocalyptic vision of a more humane world a powerful and inspiring myth.

Further reading

D. Apter, J. Joll, *Anarchism Today*
G. D. H. Cole, *History of Socialist Thought*
J. Joll, *The Anarchists*
B. Russell, *Roads to Freedom: Socialism, Anarchism, and Syndicalism*
W. Woodcock, *Anarchism*
IN ENGLAND
  J. Quail, *The Slow Burning Fuse*
IN FRANCE
  J. Maitron, *Le Mouvement Anarchiste en France*
IN SPAIN
  G. Brennan, *The Spanish Labyrinth: An Account of the Social and Political Background of the Civil War*
  H. Thomas, *The Spanish Civil War*
IN RUSSIA
  R. Avrich, *The Russian Anarchists*

Anti-Colonialism:
India and Sub-Saharan Africa

At its simplest level, Anti-Colonialism has been characterised by radical and national protest, often styled 'anti-fascist', with strong Marxist undertones. At a deeper level, however, Anti-Colonialism has to be seen in the context of a cultural encounter, a clash between a modernising 'Western' culture and the traditional ancient cultures of India and Africa. There can be no simple model. The West presented the seemingly contradictory faces of the Enlightenment (see ENLIGHTENMENT), with its ideals of rationalism, secularism and its cult of science alongside the missionary, evangelical zeal of European religions. Some distinction must be made between indigenous cultures based on the world religions of Hinduism and Islam and those rooted in less universal and less literate religions, though any simple contrast between high and primitive cultures would be misleading. In India and Africa, Anti-Colonialism turned against both the cultural arrogance of the West and the constraints of traditional culture. Such potentially conflicting loyalties arguably proved less problematic for African intellectuals, less hamstrung by their traditions and readier to assimilate the technology and material benefits of the West. In India, however, the challenge to traditional values set up far more ambivalent response. Those intellectuals in India who shaped the ideology of Anti-Colonialism experienced a deep conflict of loyalties between the claims of a 'modernising' West and their traditional culture. This amounted to a crisis of identity that created a spectrum of response, all the way from an uncritical acceptance of all things western to a narrow-minded revivalism of tradition.

Anti-Colonialism has always run the risk of degenerating into an xenophobic and fanatical Nationalism (see NATIONALISM). Such protest may more accurately be described as communal rather than national, and reflects a turning inwards of the political struggle against indigenous rivals, in the name of religion, language, caste or tribe. This may derive from long-term cultural or social loyalties, but originates in practice from the ambitions of sectarian politicians in the succession struggle to Empire. Such communal movement can turn overtly Fascist, as in the paramilitary organisations, the RSSS (Rashtrya Swam Sevak Sangh) of the Hindu *Mahasabha,* and the Khaksars of the Moslem league. Tribal expression of such communalism weakened African freedom struggles, and in the case of Nigeria led to Civil War.

The most intriguing, if not necessarily the most influential, response to the challenge of the West came from intellectuals who sought a synthesis – anxious to incorporate modernising elements from the West not by simple emulation but rather by a modernising of their own traditions. Seen in the overall context of so extraordinarily complex a cultural encounter, it becomes increasingly difficult to describe Anti-Colonialism as simply 'left-wing'.

If the ideology of anti-colonialism inevitably emerged first in India rather than in Africa, for India experienced sustained contact with the West from the 1760s whereas the full weight of imperialism in Africa only dates from the 1880s, it should be mentioned at the outset that it was as a result of his experience of both British and Boer racialism in South Africa that the leading figure in this ideology, Mohandas Gandhi (1869-1948), both resolved his own cultural identity and fashioned his new method of opposition to colonial oppression, *Satyagraha.*

The roots of Gandhi's anti-colonial ideology lay in a fascinating inter-civilisational encounter in the Presidency of Bengal, above all in Calcutta, described somewhat idealistically as the 'Bengal Renaissance'. Social reform, rather than political change, tended to dominate Indian thought in the early nineteenth century, a consequence in part of the absence of any all-Indian national consciousness. Even when all-India political organisations of a nationalist character appeared, above all the Indian National Congress in 1885, and shifted attention to political aspects of Anti-Colonialism, problems of social reform continued to attract considerable attention. There were two main stands in the Indian response to the West. One favoured its impact on Hinduism and sought both to modernise Indian society in the light of western ideals of humanism, above all through the emancipation of women, and to develop Indian political institutions along the lines of European Liberalism (see LIBERALISM). This moderate movement was inspired by Ram Mohun Roy (1772-1833) and his society, the *Brahmo Samaj*. Gandhi's political guru, Gokhale (1866-1916), belonged to this tradition. Another response placed more emphasis on the intrinsic merits of Hinduism, and, whilst not rejecting social reform, reacted more vigorously to missionary evangelicalism and to the racism of the West, took on more the character of a Hindu revivalist movement, which in turn sought a wider popular involvement in national politics. This outlook was inspired by Dayanand Saraswati (1824-1883), and his society, the *Arya Samaj,* a movement that began in the Punjab but found a parallel development in Bengal under the mystic Ramakrishna (1836-1883), and his disciple, Vivekananda (1863-1902). The person who did most to create a shift from an intellectual to a popular approach, however, was the Bengali novelist, Bankim Chandra Chatterjee (1858-1894). This movement bred a more militant nationalism, mainly under Auribindo Gose (1872-1950) and Tilak (1856-1920), which came to a climax in the violence which greeted the partition of Bengal in 1905. Tragically, this early nationalist movement, whilst pointing the way to Indian independence in 1947, also laid the seeds of the Hindu-Muslim communal conflict which led to the partition of the sub-continent into the states of India and Pakistan.

Gandhi's was the outstanding attempt to lead Anti-Colonialism away from the merely embittered protest of indigenous élite groups at the imperialist monopoly of power towards a genuine popular nationalist movement. He resolved the conflict of his cultural identity and at the same time made possible a charismatic appeal to a custom-bound peasantry by rearticulating in twentieth century political terms the traditional role of the *Sanyasi,* the peripatetic holy man of Hinduism. Gandhi sought social reform together with national liberation, and indeed doubted if India deserved to be free should the social diseases of untouchability and communalism not be overcome. He stood for a rejection of the industrialism and class conflict of the West in the name of a return to craft-industry, manual labour and a simple village economy. There was more of the anarchist than the socialist in Gandhi. His concept of 'trusteeship' was no more than the extension of the Indian ideal of the extended family to property-relationships. The hallmark of his political philosophy was non-violence,

13

learnt as much from the Jainism of his native Kathiawar as from his readings of Thoreau and Tolstoy. His political strategy of *satyagraha* has rather misleadingly become known as passive resistance. This implies weakness. In fact *satyagraha* (in translation 'soul-force', or 'truth-force') was based on moral strength. Admittedly Gandhi owed much to Indian liberalism and his political guru, Gokhale, and a *satyagraha* is based on the premise that the first attempt to solve any political dispute should be through a reasonable dialogue. Should reason fail to win over one's opponent to one's higher moral position, however, then protest should proceed to individual *satyagraha,* in its highest form the fast unto death, and beyond this to wider forms of collective protest, from non-co-operation to full-scale civil disobedience. *Satyagraha* worked best for limited objectives, such as the entry of untouchables to Hindu temples or the abolition of the salt-tax. Gandhi's rigid insistence on non-violence posed extraordinary problems of self-control and organisation for the much broader objective of *Swaraj,* or independence, and his leadership and political approach posed terrible dilemmas of loyalty for more straightforward radical nationalists like Jawaharlal Nehru (1889-1964). Yet Gandhi's leadership proved indispensable for forging an all-India nationalist movement and for achieving independence.

Nehru stood for a more radical socialist orientation of the Congress Party, inspired both by Fabian socialism and his visit to Russia in 1927. His essentially liberal and democratic temperament responded more readily to the gradualism of Lenin's New Economic Policy than to the draconian totalitarian changes initiated by Stalin in 1928 (see COMMUNISM SINCE 1917). But Nehru endorsed a far more radical peasant protest, if more by rich peasants than poor, against the high rents imposed by the private landlords or zamindars, and by the state. He sought a programme of industrialisation through a planned economy. He also believed that any widespread social reform would only become possible after independence. He remained essentially loyal to Gandhi's non-violent strategy however. He rejected terrorism. He never joined the communist party, though his relationship with the Congress socialist party in the 1930s suggested some sympathy for popular front tactics. He saw in time that Subhas Bose's (1897-1946) particular kind of militant Nationalism led to Fascism (see FASCISM). It was Nehru's continuing readiness to support Gandhi's political philosophy of non-violence that does much to explain its international appeal and its adoption by nationalist leaders, such as Nkrumah in sub-Saharan Africa.

If Indian independence in 1947 paved the way for independence elsewhere, it was the fiasco of the Anglo-French Suez expedition of 1956 which proved the immediate catalyst for the end of Empire in sub-Saharan Africa (see AFRICAN NATIONALISM). Intellectuals in Francophone West Africa, through the more aggressive chauvinism of French culture, had experienced a more serious crisis of identity than their counterparts in Anglophone West Africa. The roots of their Anti-Colonialism lay in Senghor's philosophy of *négritude* (see BLACK CONSCIOUSNESS). (The Nigerian author, Wole Soyinka, mockingly asked if the tiger had to assert its tigritude.) Where there was no settler community, Anti-

ColColonialism took on the form of only a relatively mild protest. If most nationalist leaders pronounced themselves socialist, it was often, as was the case with Senghor and Nyerere, in the form of a pragmatic socialism, seeking in the communal tradition of African society some quasi-socialist ideals, laying particular stress on agrarian co-operatives. Nkrumah (1909-1972) stood for a bolder programme of state-controlled industrialisation. In non-settler colonies, Anti-Colonialists could afford to be non-violent, for here the metropolitan powers chose a peaceful transfer of power. In the settler colonies, however, the struggle for independence had to be quite otherwise, and the Algerian freedom struggle inspired an entirely different, far more scathing and passionate Anti-Colonialism in the mind of the West Indian psychiatrist, but adopted Algerian, Frantz Fanon (1925-1961) (see ANTI-COLONIALISM). He was savagely critical of the new African nationalist leadership, above all Houphuet-Boigny, but also Nkrumah. (He was the ambassador of the provisional Algerian government to Ghana in 1961.) There are strange convergences between Fanon's thought and Gandhi's. Fanon also believed in a simultaneous social and national regeneration. His focus was also on the peasantry. Fanon likewise believed that the party should separate itself from government. But here they part company. Fanon believed that only a violent upheaval could release the colonised from the traumatic experience of colonialism and drive the nationalist movement forward into a genuine socialist revolution. His proved to be the most unsparing critique of neo-colonialism. If neglected in equatorial Africa except in Guinea-Bissan, Fanon's views may have done something to shape the more radical Nationalist movements in southern Africa, with their more overtly Marxist leadership.

The politics of Anti-Colonial freedom struggles of the African majorities in Southern Africa took a different complexion through the replacement of Empire as the oppressive agency by indigenous white élites. Such rule itself contributed a form of Anti-Colonialism, quite clearly so in the case of Afrikaaner nationalism in South Africa which under the National Party came to power in 1948, less, if not entirely spuriously so, under the Rhodesian Front which declared independence (UDI) on behalf of the white minority in 1965. Two debates have dominated the African liberation struggle in South Africa. The first was over the respective claims of a multi-racial struggle against *Apartheid,* linking African resistance to that of progressive whites, coloureds and Indians, in association with the Communist Party, and this remains the continuing policy of the African National Congress (ANC) and a négritude-style Africanist movement, asserting African control of the liberation movement which led to the breakaway of the Pan-African Congress (PAC) in 1959 (see AFRICAN NATIONALISM), and was later to be in part echoed by Steve Biko's Black Consciousness movement (see BLACK CONSCIOUSNESS). The second concerned the role of non-violence, with both the ANC and PAC by the early 1960s, rejecting the constitutional non-violent resistance of the 1950s in favour of sabotage. White rule in Rhodesia drove Zimbabwean nationalism into a peasant-based guerilla war, under the uneasy partnership of the moderate Joshua Nkomo (b. 1917) and the more radical, Marxist, Robert

15

Mugabe (b. 1924) which led in 1980, aided by the intervention of the former colonial power, to the constitutionally elected government of Robert Mugabe of the independent state of Zimbabwe.

Further reading

G. Barraclough, Ch. VI 'The Revolt against the West', *An Introduction to Contemporary History*

R. von Albertini, *Decolonisation*

K. Minogue, *Nationalism*

E. Kedourie, *Nationalism*

E. Gellner, *Nations and Nationalism*

Susobhan Sarkar, *The Bengal Renaissance and Other Essays*

D. Kopf, *The Brahmo Samaj and the Shaping of the Modern Indian Mind*

Kenneth W. Jones, *Arya Dharm: Hindu Consciousness in Nineteenth century Punjab*

Ashis Nandy, *The Intimate Enemy: Loss and Recovery of Self under Colonialism*

S. Wolpert, *Tilak and Gokhale*

M. Gandhi, *Autobiography*

Raghavan Iyer, *The Moral and Political Thought of Mahatma Gandhi*

Joan Bondurant, *Conquest of Violence: the Gandhian Philosophy of Conflict*

George Woodcock, *Gandhi*

Erik H. Erikson, *Gandhi's Truth*

L. I. & S. H. Rudolph, *The Modernity of Tradition*

Jawaharlal Nehru, *Autobiography*

S. Gopal, *Nehru: A Biography* (Vols I – III)

C. Haithcox, *Communism and Nationalism in India*

Albert Memmi, *The Coloniser and the Colonised*

J. Reed & C. Wake, *Senghor: Prose and Poetry*

Leopold S. Senghor, *On African Socialism*

K. Nkrumah, *Autobiography*

J. Kenyatta, *Facing Mount Kenya*

T. Mboya, *The Challenge of Nationhood*

Julius K. Nyerere, *Ujamaa – Essays on Socialism*

K. Kaunda, *Zambia Shall be Free*

Frantz Fanon, *The Wretched of the Earth*

D. Caute, *Fanon*

T. Lodge, *Politics in South Africa since 1945*

Nelson Mandela, *No Easy Walk to Freedom*

D. Woods, *Biko*

M. Meredith, *The Past is Another Country*

Anti-Semitism

Since the end of the Second World War, our view of Anti-Semitism has been coloured by the spectre of the Nazi extermination camp and the Arab-Israeli conflict. It is often forgotten, however, that its history dates back to the nineteenth century.

Anti-Jewish attitudes and policies have been common in Western Society since the dispersion of the Jews in the first century B.C.. In medieval Europe they were sanctioned, encouraged and institutionalised through the interaction of Christian doctrine and feudal practice. As a consequence, the Jews of Europe (Western Christendom) became a physically, as well as socially and politically, encapsulated minority. Their existence became progressively more and more centred around their ability to perform certain specialised tasks in trade and commerce, mostly as middlemen and moneylenders. A social context was thus given for prejudice and resentment against Jews to grow.

Legal emancipation began to take place at the end of the eighteenth century in the wake of the transition from a traditional feudal society to a bourgeois capitalist society. Under the influence of Enlightenment (see ENLIGHTENMENT) notions of humanity and toleration, it lowered the walls of the Ghetto and encouraged the Jews of Western and Central Europe to embark on the road towards assimilation. It did not, however, eliminate prejudice and discrimination against Jews.

More importantly, in Central Europe at least, emancipation took place in conditions of uneven political, social and economic change. This not only resulted in its completion for the most part being substantially delayed but also meant that the basic premises on which it was based were constantly challenged. Instead of emancipation paving the way for the integration of the Jews into the rest of society and the 'Jewish Question' being solved, it was re-cast into a different mould. From the outset, the traditional middle strata in Central European Society – the smallholders, artisans and shopkeepers – opposed the granting of legal equality to the Jews for fear that they would thereby be exposed to the threat of further competition and exploitation. Needless to say, the landed nobility and the clergy, who for the most part resisted reform of any kind, were also against Jewish emancipation.

When in the 1860s, during Central Europe's short-lived age of Liberalism (see LIBERALISM), the legal emancipation of the Jews was finally completed, these tensions and inconsistencies, instead of being eliminated, were merely brushed aside.

In France, on the other hand, emancipation was carried out as a matter of principle and as part of the general dismantling of the Ancien Régime following

17

the Revolution. Even the restoration of the monarchy in 1815 and the upheavals which followed later in the century did not bring about a reversal of this. Still, even in France, Jewish emancipation was by no means universally welcomed. Charles Fourier, the Utopian Socialist (see SOCIALISM), was one of its opponents, as were his followers Alfonse Toussenal and Pierre-Joseph Proudhon (see ANARCHISM), the founder of modern Anarchism. In their eyes, the Jews were the main proponents and beneficiaries of capitalism and bourgeois individualism, which they held to be responsible for the disintegration of contemporary society. In a sense this was a similar argument to the one pursued by Karl Marx in his well-known essay *On the Jewish Question*, published in 1844. Unlike Fourier and the others, however, Marx was not an opponent of Jewish emancipation as such, but felt rather that it could only be achieved within the context of the overthrow of capitalist society as a whole.

Although anti-Jewish feeling made itself felt during the period of emancipation, it was only after its completion that Anti-Semitism emerged as a distinct ideological and political force. It is generally recognised that the word itself was coined by the German publicist Wilhelm Marr (1819-1904) at the end of 1879, in the heat of Imperial Germany's first wave of anti-Jewish agitation.

This was partly an outgrowth of the financial crash of 1873 for which Jewish bankers and stock brokers were erroneously held by many to have been responsible, and partly the result of the widespread disenchantment amongst intellectuals with the fruits of national unification and the advent of industrial society.

The term 'Anti-Semitism' not only attempted to give anti-Jewish invective an ideological and programmatic quality, but bore witness above all to its increasingly racialist content. Marr's own writings left no doubt where he stood. In his notorious pamphlet, *Der Sieg des Judentums über das Germanentum* (Jewry's Victory over Germandom), which went through twelve editions in six years from its first publication in 1873, he blamed the Jews not as individuals but collectively for all the ills and weaknesses of the German Nation. The time had come, in Marr's view, for all good Germans to resist Jewish influence wherever it was felt. Although he admonished his supporters to pursue their campaign by legal means, his writings emphasised the element of struggle, which was seen exclusively in racial terms: 'There must be no question here of parading religious prejudices when it is question of race and when the difference lies in the "blood". . . .'.

Despite having founded the Anti-Semitic League in 1879, it was not Marr but the Court Chaplain of Berlin, Adolf Stoecker (1835-1909), who brought the struggle against Jewry into the political arena of Germany. He started the so-called Berlin Movement in the wake of Bismarck's rejection of liberal support in the Reichstag and the passage of the anti-Socialist laws in 1878. Stoecker's Christian Social Workers Party was conceived as an alternative to the budding Social Democratic Party. It identified 'Manchesterite Jews' with *laisser-faire* economics and liberal politics, which were in turn blamed for the financial crash of 1873.

Stoecker, significantly, received most of his support not from the working class but from the disaffected middle of German society – the still almost pre-industrial strata of artisans, employees, small-holders and shopkeepers associate ' with the German term *Mittelstand*. Together with disenchanted intellectuals, it was this group, fearful of the advent of industrial, urbanised society and mass-politics, which provided the bulk of support for Anti-Semitic movements throughout Europe.

While sharing Marr's views regarding the pernicious influence of the Jews in German society, Stoecker actually had a legislative programme of sorts to bring it to a halt. It proposed, amongst other measures, the removal of Jewish teachers from primary schools, and the limitations of Jewish appointments to the judiciary in proportion to their percentage of the total German population. It also put forward the introduction of special census techniques so as to discover the'true' extent of Jewish involvement in the professions, industry and finance. His other proposals, which dealt with the control and reform of the nation's banking and financial system, including rural credit, were implicitly Anti-Semitic since Jews were identified in the popular mind with high finance and small-time wheeling and dealing. These were demands that were to appear in slightly amended form in all Anti-Semitic programmes, right down to the advent of National Socialism in the 1930s.

Although the influence of Stoecker in the development of Anti-Semitism cannot be underestimated, it was virtually equalled by that of the German historian and professor at Berlin University, Heinrich von Treitschke. His series of articles in the *Preussische Jahrbücher*, starting at the end of 1879, probably more than anything else, gave Anti-Semitism the stamp of legitimacy it would otherwise not have had. When he proclaimed 'the Jews are our misfortune', the unspeakable had become speakable. What German students and academics had thought to themselves had become the subject for open discussion.

Another figure whose intellectual (and artistic) prestige contributed to the spread of Anti-Semitic ideas amongst the educated classes of Central Europe was the German composer Richard Wagner (1813-83) His *Jewry in Music* (1869) leaned heavily on the racial theories of the French diplomat and scholar Count Arthur de Gibbinneau (1816-1882) (see NATIONALISM). It not only did much to propagate notions of Jewish racial inferiority but dismissed outright the possibility of Jewish participation in German or, for that matter, Western, culture. His views in this regard continued to live on after his death among the members of the notorious *Bayreuther Kreis* (Bayreuth Circle) which included his English son-in-law, Houston Stuart Chamberlain, whose *Foundations of the Twentieth Century* (1899) became a veritable textbook of Germanic racist and Anti-Semitic ideology.

The 1880s were marked by an increase in Anti-Semitic agitation in Germany as well as in Austria, Hungary and elsewhere in Central and Eastern Europe. but it was not until the 1890s, with increasing political and social tensions, that political parties and movements of avowedly Anti-Semitic views gained sufficient following to present a challenge at the ballot-box. Although their success in electoral terms was seemingly both limited and short-lived, they left a legacy of hate which it proved impossible to eradicate and which was to have calamitous consequences in the future. Almost without exception, the political parties of the right attached various anti-Jewish planks to their platforms and a host of extra-parliamentary organisations and pressure groups which took Anti-Semitism for granted came into existence. In addition, most German and Austrian student fraternities and other organisations banned Jews from membership. A large proportion of Central European society had turned its back on liberalism (see LIBERALISM) and its cherished notion of Jewish emancipation.

For a time, much the same also seemed to be happening in France. Initially, Anti-Semitic sentiment was a by-product of the scandal of 1893 surrounding the failure of the French company's attempt, involving a number of Jews, to build a canal across Panama, and the Nationalist agitation associated with the ill-fated attempt by the right-wing General Boulanger to gain power. It drew most of its support from the monarchist and clerical right, whose hostility to Jews was centred around their resentment of increased Jewish participation in the social and economic life of France as well as their opposition to the Republic, with which it was identified. None the less, unlike the situation in Central Europe, it also found support amongst elements in the Socialist movement who, in the tradition of Fourier and Proudhon, saw the Jews at the root of the evils of the capitalist system.

Despite the popularity of such Anti-Semitic works as Edouard Dumont's *La France Juive* (1886), Anti-Semitism remained only an undercurrent in the political life of France until the catalytic Dreyfus Affair in the late 1890s, when a young Jewish officer of the French Army was accused of and then convicted for, spying for Germany. The public controversy concerning his guilt or innocence unleashed a wave of anti-Jewish rhetoric and violence, and brought out into the open the split in French society between those who defended the Republic and those who sought its demise. As was the case in Germany, Anti-Semitism now came to mean more than a socially, racially, culturally or religiously motivated Jew-hatred. It became a cultural code for the rejection of bourgeois Liberalism and industrial society. In the eyes of those who opposed the republican order, the guilt or innocence of Dreyfus was immaterial. He was, in their eyes, guilty because of his Jewishness and what that represented. The espousal of Dreyfus' guilt, in other words, became a vehicle for mobilising opinion against the Republic and in favour of the traditional pillars of French Society – the Monarchy, the Church and the army.

Likewise, the espousal of his innocence became for the *Dreyfusards*, as the champions of his cause were called, not simply a matter of righting a wrong committed, but of defending the very principles on which the Republic was based. By arousing the liberal conscience of France as well as appealing to the pro-republican feeling of the French masses, the Dreyfusards nevertheless contributed significantly to the defusing of Anti-Semitism as a potent force in

French political life. Even so, partly through the efforts of such publicists as Charles Maurras and Maurice Barrés, racial Anti-Semitism has remained an integral component in the ideology of the far Right in France to this very day. Up to the outbreak of the Second World War its main exponent was the magazine *Action Française* founded by Maurras at the time of the Dreyfus affair. Today, it is the *Nouvelle Droite*.

Notwithstanding the furore caused by the Dreyfus case and the particular virulence of German and Austrian Anti-Semitism, it was in Eastern Europe and the Russian Empire, where the majority of European Jewry lived, that a Jew-hatred became almost endemic and took on its most violent form. In the period before the First World War, the situation was worst in the so-called 'Pale of Settlement'. This was the area of Southern and Western Russian originally created in 1791, but its boundaries had since been modified. It had for the most part been newly acquired through the partition of Poland, and the majority of the Jewish population lived and was forced to reside in this area.

In the years of turmoil and reaction following the assassination of Tsar Alexander II in 1881, right-wind elements within the Russian Government encouraged and abetted successive waves of anti-Jewish violence on a scale unknown in Europe since the Ukrainian uprisings of the mid-seventeenth century. In these excesses, which became known as *pogroms* (= Russian, destruction), rioting mobs burnt and looted Jewish property, and attacked individual Jews, including women and children. In one of the worst *pogroms*, at Kishniev in 1903, forty-two Jews were killed, four hundred injured and one thousand three hundred and fifty homes and businesses destroyed.

Their importance in the development of the 'Jewish Question', not just in Europe but in the world at large, cannot be over-estimated. Combined with the discriminatory legislation introduced by successive Russian Governments, beginning with the infamous *May Laws* of 1882, which led to increasing Jewish pauperisation, the pograms were responsible for the massive emigration of Jews from the Russian Empire to North America, Western Europe and South Africa. In addition they resulted in the rise of Jewish nationism and Zionism. In Western and Central Europe Anti-Semitism seemed to make the solution of the 'Jewish Problem' through emancipation and assimilation increasingly difficult if not unlikely. In Russia and elsewhere in Eastern Europe, where the majority of European Jewry lived, the problem became one of sheer physical survival.

When looking for the causes of Anti-Semitism in Russia, as elswhere, the tension and confrontation brought about by the gradual demise of traditional corporate-feudal society should be considered. Russia's relative backwardness, the stubborn resistance to change shown by its ruling élites, as well as the sheer size of its Jewish population (three million souls according to the census of 1905), gave it a character very much its own. Anti-Semitism became a veritable instrument for social control. The authorities used anti-Jewish measures and violence as escape valves to relieve or stave off popular pressure for change. Given the amount of popular hostitlity to Jews, for religious as well as social reasons, especially in provinces such as the Ukraine and White Russia, this never proved very difficult to achieve. With time, moreover, anti-Jewish feeling became increasingly intertwined with Nationalism (see NATIONALISM). Most of the Jewish population of the Russian Empire was concentrated in non-Russian areas, such as the Ukraine and Lithuania, where Jews were identified as much with the Tsarist policy of Russification as with economic exploitation.

Indeed, nationalism played an important part in the rise of Anti-Semitism throughout Eastern Europe, where Jews tended to identify themselves, at least in political, economic and cultural terms, with the ruling élites of the dominant power. So it was that in the part of Poland under Russian domination, in the Ukraine and Lithuania, they were regarded as instruments of Russification. In the largely Slavonic areas of Austria-Hungary they were seen as instruments of Germanisation or Magyarisation as they did in some parts of the Pale of Settlement. The Jews of these areas functioned as intermediaries in the economies of rural districts and played a significant role in the region's first hesitant steps towards industrialisation. This meant that Jews were, for the most part, regarded not just as the accessories of national oppression but as economic exploiters and competitors. Only in independent Roumania, however, were Jews officially persecuted on a scale akin to that in the Russian Empire.

Although by the turn of the century Anti-Semitism had become an all too familiar component of Eastern European Nationalism, it continued for the most part to lack the strong content of Racism that it had in Germany and Austria, or even France. That is not to say that there were not instances of racist ideology and stereotypes entering the Anti-Semitic writing and agitation of the Czechs, Magyars or Poles, but this tended to be an expression of deep-seated prejudice rather than of a pseudo-scientific theory of race.

By 1914 Anti-Semitism was fully ripe in ideological terms. The First World War and its aftermath marked a watershed in its development as a political force. In Germany and Austria, the turning point came in 1916, with an end to hopes of an easy victory and the beginning of serious economic hardship. Until then, the relatively pro-Jewish behaviour of the German Army on the Eastern Front as it advanced into the Russian Empire gave hopes that a victory by the Central Powers would even herald a solution to the plight of the Jews under Tsarist rule.

Worsening conditions on the battlefields and at home soon proved these hopes unwarranted. Right-wing nationalist agitation increased and Jews once more became its favourite scapegoat. Matters were not helped by the considerable influx into Germany and Austria of Jewish refugees from Eastern Europe, some of whom quickly managed to establish themselves as petty traders and businessmen. Their exotic appearance and their religious orthodoxy had already made them a popular target for Jew-baiting before 1914.

In Central and Eastern Europe, the end of the war and the effects of the collapse of the Russian and Austrian empires only served to make an already bad situation worse. The Jews soon found themselves in the midst of the political and social upheaval which ensued. In Eastern Europe, they became the targets of popular revenge as the supposed accomplices of both German, Austrian and Russian domination and exploitation. Although by far the worst violence occurred in the Ukraine, with the slaughter of many thousands of Jews, there were also serious outbreaks in Poland and Roumania. Not even the enlightened and relatively experienced leadership of Czechoslovakia could prevent several series of anti-Jewish attacks. Amongst the opponents of reform and revolution, whether in Russia, Germany, Austria, Hungary or, for that matter, in Britain or the United States, Jew and Bolshevik were regarded as being synonomous, because of the prominence of persons of Jewish origin, such as Trotsky, Belu and Rosa Luxemburg, in left-wing movements generally.

It was within this context that anti-Communist Russian emigrés were able to purvey the myth of a world-wide Jewish conspiracy. This was done by means of a forgery – *The Protocols of the Elders of Zion* – brought to Germany in 1920. Based on a German novel entitled *Biarritz*, written by Hermann Goedsche under the pseudonym of an English diplomat, Sir John Redcliffe, and originally published in 1868, it had become part of the anti-Semitic propaganda arsenal of the Russian Secret Police (the *Okrana*) long before the Revolution of 1917. Purporting to reveal the existence of a secret international Jewish government, known as the *Elders of Zion*, ever plotting world domination, it supposedly depicted that two of its most potent weapons were Liberalism and industrial capitalism. Both, accordings to the myth, were intended to create political and economic chaos as the necessary pre-conditions for a Jewish takeover of the world.

While the return to more settled political and economic conditions in the 1920s led to a decline in the level of anti-Jewish agitation throughout Europe, the underlying attitudes and prejudices which brought it about were not easily eradicated. The *Protocols* continued to be published even in Britain, where Anti-Semitism as such lacked the political impact it had in Central or Eastern Europe.

The stability of the 1920s was to prove short-lived and no sooner did the Wall Street Crash throw the world economic system into disarray than Anti-Semitism emerged as the most potent weapon of the extreme Right. Once more, the 'international Jew' became the scapegoat for economic despair. Anti-Semitism perhaps came to be the most common element in the doctrines of the Fascist and other extreme right-wing Nationalist movements which soon proliferated throughout Europe. Not even Britain and the United States remained unscathed by this new and ultimately disastrous wave of Jew hatred.

That it had its most calamitous result – the physical extermination of some six million Jews – by Nazi Germany hardly needs telling. What is not always realised, however, is the central role 'the struggle against the Jews' played in both the doctrine and programme of National Socialism. Not only was it Hitler's most effective means for obtaining and maintaining popular support for the Nazi regime and *Weltarschauung*, but it remained till the very end of the

Third Reich the element of policy which took precedence above all others. The Nazi leadership and a fair proportion of the German people wholeheartedly accepted the basic tennets of racial Anti-Semitism. In their eyes, the struggle was not simply against the Jewish people, but against the 'Jewish' spirit, whether it be in religion, art, literature, music, political thought or medicine. All and everything Jewish, in their view, had to be eliminated in order to affirm the superiority of the Aryan German race.

Despite the enormity of the crimes against humanity committed by the Third Reich, Anti-Semitism remained not just a German but a European phenomenon. Even if not in its extreme racialist form, for economic reasons it was by the mid-1930s common almost everywhere. In Poland, Roumania, Hungary and Lithuania, for example, it resulted in anti-Jewish legislation being implemented long before occupation by the Germans. Although some emulation of Nazi Jewish policy was involved, it was almost exclusively the consequence of internal rather than external pressure. The sad fact remains, moreover, that the existence of widespread popular animosity against Jews in the countries under German occupation for the most part assisted them in implementing the 'Final Solution' – the physical extermination of the Jews. It has been suggested that this was also the case in the United States and Britain, where officials in both governments often showed themselves to be effectively indifferent to the plight of the Jews in occupied Europe.

The term Anti-Semitism still tends to be associated primarily with the horrors of Nazi extermination camps of Auschwitz, Treblinka and Maydanek. Since 1945, moreover, it has become freely used to describe all types of animosity, prejudice and discrimination directed against Jews. In part, this stems from the fact that in the 1930s and 1940s the dividing line between Jew-hatred and physical persecution virtually ceased to exist across a wide area of Europe. Today in Europe and the Americas Anti-Semitism can only claim the support of a small but dedicated number of fanatics, but Anti-Semitic attitudes persist to a much wider degree. Furthermore, they have been exploited by the ruling Communist parties in the Soviet Union and Eastern Europe (see COMMUNISM SINCE 1917) to justify both internal party purges and the persecutiion of dissidents, as well as to muster public support, since the six-day Arab-Israeli War of 1967, for their strongly anti-Israeli foreign policies. In the early 1950s such tactics proved fairly successful in the Soviet Union itself and in Czechoslovakia and Hungary, but since the late sixties they have tended to backfire somewhat and have even created sympathy for Jews where it did not previously exist. Anti-Jewish attitudes have also been used by Arab and Palestinian groups in their propaganda against Israel, especially amongst the European Left and black Americans. In both cases, unfortunately, a great deal of mutual animosity and recrimination has resulted.

Further reading

Jean-Denis Bredin, *The Affair: the Case of Alfred Dreyfus*
L. Davidowicz, *Hitler's War Against the Jews*
S. Gilman, *Jewish Self-hatred*
R. Hilberg, *The Destruction of European Jewry*
Jacob Katz, *From Prejudice to Destruction*
Leo Poliakov, *The History of Anti-Semitism*
P. J. G. Pulzer, *The Rise of Political Anti-Semitism in Germany and Austria*

Appeasement

The word Appeasement is one of the clearest examples of a word which once enjoyed the highest reputation as an aim towards which the efforts of all statesmen ought to be directed, and which then, as a result of its application to one particular policy against which public opinion turned, came to acquire an entirely pejorative quality. In its original use it meant the attainment of peace, the settlement of strife, the alleviation of discord, the tranquilisation of relations between states. More specifically it came in the 1920s to mean the removal of the tensions established in Europe by the events of the First World War and the Versailles peace settlement. In 1921 Winston Churchill, then addressing the Imperial Conference, said 'our aim is to get an appeasement of the fearful hatreds and antagonisms which exist in Europe and to enable the world to settle down'. The Treaty of Locarno (1925) concluded between France, Belgium and Germany, with Britain and Italy acting as guarantors, was welcomed by the British people, said Lord Balfour in the House of Lords, 'because they have always been anxious for appeasement'. The Soviet Foreign Minister, Maxim Litvinov, speaking to his British counterpart Anthony Eden in 1935, said that the signature of a Locarno-style agreement in Eastern Europe by Germany was 'an essential condition for the appeasement of Europe'. Mr Eden himself, in his speech to the House of Commons on the occasion of his resignation as Foreign Secretary in February 1938, said that his policy had been a search for the appeasement of Europe.

With the rise in Germany of ultra-right-wing anti-parliamentary nationalism (see NATIONALISM) from 1929 onwards (Nazism being only the most successfully organised expression of this spirit) with its bitter hostility towards the peace treaties, the Weimar republic and its governing figures, the idea rose in Britain of going some way to conciliate nationalist grievances, partly to forestall that nationalism developing into aggressive militarism, partly because the financial and economic weakness of Britain and the popular revulsion against war and armaments made more forceful diplomacy out of the question. Thus 'Appeasement' came to acquire a second meaning, not merely the pacification of disputes *per se*, but the pacification of disputes by the satisfaction of the demands

25

of the disputants. From this the meaning of the term slid easily and imperceptibly into a third meaning, the pacification of disputes by the satisfaction of the demands of the most violent and threatening of the disputants. This development was rendered more easy by the general revulsion of British opinion from 1920 onwards towards the Treaty of Versailles and the territorial and strategic *status quo* it had established. The Treaty was believed to be one-sided in its application of principle, so that whatever principles were applied, national self-determination, economic self-sufficiency, or the strategic defensibility of a particular frontier demarcation, the application was always to Germany's disadvantage. Hence those who benefited from the Treaty, to the revision of which even official German foreign policy was directed, could only too easily appear as obstacles to appeasement.

Contemporary British opponents of the policy of appeasement tended to fall into one of four categories: members of the official Labour and Liberal opposition to the National and Conservative governments in power from 1931 onwards; rebels within the Conservative, national Liberal and national Labour coalition party ranks; members of the left wing of the Labour party and of the Communist party of Great Britain in the country; and supporters of the League of Nations and of the Treaty of Versailles into which the Charter of the League was incorporated who objected less to the principle of appeasement than to the methods by which it was advanced. The dictators' hostility to the League meant in practice that diplomatic measures to advance appeasement were conducted outside the framework of the League; while those states who felt their interests threatened by such measures tended to turn to the League and to the principle of collective *security* embodied in the Charter for protection. Both the coalition National Government and its Conservative critics believed that Britain's military weakness needed to be repaired both because it encouraged intransigence among the dictators and as a protection lest the policy of Appeasement failed. The Labour and Liberal opposition, joined after 1935 by the left-wing and Communist movements in the country, opposed rearmament as unnecessary, as a measure designed to increase the wealth of those sections of heavy industry which would benefit from armaments expenditure and as a demonstration of lack of faith in *collective security*.

In its original form the principle of collective security was introduced into the covenant of the League of Nations on the initiative of the British delegates as a modernisation of the Anglo-Saxon principle of the 'hue-and-cry'. Aggression and the resort to aggressive war in their view threatened not only the peace of the immediate victim but the civil peace *per se*. It therefore became the duty of all citizens, that is of all the members of the League of Nations, to unite against the aggressor. An aggressor state was to be restrained from aggression by the application against him of economic sanctions, that is to say all trade with the aggressor state would cease. If these failed the question then arose of military sanctions. The populer view was that economic sanctions alone would probably be enough. Military sanctions carried out by all the member states of the League would be so overwhelming that any great measure of national expenditure on armaments would be unnecessary. Competition in national armaments, it was firmly believed, was a major cause of war. Military advisers of governments, on the other hand, aware that the Covenant authorised self-protection, were concerned that the burden of military sanctions would fall most heavily on the major powers, and that the obligation to support military sanctions on a global basis meant the addition of open-ended commitments to those of national self-defence which they were supposed to have answered anyway. Anxiety on this score led to the reservation by the individual members of the League of the choice of how and whether to meet the call for the application of sanctions against an individual state which was declared to be in breach of the Covenant. And all proposals advanced in the first six years of the League's existence to weaken or remove their reservations were defeated by the reluctance of governments, those of Britain and the Dominions being particularly strong, to take on obligations likely to commit them to the maintenance of the territorial *status quo* established in 1919, particularly to that in Eastern Europe.

League of Nations action was successful in terminating the Greek–Bulgarian conflict in 1925. Where other conflicts were concerned however the sanctions device for deterring a restraining aggression turned out to suffer from various crucial weaknesses. The impact of economic sanctions fell strongly only on those states whose international trade satisfied a high percentage of their economic needs. If economic sanctions were anticipated, a would-be aggressor could prepare to reduce their impact by stockpiling. The cessation of trade damaged trade relations to both parties, the target of sanctions and the appliant of sanctions, and could damage the economy of the appliant more severely and more rapidly than it did that of the target state. Also, the United States, a major element in international trade, especially in such crucial materials of war as oil and petroleum, vehicles, steel scrap etc., was not a member of the League. The application of military sanctions was equally subject to weaknesses. To challenge a major power ran the risk of prolonged war, precisely the evil which the League was designed to prevent. To bring military power to bear required the availability of bases close enough to the aggressor state's home territories to be effective. In the case of the wars in Latin America in the inter-war period, and in the case of the Japanese attack on Manchuria in September 1931, the military conditions for the successful and speedy application of armed force, especially against Japan, a power which itself maintained very substantial naval, military and air forces, were simply not present. In the case of Italy, against whom economic sanctions were applied in 1935 when Italian troops invaded Ethiopa, the will to extend those sanctions to include oil was not present and the American position remained sufficiently unclear to justify anxiety as to whether the cessation of American oil supplies could be relied on: while Italy made it clear that the application of oil sanctions against her would be answered by military action.

The failure of the application of economic sanctions to prevent the Italian conquest of Ethiopia marked the end of any serious belief in 'collective security' at the official level. Minor members of the League, especially the Scandinavian and Benelux states, made it clear that they could not take part in any further measures of sanctions, binding themselves together under the *Copenhagen Declaration* (1938). The liberal and left opponents of appeasement began to accept the necessity for rearmament but urged an alignment with Soviet Russia in a 'Grand Alliance', a 'popular front' of the kind which had rallied the anti-Fascist forces in the Spanish Civil War against the nationalist insurgents led by General Franco. The British Government remained determined to avoid a confrontation until its rearmament programme had begun to narrow the armaments gap between itself and Germany; but faced with the possibility of war with Germany in Europe, Italy in the Mediterranean and Japan in the Far East – which it felt to be beyond Britain's strength to fight without certain defeat – it redoubled its efforts to 'appease' at least one of the three aggressor states. In April 1938 the Anglo–Italian Mediterranean Agreements secured an alleviation of Anglo–Italian tensions, but the opening of German pressure designed to use the cause of the German minority in Czechoslovakia to destroy the Czech state confronted them with the danger of a major European war that very year. British intervention eventually prevailed on Mussolini to persuade Hitler to accept satisfaction of his ostensible demands, the annexation to Germany to the Sudeten German areas, after the British prime minister had twice flown to Germany to persuade Hitler of Britain's willingness to engineer a settlement. The agreement which secured this, signed at Munich on 30 September 1938 was hailed at the time as the ultimate justification of appeasement and denounced by its opponents as dishonourable and a weakening of Britain's moral cause. Its manifest failure to satisfy Hitler's expansionism (which Britain in September 1939 chose to oppose by force) turned appeasement into the pejorative concept it has remained ever since. In 1941 a settlement with Japan was defeated by American fears that it would constitute a 'Far Eastern Munich'. In American opinion particularly, the adage 'appeasement never pays' struck so firm a root that it played a major part in post-war American foreign policy (see COLD WAR). In fact, however, the appeasement of Italy was a factor in preserving Italian neutrality in 1939, just as the avoidance of conflict with Japan in that year over the Tientsin issue equally contributed to Japan's not entering the war until December 1941.

The concept of collective security and the belief that it had not been properly applied found its expression in the Charter of the United Nations. This belief played a very strong part in the reaction by the United States and by the majority of members of the United Nations (excluding, of course, the Soviet bloc) to the outbreak of the Korean conflict in 1950, and though other motives were undoubtedly present, played an important part in the establishment of a United Nations command in Korea and in the dispatch to Korea of contingents of troops and other armed units from Britain, the Commonwealth and other western states. Arguments derived from the wrongness of appeasement thereafter ceased to exercise so universal an appeal, the United States failing to respond to such arguments when the British and French governments advanced them to justify their action against Egypt in 1956 and the Americans failing to find any support for them in their intervention in Vietnam from 1960 onwards, save from Australia. The United Nations switched its policies towards the limitations and fencing around of conflicts rather than their universalisation.

Black Consciousness

Black consciousness is not quite an ideology, nor quite a political movement. It is best explained as the common trait of some half a dozen political movements of the late twentieth century. As a general label the phrase is indispensable, for it identifies one of the most important themes of the age: the attempt of all the various peoples of black African descent to overcome their divisions in the face of history, geography and white oppression.

The expression first became current in the United States during the 1960s, and retains a strong Afro-American flavour, although Steve Biko gave the name 'Black Consciousness' to his attempt to transcend tribalism (see AFRICAN NATIONALISM). Black consciousness as the corrective to white consciousness – or prejudice, or arrogance – makes excellent sense in white-dominated multi-racial societies, such as the United States, South Africa, or Great Britain. It is an assertion of self-respect, whether in the individual or in his race, and may be expected to manifest itself so long as whites are tempted to abuse their power over blacks.

The growth of black consciousness began long before anyone gave it a name. As early as 1903 the New York journalist, John Edward Bruce, proclaimed exultingly: 'I am a negro and all negro. I am black all over, and proud of my beautiful black skin. . .' and he was certainly not the first to express this response to hateful conditions.

This form of black consciousness manifests itself in today's United States as black nationalism: for as Eugene Genovese, the historian of slavery has remarked, Afro-Americans are 'not so much a class as a nation' – still barred from full acceptance as Americans, whatever their economic status, because of their colour. The most famous slogan of black nationalism has been 'black is beautiful'; the most famous leader Malcolm X (1925-1965), whose most signifi-cant contribution was his insistence on black self-help as a means of achieving black self-respect. His energy, eloquence and intelligence were such that not even his assassination by rival blacks could silence his message. Although he seemed superficially to be advocating race war, Malcolm claimed that he was merely stating the facts of racial relations in America and his theme was essen-tially one of spiritual redemption: not for nothing had he been rescued from

29

the life of a petty criminal by the Black Muslims.

To insist, in the face of denigration, on the value of one's race, is sensible and laudable; but it is only a beginning. Black consciousness is also characterised by an insistence on the historical importance of its mission. At the first Pan-African Congress in 1900 W. E. B. Du Bois (1868–1963) (see AFRICAN NATIONALISM), the distinguished American scholar and black leader, prophesied that 'the problem of the twentieth century is the problem of the colour-line – the relation of the darker to the lighter races of men in Asia and Africa, in America and the islands of the sea.' This statement has been largely vindicated by events. The non-European races dealt a series of heavy shocks to the briefly-dominant whites; for many Old and New World Africans, black consciousness has been a means of claiming a place in a great movement, and of announcing it to the white world.

Characterisation only becomes problematic when the attempt is made to give black consciousness a meaning beyond resistance and reassertion. There is a crisis in black consciousness (to use the term in a simply descriptive sense) which so far neither ideology nor history have been able to resolve. Yet at least the struggle for resolution has produced a long list of movements, leaders and ideas, all with something valuable to contribute. Perhaps it is in its failures (few of which have been absolute) that black consciousness is most interesting, most clearly itself.

At the root of the problem is the fact that the urgent problem of establishing a black identity cannot be solved by simple assertions of blackness or négritude. The black race is deeply divided – one of the baleful after-effects of slavery in the Americas and colonialism in Africa. The dearest wish of the proponents of black consciousness is to surmount this division, but so far the obstacles have largely defeated them.

In spite of the many cultural traits carried by the slaves from Africa to America, the individual Afro-American suffered an irreparable breach with his ancestry. He is without a history, culture, place, language, or even a name, that he feels able fully to call his own. He feels stranded, 'out of time', as the poet Claude McKay put it, in a white man's alien culture. This experience resembles that of white immigrant groups in the United States; but it is far more overwhelming, and the efforts to overcome it have had to be far more intense. The most conspicuous recent attempt has been Alex Haley's, which found expression in his book *Roots*. More and more Afro-Americans now visit Ghana and Nigeria in search of their past; and many have even settled in West Africa. Du Bois himself did so at the very end of his life.

Subject races have always turned for vindication to history, often crying up the glory of their ancestors and (in the case of emigrant groups) of their homelands. Black Americans have naturally felt this impulse: for example, Bruce's assertion of his blackness was stimulated by his meeting with a West African, Majola Agbebi of Nigeria. The idea of Africa has thus always been a potent myth and a source of support and consolation. This partly accounts for the foundation of Liberia as a colony of freed slaves in 1822. It explains the *Back-to-Africa* movements of Bishop Henry McNeal Turner (1834-1915) and Marcus Garvey (1887-1940) who proclaimed himself Provisional President of the Empire of Africa; it explains fervent cries for a *return to Africa* (or Black Zionism) of the past forty years; and finally explains the part played by Afro-Americans in launching Pan-Africanism (see AFRICAN NATIONALISM). For Afro-Americans, black consciousness can mean acting on the belief that the African heritage can be retrieved, that the physical evidence of African descent can be used to undo the cruel work of history, and that a full sense of identity must be restored to the children of the slaves. In this sense it is an alternative to that other slogan of the sixties, 'Black Power', which was a movement directed to winning autonomy for black Americans (though of course the sense of an African heritage could greatly strengthen the determination and self-confidence of Black Power exponents).

In some respects the experience of blacks who remained in Africa was analogous to that of the slaves. The indignities of colonisation resembled those of slavery and both had a similar origin in the white man's unscrupulous readiness to exploit other races. But the colonial experience also differed from that of slavery in a great many fundamental respects: for example, it left the traditional organisation of African society into tribes and villages intact, and in doing so preserved African identity. The indigenous African therefore possesses a sense of identity and cultural rootedness that the Afro-American, saturated with the culture and values of the prosperous West, has lost. The myth of black consciousness proposes that African descent can and will override all other considerations to create, as it were, a black commonwealth. But the reality is that skin colour, or the knowledge of black ancestry, are nowadays the only things that can define an Afro-American: in every other way he seems indistinguishable from his fellow-Americans, and is thereby alienated from Africa. The same is largely true of British and West Indian blacks.

In the face of such problems a tendency arises for black consciousness to be thrust back upon its American origins, and on the old debate between those who think, with Garvey (who at one time actually endorsed the Ku Klux Klan) that Afro-Americans should live separated from whites, and those who think, with Du Bois (a founder of the bi-racial National Association for the Advancement of Coloured People) that they should struggle for full integration. The integrationists enjoyed spectacular successes during the sixties, with the passage of a series of civil rights acts, especially the voting law of 1965; their gains have been a permanent accretion of affluence and political power to the middle class. Most Afro-Americans, however, are working class, and among them separatism remains strong, which explains the success of the Nation of Islam ('Black Muslims') founded by Elijah Muhammad (1897-1975), who required his followers to give up their possessions, their Christianity, their very names (thus Malcolm Little became Malcolm X and Cassius Clay became Muhammad Ali). But the North American black community is too large, too heterogeneous,

31

and too fundamentally Christian for more than a fraction ever to come under the Black Muslim umbrella. The memory of the Christian minister, Martin Luther King Jr. (1929-1968) is more potent than Muhammad's, and stands for integration.

The myth of Africa is not yet exhausted, however, as is demonstrated by the story of the Rastafarians. This sect came into being as a result of a prophecy by the Jamaican-born Garvey that a black king would shortly be crowned in Africa. When, soon after, Ras Tafaris mounted the throne of Ethiopia as Emperor Haile Selassie, the prophecy was fulfilled. Many poor Jamaicans have ever since made a cult of the Emperor, even though he was eventually dethroned and died a prisoner. A few of them have made their way to Africa, as their religion promised them; for most the cult has chiefly been a means of combatting the grim poverty of life in the Caribbean and British cities. Some sort of accommodation has been reached between the government of Jamaica and the Rastafarians; but the cult's millenial promises remain as unattainable as those of the Black Muslims, or the obscure sect of Black Hebrews. They can hardly be reconciled with African realities. In short, Rastafarianism, like the Nation of Islam, though it is a testimony to the imagination of black consciousness, must be seen as an evasion of the problem of Afro-American identity rather than as a solution.

An alternative approach, foreshadowed by Du Bois in his prediction about the colour-line, was explored by the Martinique-born Frantz Fanon (1925-1961). In his short life Fanon moved rapidly from claiming integration and equality to being an active leader of the Algerian revolt against the French (1954-1962) and an advocate of pan-African (see AFRICAN NATIONALISM), if not pan-black, revolution. (It is worth remembering that Du Bois was a Communist during the last years of his life.) But Fanon's writings not only include what Genovese has called a 'psychopathic panegyric to violence'. They display, rather than bridge, the gulf between Africa and America. His over-simplified picture of African history had great appeal to rebellious young blacks in the United States during the 1960s, but meant little or nothing to the new nations, which Fanon thought had got onto the wrong track. In the seventies his attraction seems to have waned even in the United States.

Caught between countries, continents, classes, religious and political creeds, black consciousness cannot yet be said to have matured as an international ideology. Yet the fact remains that in the present world a black skin is indeed an indication of a common interest. For every black, the way forward is impeded by white men. While that is so, black consciousness will retain its validity. And it may yet be transmuted. The West Indians, for instance, who know both urban and rural poverty; who remember both slavery and colonisation; who know both the sterility of the past and the frustrations of modern life; who have gone out from their over-crowded islands to Britain, America, and Africa; may yet find the route by which black consciousness will emerge as something more potent than a defence against racism.

Bonapartism

Relegated to St Helena after his defeat at Waterloo, Napoleon I became the centre of a cult, assiduously fostered by himself and disseminated by those around him. The Emperor's thoughts on his past, together with his supposed plans for the future of France, set against the background of his captivity and death, became the basis of the Napoleonic legend. This legend, well publicised, disturbed French governments by its force, and in 1840, in the hope that official patronage would both capture and neutralise its effects, Napoleon's body was brought back from St Helena to Paris.

The attempt failed because there existed an heir – Louis Napoleon, nephew of Napoleon I – who was determined that not only should his uncle's remains be brought back, but also that his political system should be restored and reinvigorated.

His task was facilitated by the existence of the Napoleonic legend, and even more by the fact that so many of France's institutions were as Napoleon I had left them. All that was needed was to restore the political machinery. In 1839 Louis Napoleon published *The Napoleonic Ideas,* and in 1840 *The Napoleonic Idea,* two works which transformed the Napoleonic legend into a political doctrine. While embracing the legend, the new Bonapartism went further, promising a government which would be strong and authoritarian in the Napoleonic tradition, but which would also provide direct democracy through universal suffrage and which would aim for social justice.

In 1844, in *The Suppression of Poverty,* Louis Napoleon appealed directly to the peasants and to the workers – the latter now becoming a factor in French society as industrialisation increased. At the same time he stressed that, as his uncle's heir, he would heal the social and political wounds in French society which had been deepening since 1815, because Bonapartism would be non-party and would be neither exclusive nor intolerant. 'I shall always govern in the interests of the masses.' For him, government must be based on authority from above, confidence from below, which would be maintained by a dialogue between ruler and people. By means of the plebiscite, this would restore to the people the rights which had been theirs since the Revolution of 1789.

The Revolution of 1848 enabled Louis Napoleon to return from exile in England and to be elected first a deputy, and then President of the new Republic by five and a half million votes. The legend, the doctrine and the power had fused together.

By 1852, the Empire was restored, endorsed by seven million votes, a ratification of Louis Napoleon's *coup d'état* of 1851, which had also been endorsed by seven and a half million votes. The power of the political oligarchies was

33

broken by these two events and until 1870 France was governed by an authoritarian constitution which fulfilled the tenets of Bonapartism.

Napoleon III created a strong economic basis for France by the extension of railways, banking, and commerce generally – he was a staunch supporter of free trade – while attempting important social reforms with a view to improving the lot of both peasants and workers. The Empire was a period of economic, political and social stability in nineteenth century France, but, with its defeat in war in 1870, the regime was discredited.

Christian Democracy

Christian Democracy as an organised political movement is a child of the Second World War. Unlike earlier movements of political Catholicism in Europe, Christian Democracy claimed to represent Christian values in general, an ideal which has been realised in West Germany although largely not elsewhere. Also, the movement was self-consciously democratic, wishing to demonstrate its hostility to and distance from the period of Fascism (see FASCISM). In France, the Christian Democrats of the *Mouvement Républicain Populaire* drew heavily on their identification with the Resistance and it is no accident that West Germany and Italy have been the countries with the most successful Christian Democratic parties.

The roots of Christian Democracy as a set of ideas, however, go back to the French Revolution, and they are essentially Catholic rather than Protestant or interdenominational. The revolution broke the link between Church and State in France, and challenged the position of the Church elsewhere in Europe. It required both clerical and lay Catholics to formulate responses to a changed political life and civil society. From around 1830 (also a year of revolutions) a distinct strain of liberal Catholicism became evident in France, associated with the names of Montalembert, Lacordaire and the maverick figure of Lamennais. Similar movements emerged during the same period in Belgium, Ireland and other countries. Their liberalism was less theological than political: it involved a recognition of the new kind of society and public discourse created by the revolution, and a willingness to use subsequent advances in parliamentary forms and civil rights in the defence of Catholic interests. An explicit claim of this kind was made by Lacordaire following the 1848 revolution in France, when he began a new journal which sought to 'reconcile the Church and democracy'.

At the same time, industrialisation, urbanisation and the growing conflict between social classes posed a parallel challenge. Such profound changes were seen as a threat to Christian family life and belief. They were also regarded as the product of a dangerous and heartless *laisser-faire* liberalism (see LIBERALISM), which was allegedly responsible for unleashing a war of all against all in society and for fostering crudely materialistic values. The growth of a secular socialism (see SOCIALISM) was seen as an equally (and potentially more) dangerous symptom of social ferment. English Christian Socialism was one response to this. On the continent the Protestant response to the social question was sluggish, but a developing 'Social Catholicism' increasingly drew attention to the twin evils of liberal capitalism and socialist collectivism. Social Catholics also characteristically attacked the state not only for its anti-clericalism, but also for its alleged indifference to social evils. All of these strains of thinking can be seen around the middle of the century in the pioneering work of Adolf Kolping, a German priest who extended the concept of pastoral care to the formal organisation of young journeymen. Such views are also evident in the writings of his influential contemporary, Bishop Ketteler of Mainz.

Initiatives of this kind, both lay and clerical, were evidence of a new recognition that Catholics could not simply stand by, but must use the methods of the Church's opponents to harness political support in a hostile world. The papacy of Leo XIII, with his important encyclical *Rerum Novarum* (1891), offered support for political movements that proved to be the precursors of modern Christian Democracy. From about the 1870s, organised political Catholicism became a significant force in Germany, Belgium, Switzerland and Austria, although it failed to take off in France or Italy, as a result of domestic political circumstances and the hostility of Leo XIII's successor, Pius X. These movements had much in common, both ideologically and socially. They opposed liberal secularism, together with innovations such as civil marriage, and they resisted the incursions of the state into various areas of religious life, most notably education.

They also tended to be internally divided along similar lines when it came to large economic and social questions. One important strand in the ideology of political Catholicism was a simultaneous hostility to both capitalism and socialism. Politicians, publicists and priests who took this stance saw the self-sufficient peasant or guild-organised craftsman as an ideal. This was a position they shared with some anarchists (see ANARCHISM) and early socialists (see SOCIALISM), and it owed much to the nineteenth-century rediscovery of 'medievalism'. Similar views animated a new generation of Christian socialists in England, and underpinned the concept of *distributism* (or distributivism) espoused by the social-Catholic English intellectuals Belloc and Chesterton. For Belloc, capitalism and collectivism were equally suspect for their materialistic tendencies, and 'distributism' among a population of simple, self-sufficient property owners provided the basis for an early 'small is beautiful' philosophy. On the other hand, the far more important movements of political Catholicism on the continent tacitly retreated from many of their anti-capitalist positions in the decades before 1914. They came to accept the prevailing economic system, while increasingly organising Catholic workers, peasants and other groups to defend their interests within that system. Where an anti-capitalist rhetoric remained, it was largely directed against finance or 'mobile' capital. As in the

35

case of the Christian-Social mayor of Vienna, Karl Lueger, this often had anti-semitic overtones (see ANTI-SEMITISM).

While organised political and social Catholicism achieved considerable importance in the countries mentioned above (and, after the First World War, in Italy), these remained essentially movements of the faithful, castigated as 'Black' by their opponents. They were also compromised by their political record in the interwar years, either failing abjectly in the face of Fascism (see FASCISM) (like the German Centre Party and the Italian *Popolari)*, or carrying a more direct responsibility for the success of Fascism (as in Austria and Slovakia).

Post-war Christian Democracy has been different in a number of respects. While the core of the movement in most countries has remained Catholic, it has often been able to broaden its political base and become a powerful inte-grating force on the Right, notably in West Germany and Italy. There, the CDU/CSU and *Democrazia Cristiana* have also proved generally more reliable than their predecessors as supporters of formal political democracy. They also share with post-war Christian Democratic parties elsewhere some other 'modern' features: a general commitment to European unity, for example, and a broad acceptance of liberal capitalism (along with a sometimes virulent anti-com-munism). The largest Christian Democratic parties, those of West Germany and Italy, are hybrids, combining traditional religious and social values with whole-hearted acceptance of western capitalism and of modern political techniques. Indeed, their very size and heterogeneity have sometimes made it difficult to define exactly what they do stand for, beyond looking for political power. The values of political and social Catholicism had been fairly clear-cut; by the 1980s perhaps the most important single thing which can be said of the 'ideology' of Christian Democratic parties is its lack of importance.

Further reading

M. P. Fogarty, *Christian Democracy in Western Europe, 1820-1953*
H. Maier, *Revolution and Church. The Early History of Christian Democracy, 1789-1901*
G. Pridham, 'Christian Democracy in Italy and West Germany: A Comparative Analysis', in M. Kolinsky and W. E. Paterson (eds.), *Social and Political Movements in Western Europe.*

Coexistence

The term 'peaceful cohabitation' *(mirnoe sozhitelstvo)* was originally used by the Bolshevik revolutionary leader, Leon Trotsky, on 22 November 1917 to cover relations between the Soviet and non-Soviet world, and continued in Soviet practice until December 1927 when the term coexistence *(sosushchestvovenie),* which has a somewhat more passive sense, officially replaced it. The term was originally part of a Soviet propaganda offensive designed to mobilise opinion in the non-Soviet world against those who argued that the Bolshevik revolution was so great a threat to order and peace everywhere that intervention to suppress it was justified. The gradual recession of the fear of intervention as Soviet relations with the non-Soviet world became more settled and normalised was coupled with the victory of Stalin, with his doctrine of 'Socialism in one country', over Trotsky's doctrine of 'permanent revolution'. As the Soviet Union began to feel threatened by the rise to power of Nazism in Germany, with its violent anti-Communist propaganda, the phrase fell into desuetude. It was revived after Stalin's death by Nikita Khrushchev, who dominated Soviet political life between 1956 and his fall from power in 1964. Khrushchev argued, especially against the then more militant Chinese leadership, that the acquisition by the Soviet Union and the United States of substantial arsenals of nuclear weapons and intercontinental missiles, giving each side the capacity to destroy the other utterly and completely, made open war between the two sides unthinkable and unacceptable. Disagreement on this issue, dramatised by the signature of the Test Ban Treaty in 1963 and the earlier Soviet refusal to aid China develop her own nuclear forces, played a major part in the Sino-Soviet doctrinal schism which broke out in public that year. Khrushchev made it plain that coexistence did not alter the essential state of competition between the 'socialist' and the 'capitalist' state systems which would continue until the historical process inevitably brought about Communist triumph and the 'burial' of capitalism. And part of that competition inevitably involved Soviet support for the revolutionary side in 'wars of national liberation', i.e. civil wars in third world countries in which one side seeks Soviet aid.

As part of the processes of peaceful coexistence, the Soviet authorities had for long been seeking a settlement of those issues in Europe outstanding since the end of the Second World War which had played so large a part in fermenting the 'Cold War' (see THE COLD WAR) between the United States, in support of its west European associates, and the Soviet Union, from 1945 onwards. This search was conducted under the slogan of *detente,* a technical term borrowed from the vocabulary of nineteenth-century diplomacy covering the reduction in tension (and thus of the risks of the outbreak of war) between states. The process began in earnest with the signature of the Nuclear Arms Non-Proliferation Treaty in 1969, and continued in direct Soviet-American talks on the limitation of strategic weapons (SALT agreements) as well as in talks on security, co-operation and the mutual and balanced reduction of standing forces under arms in Europe. The first set of talks resulted in the Final Act of the Helsinki Conference of August 1975, which set out principles guiding relations between states and measures governing aspects of security and disarmament, as well as a series of areas in which economic and technological co-operation could be developed and confidence and human contacts between the participants be encouraged. Signatories bound themselves to recognise the sovereignty and territorial integrity of states and the right to self-determination of their peoples.

The Cold War

The 'Cold War' is a term coined by the American financier Bernard Baruch in April 1947 which passed very quickly into general currency. It was invented to describe a state of hostile relations between states whose efforts to defeat and thwart each other are manifested in economic pressures, propaganda, covert and subversive activities, political action at the meetings of international organisations, measures which always stop short of actual fighting, 'hot war' or 'shooting war'. The term presents considerable difficulties to historical analysis. It has been loosely used to describe the whole period of relations between the Soviet Union and the major western powers from the Bolshevik revolution in November 1917 onwards. But the majority of uses confine it to the period of Soviet relations with the West, especially with the United States, after the end of the Second World War. The real difficulties arise as soon as questions are asked as to when the Cold War began, what were its causes, and when did it end. Confusion between the period in which a war can be said to have originated and its early stages is avoided in the case of recognisable 'hot' wars, as the transition from antagonism to open hostilities can always be marked, if not by a formal declaration of war, at least by some overt move. But an undeclared 'war', which stops short of actual fighting, is more difficult. Further confusion is caused when the global spread of the Cold War is considered and the question is asked whether one single conflict or several parallel conflicts are involved. Consensus among historians can be said to be moving slowly towards the view that sees the equivalent, in Cold War terms, to a declaration of war to be contained in the declaration made by President Truman on 12 March 1947, declaring it to be American policy to 'support free people who are resisting subjection by armed minorities or outside pressures', justifying thereby the vote of $400 million to support Greece and Turkey against Soviet pressure and, in the case of Greece, against internal insurrection backed by the Greek Communist party and supported from across the Yugoslav and Bulgarian frontiers. After Stalin's death in 1953 came a period of 'thaw' ending with the opening of the second stage in Europe, the Berlin crisis of 1958-63, and which ended with the Cuban missile crisis in October 1962, the subsequent negotiation of the Test-ban Treaty and the establishment of a direct telephone line between the White House and the Kremlin, the so-called 'hot line'. The Cold War was continued in Asia, however, until the diplomatic revolution of 1969-73 which saw the recognition by America of Communist China, the American withdrawal from Vietnam, the Four Power Agreement over Berlin and the non-proliferation treaty, a period on which the Helsinki agreements on *détente* in Europe of August 1975 seemed for a time to have set the final stamp. The deterioration of relations between the United States and its allies after the introduction of Soviet troups into Afganistan has led to claims that a new Cold War has opened.

One of the tactics of the 'Cold War' inevitably became to approach real war so closely as to restrain or alarm the opposing side from any step likely to 'escalate' the crisis further. This tactic was given the title 'brinksmanship' by Professor T. C. Schelling of Harvard (1963), from a speech made by the US Secretary of State, John Foster Dulles, in January 1956, on the art of 'going to the brink of war'. 'Brinkmanship' involves the deliberate creation of a recognisable risk of war, of deliberately letting the situation get out of hand, to force the other party, through fear of the consequences, into withdrawal and accommodation. The Cuba missile crisis, when, as the then Secretary of State, Dean Rusk, put it 'we were eyeball to eyeball and the other man blinked', Soviet nuclear missiles being withdrawn from Cuba under American pressure, is probably the extreme example of this tactic.

Collaboration
and Resistance

There was resistance against the armies of Napoleon by the people of Spain and Portugal; there was resistance against British imperialism by many people in India, and there was resistance against the Prussians by Paris Communards in 1871. But it was not until the Second World War that the term 'resistance' took on the meaning that it has today: action, mostly clandestine, against Nazi Germany (see FASCISM) by the peoples of the occupied countries, sometimes on their own and sometimes with the help of the Western allies, Britain and America, or Soviet Russia. The term is also used in a more limited way to refer to the resistance of the Chinese and other South-East Asian people against Japan during the same period.

In many ways collaboration was simply the opposite of resistance – actions by people in the same occupied countries that helped and supported the Nazi, or Japanese, occupiers. But the contrast is also one of chronology. Collaboration in most of the occupied countries was strongest in the years 1939-42 when it seemed possible, if not probable, that Germany and Japan would win the war. Resistance, on the other hand, was strongest in the years 1942-5 when the Allies first contained their enemies and then began to defeat them. Not surprisingly, those who collaborated in the earliest part of the war and those who only resisted at the very end have been equally accused of opportunism, though this accusation begs many complicated questions about the different impact of occupation in different countries at different times. Due to this diversity it would be unwise to try and characterise the model resister or the typical collaborator. Nevertheless, Jean-Paul Sartre, in an essay full of perceptive half-truths, answered his own question 'What is a Collaborator?' by giving a picture of someone who had been an outsider in pre-war society and who welcomed the arrival of the Nazis as an opportunity to become a person of status and influence. It is interesting that some resisters maintain that they too had been outsiders, rebels or non-conformists, before the war. If they had not been so individualistic, they say, they would have submitted to the Nazis in the same way as the vast majority of the population who, whether in France or Norway, Holland or Denmark, were too stunned by the occupation and too intent on day-to-day survival to imagine that anything could be done to alter the situation. Whatever the general truth of this 'outsider' explanation, it is certainly accurate to say that both active resisters and active collaborators were usually a minority among the occupied populations. The sole exception to this was in Poland, where more than a century of resistance to the imperialism of Central and Eastern European powers had established a historical tradition to which most of the population remained faithful; indeed, resistance in Poland was so widespread that the Germans made no attempt to encourage even an appearance of collaboration.

Elsewhere in occupied Europe the dominant reaction to the early victories of the Nazi *Reich* was the attitude and policy of *attentisme*: waiting for things to change and concentrating on survival. Later in the war certain resisters, who wanted immediate military action against the Germans, used the same term to denote the attitude of other resisters who were waiting for the arrival of the Allies before launching their attacks. The earlier use of the term originated in France, where an Armistice had been signed between the German occupiers and the new French government under Marshal Pétain. This Armistice was regarded as a fragile state of peace which would be jeopardised by any form of hasty action, and most of the population saw no alternative to *attentisme*.

The government of Pétain went further in this understanding of the Armistice and encouraged the French to see it as an honourable settlement, securing not only a continued measure of self-government for the southern part of France based in the town of Vichy, but also a vital opportunity for national reassessment and moral revival. In return the French responded by a religious veneration for the eighty four year-old Marshal, whom they saw as the saviour of France in its worst moment of humiliation and disaster.

Pétainism was both the policy and creed of national regeneration proclaimed by the Vichy government and the immense public response to the person of Pétain himself. 'Greater than Joan of Arc' was the widely accepted estimation of this paternal, handsome and narcissistic leader of France, whose record in the First World War as the 'Victor of Verdun' assured him the devoted discipleship of millions of old soldiers and their families. Under the protection of Pétainism the Vichy government was able to create an authoritarian state which more and more resembled the fascist regimes of Italy, Spain and Portugal and drew gradually closer to the Nazis. The policy of collaboration, announced to the nation by Pétain in October 1940, shifted from one of coexistence to one of co-operation. Finally, in 1944, it led to assimilation when the rump of Vichy collaborators, with Pierre Laval at their head, took refuge inside the Nazi *Reich* as the Allied armies and the French Resistance liberated the country.

Pétain was one kind of collaborator – the national hero using defeat and occupation as the opportunity to impose a reactionary political system, and drawn, part reluctantly and part willingly, into collaboration with the national enemy. Pierre Laval was another – the opportunistic politician, trading certain French interests in order to protect others, a policy which he tried to present at his trial as a calculated *double-jeu,* a double game which made no friends among either the idealistic collaborators or the dedicated resisters.

A third kind was exemplified by Vidkun Quisling in Norway. As head of the fascist *Nasjonal Samling* (national unity) party Quisling became an enthusiastic supporter of the Nazis, and in December 1939 urged Hitler to occupy Norway so that he could establish his own form of fascism in close partnership with the Nazi *Führer.* The goal of a puppet existence was finally realised in February 1942 when Quisling became the Nazi-sponsored leader of Norway, free to promote his racial ideas about the 'Aryan bond' between Scandinavians and Germans. Within a year 'Quisling' had become synonymous with treason and was universally used to denote any government leader of an occupied country who collaborated closely with the Nazis. Like Laval, he was executed on the liberation of his country, but, unlike Laval, no historian has come forward with an apologia for his action. In retrospect the *double-jeu* type of collaborator has gained some form of credibility: the *Quisling* of any country has none.

The fascist enthusiasm which possessed Quisling was also the hallmark of lesser-known fascists in other occupied countries, who responded to the Nazi occupation with the hope that they would become the leaders of their countries within the *New Europe* or *New Order* established by the triumph of international fascism. Mussert in Holland, Degrelle in Belgium and Doriot and Déat in France are all examples of this fascist collaboration, but in all four cases their dedication to the Nazis was not reciprocated by the Third Reich. Hitler was more interested in Germanic expansion and Aryan domination than in international Fascism, and even when Doriot wore a Nazi uniform to serve in the volunteer legion which French collaborators sent to the Eastern Front, he remained no more than a useful pawn, manipulated by the Germans for their own ends. Whereas most early collaborators hoped for mutual co-operation, Hitler and Goering had no such intentions, and the 'New Europe' of Nazi propaganda and fascist hopes never became a reality (see FASCISM). The populations of the occupied countries were there to be dominated, exploited or even exterminated, a fact which was eminently clear by the middle of 1943, leaving only the most fanatical or desperate collaborators with any sympathy for Nazi Germany.

By 1944 there was widespread disillusionment and resentment among the many would-be partners of Nazism. Even the economic collaborators, industrial and commercial, who had envisaged profits from collaboration, were facing

41

not only the hostility of resisters but also the effects of Nazi exploitation as more and more labour was drafted from the occupied countries into the Reich. Albert Speer, a late promotion to the Nazi hierarchy, tried to reverse this process and establish some form of two-way economic collaboration, but by then the Nazi empire was disintegrating: those in the occupied countries who responded to his vision of European economic integration were no more than an isolated few and had no opportunity to give the hated word 'collaboration' a fresh meaning.

The discrediting of collaboration was paralleled by a steady growth in the stature and status of resistance, which was finally accepted as the only morally defensible position within the occupied countries. Since the war no major re-appraisal of this position has been attempted though some would say that there have been certain abuses of its tradition. In some post-war circles a resistance past was, and still is, a necessary qualification for success and it is therefore not surprising that exaggeration and invention have been employed by some whose qualification would otherwise have been non-existent or at best dubious. The standing of resistance is also threatened by the frequent internal rivalries among resisters themselves, and its record is questioned by a few historians who like to reiterate the fairly obvious point that it was not the resistance but rather the Allied armies who won the war. Nevertheless the history of resistance sur-mounts these minor problems simply because it remains an astonishing fact that so many people from so many different social and political backgrounds should have co-ordinated such effective action against one of the most ruthless and efficient tyrannies of modern times. The very diversity of methods and motivations is testimony to the grass-roots origins of resistance. It was not planned and executed from above; in all the occupied countries it grew from below.

The potential of the resistance movement for disrupting the Nazi war machine was grasped at an early stage by the British who set up a Special Operations Executive (SOE) to promote and support resistance on the continent, co-ordinat-ing its efforts with exiled leaders who, like General de Gaulle, supervised resis-tance from outside. The financial and strategic help given to internal resistance made it possible for small isolated groups to become part of organised secret armies in touch with Allied Command – a link that was vital for their eventual military effectiveness. But not even the SOE, with its agents throughout Europe, could create resistance where the local population was *attentiste* or col-laborationist: its whole strategic operation depended ultimately on the readiness of local people to resist. The history of the resistance movement is therefore a part of the internal history of each country or even more specifically of each region, town or village: it is not just a note in the margin of the history of Allied strategy for defeating Nazi Germany and Imperial Japan.

The diversity of such internal histories makes it very difficult to summarise resistance. French Communist resisters differed from French Radical or Conser-vative resisters, and they differed just as much from fellow Communists in

Yugoslavia. There were also differing degrees of strength and determination among local collaborators, a factor that conditioned many of the aims and methods of resistance, and there was, even more decisively, the variation in Nazi control. Where this was weakest or most tolerant, as in the unoccupied Southern zone of France between 1940 and 1942, resistance was more considered and articulate, publishing clandestine newspapers which could indulge in the luxury of cultural and political discussion. Where it was heaviest, as in Poland, or Czechoslovakia, resistance could only be tightly geared to specific actions of sabotage and subversion.

Yet despite these substantial variations, there were certain goals and methods common to most countries. All operated networks of escape and intelligence, closely controlled and co-ordinated by Allied agents and maintained in the greatest secrecy to avoid penetration by the enemy. The use of radio as the major link between these networks and the Allies meant that the enemy could often pinpoint resistance headquarters quickly and easily by tracing a broadcast to the point of transmission. As a result the life of a wireless operator in occupied Europe was said to average no more than seven weeks. By comparison, resisters who left their homes to form combat groups led a more open and collective life, less subject to infiltration by the agents of the occupying power but naturally more liable to military confrontation and defeat. In either case those captured were invariably executed as spies or terrorists, for all resisters were regarded by both Germans and collaborators as *francs-tireurs,* irregular fighters beyond the protection of the rules of war.

The resisters who were most vigorously denounced and pursued by the German army and collaborators were those who created an alternative society in remote forests and mountains, liberating small areas and using them as bases for guerrilla attacks on enemy convoys, military targets, and any industrial enterprises that served the interests of the occupiers. In France these bands of fighters were known as the *Maquis* (the word means 'scrubland' or 'bush') but elsewhere they were commonly known as *partisans.* To the occupying power they were 'terrorists' 'bandits' or 'outlaws', while to the peasants among whom they moved and from whom they needed food they were often an uncomfortable presence inviting reprisals from the occupying army whose frustration in the pursuit of the elusive guerrillas led to the taking and shooting of increasing numbers of civilian hostages. Pitched battles were rare, for it was in the interests of the *Maquis* and partisans to avoid them, but at different moments the German army launched whole divisions in a vain attempt to eradicate them entirely. This success in engaging large numbers of troops who might otherwise have been deployed against the Allies is at the heart of resisters' claims that they were more than just an occasional irritant. Tito's partisans in Yugoslavia and Soviet partisans behind the German lines in Russia were undoubtedly strategic forces without whom the progress of the Allied and Russian armies would have been considerably slower. Similarly in France, the *Maquis* of the Vercors and the Glières in the South East and the *Corps franc* of the Montagne Noire in the

43

South West are only the best known of the many units which dislocated the German war effort and prepared the country for liberation.

The unity of so many different resisters in the fight against Nazism could not mask the most persistent internal division between those who were Communist (see COMMUNISM SINCE 1917) and those who were not. In Western Europe the split has often been exaggerated, for there were non-Communists even in the most Communist of resistance groupings. But in Central and Eastern Europe, in Yugoslavia and Greece, the divisions were crucial, leading to actual fighting between the opposing factions, supported on one side by Soviet Russia and on the other by the Western Allies. This was particularly tragic in Greece, where an internal civil war followed the liberation, and the same situation was only avoided in Yugoslavia by the effectiveness of Tito in convincing both the Red Army and the Allied Command that his form of Communism was the only practical and popular form of resistance. Eventually the events of the war decided which country fell into which sphere of influence, but the ideological split among resisters meant that there were partisans in Poland who bitterly resented the liberating Russian army just as there were Communist maquisards in France who had not been fighting for the return of a capitalist society.

At the end of the war, resisters exacted human payment from the collaborators through a series of purges and trials at local and national level. The executions which occurred, whether before or after formal conviction, were evidence of the intensity of feeling generated by the clash of these mutually opposed re-acttions to Nazi occupation. Europe had split into those who co-operated in Hitler's war and those who did not, and since Hitler was seen as a synonym for evil on an unprecedented scale, those who collaborated with him could not be judged to have served the interests either of their own country or of humanity in general.

Further reading

H. Michel, *The Second World War*
M. R. D. Foot, *Resistance*
M. R. D. Foot, *S.O.E. in France*
J. Haestrup, *Europe Ablaze*
S. Hawes & R. White (ed.), *Resistance in Europe*
H. R. Kedward, *Resistance in Vichy France*
Robert Paxton, *Vichy France*
Bertram Gordon, *Collaborationism in France during the Second World War*

Communism
since 1917

The word communism signifies a type of society in which property is vested in the community, with each citizen working for the common good according to his or her ability and being rewarded according to his or her needs. This type of society has been an ideal for a very long time. Many small communist communities in the past have been inspired by religious principles and the successors of some *Hutterite* communities still survive in North America. They originated in Anabaptist groups, operate collective farms, keep themselves apart from outside society and educate their children up until the age of fourteen at home. A modern variant is the Israeli kibbutz. During the nineteenth century socialists, notably Robert Owen and Charles Fourier, founded small utopian socialist communities based on rationalist ideas but they did not survive long. The word communism acquired its present meaning in 1848 when Karl Marx and Friedrich Engels, in their *Communist Manifesto,* used it in the same context as socialism (see SOCIALISM). The coming revolutionary victory over capitalism would usher in socialism. During its first or lower stage everyone would work according to his or her abilities for the common good but rewards would be more or less commensurate with the contribution made to the constitution of society; during the second or higher phase, called communism by Marx, Engels and their followers, the production of goods would reach such a pitch that everyone would be rewarded according to his or her needs. The state would have withered away and all instruments of coercion and oppression would have disappeared. Rational behaviour would prevail and the perfectibility of human nature would become possible.

Before 1917 all Marxist parties included the word socialist in their names and the *All-Russian Social Democratic Labour Party* (RSDRP), founded in Minsk in 1898, was no exception. However the RSDRP split at its second Congress in Brussels and London in 1903 into Bolshevik (majoritarian) and Menshevik (minoritarian) factions. The leader of the Bolsheviks was Vladimir Ilich Ulyanov (1870–1924), known as Lenin. The Bolsheviks, in 1912, claimed that they were the true RSDRP and parted from the Mensheviks. The latter, however, did not accept this and by 1917 many party members did not acknowledge the distinction between the two wings of the RSDRP. In order to underline the difference the Bolsheviks referred to themselves as the RSDRP (Bolsheviks) but when Lenin returned to Petrograd in April 1917 from exile in Switzerland he proposed in his 'April Theses' that the name of the party be changed. The new name, the *All-Russian Communist Party (Bolsheviks)* (RCP) was adopted in March

45

1918. Other parties, created in the image of the RCP, such as the Communist Party of Germany (KPD), also bore the word communist. Hence the Soviet state is referred to as being communist, as are all states of the socialist bloc or commonwealth such as Poland, Czechoslovakia and so on. The ruling parties in these countries are also called communist even though in many cases they do not have the word communist in their names, e.g. in Poland the ruling party is the *Polish United Workers' Party* and in the German Democratic Republic it is the *Socialist Unity Party of Germany* (SED). They all acknowledge Marxism-Leninism as the guiding ideology. Non-ruling parties, often taking great care not to use the word communist in their names, are also referred to as communist parties. The doctrines and practices of these parties constitute communism. This is so even though no society has yet reached the higher stage of socialism, communism. The USSR, the *Union of Soviet Socialist Republics,* acknowledges this in its name. Communist states may call themselves people's democracies, democratic republics, people's democratic republics or socialist republics. Originally, beginners were called people's democracies or people's republics. This implied that there was little industry in the state sector and little land collectivised. The East European states, except East Germany, are examples, as is China. The more developed, such as East Germany, became democratic republics. They could become socialist republics by nationalising and planning industry and collectivising agriculture. However while this may be true of Romania, which is a socialist republic, it is not true of Yugoslavia, which although a socialist republic has many private farmers. North Korea called itself the *Korean People's Democratic Republic* from the outset. Nowadays it is rare for new states to call themselves people's republics; *democratic republic* or *people's democratic republic* are more common. Ethiopia refers to itself as Democratic Ethiopia. Vietnam calls itself a socialist republic. However some states not ruled by Marxist-Leninist parties, such as Algeria, are also officially known as people's democratic republics.

'Deviation' is an ideological concept which provides a defence against and permits the banning of undesired theoretical views and political activities. Decisions taken at party Congresses are binding not only on party members but are also guidelines for state functionaries at all levels. Those who oppose Congress or Central Committee plenary decisions are labelled deviationists. There are 'right' deviations – revisionism and social democracy – and 'left' deviations – dogmatism, Maoism, Trotskyism and sectarianism. Roughly speaking, 'right' deviations are insufficiently revolutionary for the party whereas 'left' deviations are too revolutionary. If those involved do not engage in self-criticism they can be expelled from the party and removed from their positions in the party, state, economy and science. Dogmatism is holding on to outmoded patterns of thought instead of engaging in the creative development of Marxism-Leninism. Hence after the Twentieth Party Congress those who defended Stalinist ways, such as the Chinese, were accused of dogmatism. The Chinese countered by referring to the Soviets as revisionists, a term dating back to Eduard Bernstein and German social democracy at the turn of the century (see SOCIALISM). The Chinese used the word revisionism to describe anything they disliked about Khrushchev's policies. Sectarianism is refusing to work with others on the left and opposing united front, popular front or tactical alliances with other political groupings. Molotov was accused of it when he was relieved of his party and government posts in July 1957. The Chinese were often referred to as 'splitters' and 'sectarians'. Those in the Socialist Unity Party of Germany (SED) in the German Democratic Republic who refused to work with ex-Nazis were also labelled sectarians.

Socialism won many followers in Russia during the last thirty years of the nineteenth century but at least until the 1890s it was dominated by populist (see POPULISM) notions which can be traced back to Alexander Herzen. He saw in the Russian peasant commune (*mir*) the embryo of a future socialist society. In this way the capitalist stage of development could be avoided with human endeavour concentrated in co-operatives, long sanctified by Russian tradition. Individual liberty was important to Herzen; indeed he can also be seen as the first Russian Liberal. However the peasants were slow to realise that revolution should be their goal, so some young people went into the villages to show them the way. In other words, political consciousness was to be brought to them from without. It was accepted, however, that social revolution would be achieved by the peasants themselves. Nevertheless some populists did use terror to hasten the process and to undermine the monarchy. The populist movement split over this in 1879, forming radical and moderate wings. Some moderates, such as Georgy V. Plekhanov, moved to Geneva in 1880 but immediately converted to Marxism (see SOCIALISM). The assassination of Tsar Alexander II in March 1881 was a turning point. It failed to destroy the state, indeed it strengthened Tsar Alexander III's resolve to deal severely with revolutionaries.

Plekhanov was the first intellectual leader of Russian Marxism, but he operated exclusively from western Europe. The first Russian Marxist group, the 'Liberation of Labour' Group, was founded by him in 1883, the year in which Karl Marx died in London. Plekhanov, basically an orthodox Marxist in the German tradition, accepted that Russian socialism should be based on the proletariat. He rejected Herzen's belief that Russia was in some way special and placed Russia in the broad European tradition. Plekhanov bitterly attacked his former brethren, the Populists, in a series of books and pamphlets which had an immense impact in the 1880s and 1890s, not least due to their lucidity and style. Capitalism was inevitable in Russia, he told the Populists. The coming revolution would be bourgeois and this would strengthen the working class so that they would be quite capable of moving on to the next stage, socialism. He placed great stress on political organisation, however, and thought not only that a party should be ahead of the proletariat, but that orthodox theoreticians from the intelligentsia should exercise a controlling influence. Plekhanov had been shocked by the tolerant attitude adopted towards revisionism in the German Social Democratic movement (see SOCIALISM) and wanted to prevent this

47

happening in Russia. His ideas were to be further developed by Lenin.

Revolutionary activity was muted in Russia after 1881 but by the time Lenin went up to the University of Kazan in 1887 revolutionary groups were forming. He joined the populist group to which his brother Aleksandr, hanged in May 1887 for attempted regicide, had belonged.

Lenin moved to Geneva in August 1900, but did not share Plekhanov's orthodox views. He had spent the 1890s in Russia, partly in exile in Siberia, and this had a powerful effect on him. While there, in late 1897, he took issue with the 'ekonomisti', or economists, who stressed the advantages which workers could gain from piecemeal improvements. The writings of P. N. Tkachev helped him to formulate his views on political organisation. It would be conspiratorial, since political activity was illegal, rigorously disciplined because of the dangers of infiltrators, and be made up of professional revolutionaries who would dedicate themselves to carrying the message to the population. Study circles could provide a point of entry with workers being drawn in wherever possible. The backwardness of the labour movement in Russia added urgency to Lenin's ideas on organisation and when he moved to western Europe he further refined his thinking in *What is to be Done?* (1902). This was a major contribution to communist theory. He argued that, left to themselves, workers were only capable of developing a 'trade union' consciousness. Hence a professional revolutionary organisation was necessary to stimulate and mould the masses and raise the level of their political consciousness. This implied that political consciousness could be brought to them exogenously, from without, by their intellectual leaders. A party of full-time, dedicated revolutionaries, disciplined and run from the centre, was urgently needed.

After his return to Petrograd in April 1917 Lenin radically changed the direction of the Bolshevik party. His analysis of the February revolution which had placed the bourgeoisie in power led him to the conclusion that the bourgeoisie was not really ruling since it did not control the two pillars of a capitalist state, the army and the police. Hence, to Lenin, the bourgeois stage of the revolution which had begun in February could be cut short. Indeed the working class and the poorer strata of the peasantry could seize power and then begin the construction of socialism. Just as Lenin's views were approaching those of Leon Trotsky on permanent revolution, so Trotsky came to accept Lenin's thinking on party organisation. Trotsky joined the Bolsheviks in the summer of 1917 and he and Lenin became the central figures in the Bolshevik seizure of power in October 1917. Some Bolsheviks, such as Kamenev and Zinoviev, were appalled at Lenin's telescoping of the two revolutions, as were the moderate socialists, the Social Revolutionaries (SRs) and Mensheviks. Lenin proclaimed 'all power to the Soviets' – this mass organisation would be the vehicle which would carry the Bolsheviks to power. Whereas the moderate socialists regarded the soviets as popular organs which would cede most of their power to governmental organs after the Constituent Assembly (the new parliament) had established a new administration, leaving the soviets or councils with mainly supervisory functions, the Bolsheviks treated them as institutions which afforded the creative, dynamic energies of the masses full play. Lenin's views on the soviets constitute an original contribution to Marxism. The failure of the Provisional Government to end the war, alleviate the economic suffering or sanction the seizure of the landed estates radicalised the population. Lenin rose to the occasion and offered the masses everything they wanted: land to the peasants, an end to the war, workers' control in the factories and self determination for the nationalities. The concept of national self-determinaion is another of Lenin's additions to Marxism. He argued that non–Russians, after the revolution, should be allowed to decide whether they wished to join the new Soviet state or establish their own independent state. Despite being vehemently opposed by Bolsheviks such as Pyatakov, Lenin's views prevailed.

The Bolsheviks seized power in Petrograd on 25 October/7 November 1917 through the agency of the Military Revolutionary Committee of the Petrograd Soviet. The whole operation was masterminded by Trotsky. They then handed it to the Second Congress of Soviets, then in session in the capital, and in which the Bolsheviks had a majority. Hence the October Revolution was a Soviet Revolution, favoured by the majority of the population. Two key bodies were set up by the Congress, the *All-Russian Central Executive Committee,* the supreme legislative organ, and the *Council of People's Commissars, Sovnarkom.* The latter, headed by Lenin as Prime Minister, was composed entirely of Bolsheviks, although Lenin had tried to get a few left SRs to join. The All-Russian Central Executive Committee had a Bolshevik majority. Hence, within a very short time, the Bolsheviks had begun to institutionalise their power. All this was against popular expectations. The masses had made the revolution to place power in the hands of the soviets at all levels. Lenin wished the dictatorship of the proletariat to be effective after the revolution, but this was opposed by part of the working class. The Mensheviks and right SRs favoured a broadly-based socialist coalition government. Lenin's views on the economy were out of step with the aspirations of the workers. He and Trotsky were strongly in favour of state capitalism, or allowing owners to retain their factories with the workers supervising production. The workers wanted to run the factories themselves and understood workers' control to mean just that. These views were strongly supported by the 'left' communists, spearheaded by Bukharin, in the Central Committee of the party. He favoured the construction of a socialist economy immediately after the revolution. It was only with the large-scale nationalisation of industry in June 1918 that the hopes of labour were fulfilled. However, the onset of war communism, which ran from June 1918 to March 1921, destroyed their hopes of running the economy through the trade unions.

The world-wide socialist revolution, held to be indispensable if the Russian Revolution were to survive, did not occur. Soviet Russia had to battle along on its own and rely on its own limited resources. The question of concluding peace with Imperial Germany tore the party apart. In the end, Lenin was able to convince Trotsky that it was regrettable but necessary, and his vote broke the deadlock in the leader's favour. The Treaty of Brest-Litovsk was signed in March 1918. The 'left' communists were unrepentant, however. They wanted a revolutionary war, and the left SRs, who had joined Sovnarkom in December 1917 to form the only coalition government the Soviet Union has ever had, left and began to engage in armed violence. An SR murdered the German ambassador in an attempt to rekindle the war, and during the summer there were several SR uprisings. In August 1918 Fanya Kaplan, an SR, almost assassinated Lenin. A peasant revolt on the Volga in June 1918 led to the introduction of 'Red Terror' to counter 'White Terror'. The Bolshevik support base shrank and shrank. To the Civil War, which began in May 1918, was added intervention by the main world powers after the end of hostilities in the west. Dire necessity forced the emergence of the Red Army, brilliantly led by Trotsky. Under 'war communism' money ceased to have much value, so the peasants were unwilling to part with the surpluses as there were few goods to be had in exchange. Procurement squads of armed workers descended on the countryside, extracting the surplus and more besides. The Bolsheviks advised the peasants that they had a choice: support them and keep their land, or support the Whites and bring back the landlord. Industry was also in turmoil as hunger and disease spread; the cities emptied and the working class dwindled. So desperate was the situation that Lenin supported measures, adopted at the Ninth Party Congress in April 1920, that reduced the role of labour in decision making: the use of non-communist specialists, one-man management in industry and the filling of party and trade union bodies from above and not by election from below. Fortunately for the Bolsheviks, November 1920 saw victory in the Civil War and an end to intervention. The country was at bursting point, and four events in early 1921 left an indelible mark on the future shape of Soviet Russia: the peasant revolt at Tambov on the Volga, the mutiny of the sailors at the naval base of Kronstadt – both ruthlessly suppresssed; the Tenth Party Congress and the introduction of the *New Economic Policy* (NEP). Kronstadt demonstrated that democracy took second place to the retention of power by the communist party. The Kronstadt revolt is held in high esteem by anarchists (see ANARCHISM) and other ultra-leftists who stress the democratic nature of the rebel's aims. The Tenth Congress banned factionalism, which meant that there was less debate within the party and that the decisions of the top leadership became even more important.

Trotsky, in negotiating with the Germans at Brest-Litovsk, acted as if he were the spokesman of the international proletariat. The interests of Soviet Russia were not of paramount importance to him, as it was only a transitory phenomenon. This touched on the basic problem for the Bolsheviks: was Soviet Russia a revolutionary base of a state? The 'left' communists viewed it as the former, but Lenin was inclined to see it as the latter. When the Bolsheviks discovered that the British Labour Party had proposed an international socialist conference, they prepared frantically to upstage the event. The founding congress of the Third International (see SOCIALISM), the *Communist International* or

Comintern, took place in Moscow in March 1919. There were only thirty five delegates present. The Second Congress, which was much more representative with delegates from forty one countries attending, convened in Petrograd in July 1920 and then moved to Moscow. Lenin's twenty one conditions for admission were adopted at the Congress and underlined Soviet domination. Sympathisers were to break away from socialist parties and form their own parties which were to be called communist parties. Unrelenting opposition to social democracy was demanded. The new parties were to be strictly disciplined according to the precepts of 'democratic centralism', the guiding principle of the Bolshevik party; they were to create a centralised press, to carry through periodic purges and to conduct systematic propaganda in the armed forces and among workers and peasants. A primary task was to support Soviet Russia and all Soviet republics which came into existence. Decisions of the International and of its executive committee were binding, and a breach of discipline could lead to expulsion.

World revolution did not materialise, despite the fact that soviet republics had been set up in Hungary and Bavaria and prospects in Germany had appeared rosy until they were finally dispelled in 1923. The Bolsheviks were taken aback by the eagerness of non-Russians to break their ties with the new Russia. Poland, Finland, Estonia, Latvia, Lithuania, the Ukraine and Georgia – which had elected a Menshevik government – all slipped outside the 'republic of soviets'. This was national self-determination in action. The Ukraine was brought back into the fold after the Germans had left. The failure of the offensive in Poland in August 1920 was a turning point. Lenin had expected that the Polish workers would see the Red Army as liberators, but the Poles merely regarded them as invaders. The Polish experience, however, did convince Lenin that his policy of national self-determination was correct.

The revolution in the East was also disappointing. The *Congress of the Peoples of the East* in Baku in September 1920 revealed to the Bolsheviks that, if revolution came in the East, it would be informed by hostility to the western colonial powers and not based on class solidarity with the Russian workers and peasants. They drew back and concentrated on promoting revolution based on the Marxist principle of class struggle.

G. V. Chicherin, who took over from Trotsky as People's Commissar for Foreign Affairs in March 1918, had a more orthodox view of Soviet interests. The commissariat began to play a more important role in 1920 and to act independently of the Comintern. Many treaties with states bordering Soviet Russia were signed in 1920-21.

The party rank and file never accepted the New Economic Policy (NEP). It had restored capitalism by transforming grain requisitions into a tax in kind, later expressed in money terms, and this permitted the peasant to dispose of his surplus as he thought fit, thus legitimising commerce once again. A multitude of small industrial concerns fell into private hands, but the nationalisation of the banks and the state monopoly of foreign trade remained. Lenin gave the

51

impression that NEP would last rather a long time, and was to give the Soviet state a breathing space during which it could recover its strength. Lenin presented the NEP package to the Third Comintern Congress in June-July 1921. Soviet Russia needed to trade with the capitalist world and to grant concessions to foreign industrialists and businessmen. This implied a halt to revolutionary activity abroad. Correspondingly, in December 1921, the Comintern changed course: communists were to join Social Democrats and form a unified trade union movement. A united front with all Progressives was another goal.

When Stalin became Secretary General of the party in April 1922, he was not seen as Lenin's successor. After Lenin's death in 1924, Stalin saw Trotsky as his main rival and it would appear that this influenced his thinking on policy. Trotsky believed that socialism could not be built without the aid of a world revolution, and therefore placed great emphasis on the activities of revolutionary parties abroad. Stalin, on the other hand, developed the concept of 'socialism in one country' during the autumn of 1924, a doctrine he had borrowed from Bukharin. Stalin supported the view that a 'complete socialist society' could be built in the USSR but conceded that the 'final victory of socialism' would have to wait until world revolution. Trotsky, Kamenev and Zinoviev joined forces to oppose Stalin on this issue in 1925-27. They were referred to as the 'united' or 'left' opposition. (The constitution of 1936 formally brought the debate to an end by stating that the Soviet Union was a socialist state.) They also favoured higher roles of industrial growth and a squeeze on the peasants. Bukharin was an important ally of Stalin at this time. He thought that the necessary capital would come from an increasingly prosperous agriculture. The left opposition was defeated in December 1927 and Trotsky was exiled to Alma Ata in January 1928, deported to Turkey in 1929 and finally murdered in Mexico in 1940. Stalin changed course and stole the clothes of the left opposition. This gave rise to a 'right opposition', composed of Bukharin, Rykov and Tomsky. They were soon swept aside, and the First *Five Year Plan* got under way in October 1928. Plan goals rose relentlessly, however, and collectivisation was stepped up. Trotsky abroad became a focal point of opposition to Stalin both inside and outside the USSR. He never became an effective political opponent of the Soviet dictator, however. Trotskyism is the political current which derives from Trotsky's analysis of Soviet society. He attacked the 'bureaucratic degeneration of the Soviet system' and the construction of socialism in one country. He deplored the unbridled dictatorship of a communist leadership which 'had lost contact with the masses'. He underlined especially the significance of proletarian internationalism for his theory of permanent revolution. The Fourth 'Trotskyite' International was set up in 1938, and today has sections in over fifty countries. It regards itself as the heir of Lenin and Trotsky and favours the rule of soviets and workers' self-management in industry. Stalin labelled Trotskyites 'agents of fascism' (see FASCISM), 'pseudo-revolutionaries' and 'dogged enemies of socialism and progress', among other things.

The onset of the Depression in 1929 in the West led to social democratic leaderships being labelled 'social fascist and rabid enemies of the proletariat'. This applied especially to Germany, where National Socialism was seen as capitalism in its death throes. Hence the main enemy was not Fascism, but Social Democracy (see SOCIALISM), which was seen as the ally of capitalism. The term 'social fascist' implies that Social Democracy, by aiding Fascism, reaped material rewards for its 'treachery'. The view that social democracy represented 'social fascism' held until the Eighth Comintern Congress in 1935, when it had become clear that National Socialism was not a transitory phenomenon. The Congress called for united action by communists and social democrats to stem the flood of fascism, and so the concept of the *Popular Front* came into being. A Popular Front government, headed by the socialist Leon Blum, came to power in France in June 1936, but it resigned in June 1937. Blum also led a Popular Front government which held office for about a month in 1938.

The signing of a ten-year non-aggression pact by the Soviet Union and Germany, in August 1939, led to another change in Comintern policy. Opposition to Fascism was dropped and communist parties everywhere were required, until the German attack on the Soviet Union on 22 June 1941, to oppose the Allied war effort and to describe National Socialism as the 'lesser evil'. This led to the French Communist Party, to quote one instance, being banned. The policies of the individual communist parties were regulated according to the interests of the Soviet Union.

Forced collectivisation and industrialisation led to the emergence of a new intelligentsia, linked to the goals of the Five Year Plans, the re-emergence of hierarchy, uniforms and a renewed emphasis on the family. Rigorous labour discipline, show trials, purges, the rise in influence of the political police and the downgrading of the party are all part and parcel of Stalinism. The party lost its overall guiding role: this passed to Stalin, who became the universal genius and 'father of the people', possessing the monopoly of wisdom and whose thoughts could inspire great ideas. Doctrinally, Stalin developed the concept of 'socialism in one country', and also the notion of revolution from above when he described the expropriation of kulaks (rich peasants, but in reality anyone who opposed collectivisation) as having being accomplished from above, on the initiative of the state. As the Soviet Union approached socialism, so the class struggle became 'fiercer' than ever before since opposition elements were held to increase their opposition as their power bases dissolved. Hence the class struggle was at a higher level of intensity just before the advent of socialism than at any point during the dictatorship of the proletariat. A strong state was thus essential to overcome hostile class elements. The advent of socialism ended this state of affairs. Classes – the working class and the collective farm peasantry, together with the intelligentsia, viewed as a stratum – continued to exist under socialism as from 1936, but were defined as 'non-antagonistic'; the state under socialism also changed and promoted the interests of all, but as long as hostile, capitalist states remained it had to remain mighty in order to protect socialism during the transition to communism. There was also a discernible rise in Russian nationalism, and native intelligentsias throughout the country suffered grievously. Although himself a Georgian, Stalin promoted the Russians as the leading nation of the USSR. Cultural standards dropped and in non-Russian areas the slogan 'national in form, socialist in content' often meant little more than translation of what was said about Stalin and the state into the local language.

It was not necessary to impose Stalinism entirely from above, as there was much support for it from below. Many were eager to make a career for themselves, and quickly destroyed the old élites who stood in their way. This was nowhere more true than in the writing of history. Ambitious young communists attacked existing interpretations and attempted to catch the heroics of the Soviet era in prose. Party-mindedness (*partiinost*) or commitment to the party point of view was imperative. Bourgeois objectivism, or the view that writing, in order to be scientific, had to be free of value judgements, was rejected out of hand. Such writing, in communist eyes, was merely a mask to hide the class content of bourgeois ideology and the denigration of socialism.

The Stalin cult began in earnest in 1929. It gradually superceded the Lenin cult, which had developed during the 1920s when the focus of ideological legitimacy became the first Bolshevik leader. Stalin became the 'Lenin of today' and together with the personalisation of the ideology came the simplification and codification of Marxism-Leninism. This was a response to the modest level of culture of the average party member. The Stalin cult and the Stalin Marxist-Leninist code eliminated other voices, and critical or 'creative' Marxism became officially unacceptable. From being in the 1920s a body of doctrine about which there could be conflicting views, it became much more rigid during the 1930s. The touchstone became Stalin's point of view. One expression for this was the *History of the Communist Party of the Soviet Union (Bolsheviks)*, first published in 1938.

The murder of Sergei Kirov on 1 December 1934 removed the last credible alternative to Stalin, and Stalinism solidified in the late 1930s. There was great enthusiasm in the beginning, except in the countryside, for the industrial goals set for the country, but it waned in the early 1930s. Since socialism had proved victorious in the USSR, the core of opposition to it could not be inside the country. It had to emanate from abroad. Hence during the show trials, the name of Trotsky was frequently dragged in. The trials appeared to reveal the existence of a conspiracy against Soviet socialism, but in the 1950s it was admitted that most of the evidence had been fabricated and many innocents executed.

The communist party played an important part in ensuring victory during the Great Fatherland War (1941–45), but at the expense of playing down ideology and stressing nationalism and patriotism. There was a great influx of new members, many of them recruited on the battlefield, and this meant that their grasp of Marxism-Leninism was not very strong. The party began to reimpose its authority and to return to Stalinist orthodoxy from 1943 onwards, but many party members and the population at large expected a loosening of the reins after the war. They wanted to relax after their Herculean labours, and to enjoy a higher standard of living. The evolution of the party was affected sharply by the onset of the Cold War. The major problem, after hostilities had ceased, was what policy to adopt towards the United States. Stalin revealed in 1945 that he had three main options: co-operation; isolation; and aggressive foreign communist party activity to undermine capitalism worldwide, but always stopping short of provoking a war with the United States. Stalin chose co-operation until the autumn of 1947. The goals of his policy were: to attract US capital to aid post-war Soviet reconstruction; the establishment of a Soviet sphere of influence in Eastern Europe; the stabilisation of Western Europe within the capitalist system; the blocking of the advance of US capital in China by a tactical alliance of the communist party and the Kuomintang; and to ensure that if Germany and Austria did not go socialist, they would not be integrated in an American-dominated, capitalist world economy either. This policy of studied co-operation was expected to bring tangible rewards, reparations and US credits. The party had to be able to cope with the new situation, and a vigorous programme of ideological training was introduced. This may be called the reimposition of othodoxy, but it consisted mainly of Stalin's version of party history and his interpretation of Leninism. The upper levels of the party received a boost in December 1945, when the Politburo began to meet fortnightly. Then, in March 1946, the Central Committee elected a new Politburo, Secretariat and Orgburo. All this did not mean that the communist party had taken over the country: Stalin was still in control, and he ensured that the political police kept the party and government in place. Had the majority of party members had their way, there would have been a great flowering of Marxist-Leninist thought after the war, but Stalin appears to have feared that such a movement could escape his control and so he stifled it. Stalin's speech on 9 February 1946 in the Bolshoi Theatre in Moscow signalled the way ahead for the Soviet population. He praised industrialisation and collectivisation and the social system which had emerged. The way ahead was to be hard, and up to three Five Year Plans would be needed to build the economic base the Soviet state needed to make it strong enough to resist any aggressor. This analysis revealed that Stalin had come to the conclusion that the Soviet Union should do without American credits. The USSR would have to reconstruct her shattered economy using her own resources and aided only by reparations. In order to galvanise the population to undertake the onerous tasks spelled out by Stalin, a campaign associated with the name of Andrei Zhdanov was launched in 1946. The new orthodoxy involved xenophobia, anti-intellectualism and strident Great Russian nationalism. The party set out to impose its authority on science and culture – indeed, on all intellectual activities. Zhdanov, who had spent the war years in beleagured Leningrad, launched the campaign by pillorying two literary journals. One journal was stated to be 'permeated with a spirit of servility towards everything foreign'. He followed this up by attacking literature and art in general. He made it clear that the party would not tolerate 'kowtowing to the West'. The offensive was then continued by attacking the theatre and the cinema. Comparative literature was castigated for teaching that the great Russian writers had been influenced by foreign ideas. Music, especially opera, was taken to task. Philosophy was abused because it was not sufficiently critical of non-Marxist thought. The period from 1946 to August 1948 when Zhdanov died is known as the *Zhdanovshchina,* the Zhdanov times. Although the situation eased slightly after Zhdanov's death, life still remained difficult for the creative intelligentsia as long as Stalin lived.

In the world of science the man who played the role of Zhadnov was T. D. Lysenko. At best an enthusiastic amateur, at worst a nefarious charlatan; he fathered the pseudo-science of agrobiology. His activities ranged from plant physiology to animal husbandry and his success lay in his ability to elicit party, and especially Stalin's, support. He promised greater improvements in agriculture than the real scientists but, since he enjoyed party support, it was difficult to dislodge him. He championed the views of Vilyams (d. 1939) on grassland management and won party acceptance for them in 1948. They were then imposed nationally, to the discomfiture of Vilyams's opponents and especially those who favoured the use of mineral fertilisers in raising yields. Lysenko was finally toppled in 1965. Another science which suffered was genetics: indeed Mendelian genetics were banned. Relativity theory and quantum mechanics were also treated as pseudo-sciences.

When the US administration invited the Soviet Union and Eastern Europe to participate in the Marshall Plan, Stalin and his advisers were in a quandary. If they accepted, they ran the risk of US capitalism acquiring influence over the Soviet, as well as the other, economies of the region. If they rejected the offer their economic development would be slower. Stalin decided to turn down the American offer since he placed security ahead of economic advantage. This pessimistic reading of Soviet-US relations had a profound effect on ideology. The Soviets turned their backs on the Marshall Plan in July 1947, but it took them two months to arrive at a counter strategy. During the summer of 1947 the Western European communist parties were left to reach their own conclusions. The French communists were in favour of accepting Marshall Plan aid as late as September 1947, just before the founding congress of the Communist Information Bureau *(Cominform).* At the congress Andrei Zhdanov spoke for Stalin. He divided the world into two hostile camps: the imperialist, led by the United States, and the socialist, led by the Soviet Union, with countries such as India and Indonesia outside. The era of co-operation with the United States was clearly over, but at an international level the USSR still stated that it wished to come to a mutually beneficial arrangement with the United States. The French and Italian communist parties were castigated at the congress for lack of revolutionary commitment and opportunism. This was rather hard on them, since it had been Kremlin policy that they enter post-war coalition governments – this now became opportunism. They were ordered to adopt very militant tactics and, in stoking up social unrest, frightened away all but the hardcore support.

Until his death in August 1948 Zhdanov was, probably, Stalin's most influential adviser. He devised many opportunities for the expansion of Soviet influence after 1945 and consistently advocated an active, aggressive approach. Malenkov was Zhdanov's main critic and favoured a more cautious approach. The latter's death permitted Malenkov to become Stalin's key adviser, and he exacted revenge on the Zhdanovites in the 'Leningrad Affair' in 1949. Many top party and government officials in Leningrad and Moscow perished, and after 1955 Malenkov was accused of fabricating damning evidence.

The whole episode is typical of high Stalinism, when Stalin's associates fought for influence over the ageing dictator. The most effective way of routing an opponent was to accuse him of anti-Marxist or anti-Leninist views. An example of this took place in 1950 when Khrushchev propagated *agrogoroda* or agro-towns. Peasants were to be moved from several villages into a large town with modern amenities. *Pravda* printed the proposal, but it was withdrawn the following day. Someone, probably Malenkov, had convinced Stalin that the project was not ideologically sound. Khrushchev conceded in the Moscow evening newspaper that it was un-Marxist, a very dangerous admission under Stalin. Fierce infighting was typical of high Stalinism and one is left with the impression that ideology was mainly shaped by tactical considerations.

Enormous attention was paid during the Stalin era to the correct formulation of Marxist-Leninist thought. It had to reflect experience since it was conceived of as dynamic, just like life. Hence, at any one time, it was very difficult to define precisely. One can argue that Stalin took Marxism-Leninism very seriously, since he hoped to see the new Soviet man and woman emerging from the state-controlled environment. It was expected that social character would be formed mainly through the medium of language. If the state were to discover the 'objective scientific laws' of the language conditioning process, then *homo sovieticus* would emerge. These laws were never discovered, however.

When Stalin died in March 1953, his successors feared that another dictator would emerge and sought to prevent this. Malenkov appeared as the natural successor, supported by Beria, the head of the political police. One difficulty that faced Malenkov was that it was not clear whether the party or the government was the vehicle of power. Stalin had died as Prime Minister but Malenkov, assuming his mantle, did not inherit his power. The policies he adopted to strengthen his position are known as the New Course. Whereas Stalin had concentrated on heavy industry, Malenkov promised to raise living standards by switching some resources from heavy to light industry. Agriculture was provided with more machinery and mineral fertilisers. Khrushchev, using the party secretariat as his base, attacked these policies as un-Leninist and un-Stalinist. He countered by defending the primacy of heavy industry and argued that living standards could be improved by expanding the sown area; he favoured the ploughing up of the virgin lands. His industrial policy was conservative and orthodox, his agricultural policy extensive and innovative. Malenkov, on the other hand, favoured an intensive agricultural policy – greater output from the same cropped area. During the campaign against Malenkov, Khrushchev presented himself as the defender of Marxist-Leninist orthodoxy and Malenkov as the revisionist. A major factor in the struggle was that both regarded the subordination of the political police to the party and government to be of paramount importance. This was secured after Beria was executed, probably in December 1953. The delegitimation of terror was achieved in 1955 when Molotov was obliged by Khrushchev to admit that socialism had been built in the USSR. Since the country was now building communism, terror could no longer be justified by using class criteria. Stalin, of course, had claimed that socialism had been built in 1936 but, given a hostile, capitalist world, coercion against the state's enemies was necessary. The adoption of peaceful coexistence under Khrushchev did away with this argument. At the Twenty-first Party Congress in 1959 Khrushchev claimed the 'final and complete' victory of socialism. He thus proclaimed the end of capitalist encirclement and class-based oppositional political crime. This effectively repudiated Stalin's 'revolution from above'.

The conflict between Malenkov and Khrushchev was a landmark in another way. It gave rise to the first genuine policy debate, apart from the discussion on interest in 1948, since the late 1920s. The debate reached down to the local party level. There was no preordained way of deciding which protagonist would win, and neither could use the political police to stifle the opposition. If national popularity had been the main criterion, Malenkov would have won, but Khrushchev proved himself a more skilled political tactician. He secured the support of the heavy industry lobby and of the military. He had the party apparatus behind him as Malenkov attempted to strengthen the government at the expense of the party bureaucracy. The ideological differences between Malenkov and Khrushchev were more apparent than real. Khrushchev was later to adopt practically all of Malenkov's ideas.

Khrushchev's most dramatic rewriting of Marxism-Leninism took place at the Twentieth Party Congress in 1956. He denounced Stalin and admitted that the 'cult of the personality' had grievously harmed the party and the nation. Since Stalin had failed to integrate the role of the individual leader in history, he could be toppled without overthrowing Marxism-Leninism. The ideology was to be based on Leninist norms, as it had been before Stalin's malfeasance had begun. Khrushchev was careful not to question industrialisation and collectivisation, the twin pillars of Stalin's economic policy. De-Stalinisation was not intended to diminish party control, merely to rid it of its Stalinist excrescences and thereby to strengthen it. Khrushchev was attempting to break the psychological hold Stalin still had over the Soviet population so that their creative potential could be released.

Khrushchev's most serious confrontation with his opponents took place in 1957 when he defeated the 'Anti-Party Group', so called because it opposed the party running the economy and the state. Molotov was the guiding spirit and he had taken umbrage at Khrushchev's meddling in foreign affairs, especially his visits to China and Yugoslavia. He and the other critics wanted a much more orthodox Stalinist economic policy – they opposed the *sovnarkhozy* (economic councils) – and they favoured less investment in agriculture. Although he was heavily outnumbered in the Politburo, he outmanoeuvred them with the help of the secretariat. He was a revisionist, but, since he was a superb tactician, his revisionism became orthodoxy. Like Stalin, Khrushchev took ideology seriously, but he was wont to confuse Marxist-Leninist thought and his own voluntarism: in other words ideology was manipulated to suit Khrushchev's needs and desires of the momemt. An example of this was in 1961 when a new party programme was launched, promising that Soviet citizens would be living under communism in the 1980s. The driving force behind the 'leap into communism' appears to have been the Chinese claim that they would reach communism ahead of the Soviets. The Communist Party of the Soviet Union (CPSU), previously the vanguard of the proletariat, became the party of the whole people. The state – it was now the all-people's state – would begin to wither away as voluntary organisations took over more and more functions at the local level. Lack of economic success began to raise doubts about Khrushchev's prognostications of communisn in the 1980s. In his frustration at poor results, Khrushchev introduced reform after reform, including the bifurcation of the party in 1962 into industrial and non-industrial wings. His main legacy when he was removed in 1964 was that he had restored the primacy of the party in the state. *Pravda* accused him of 'hare-brained' schemes and of ignoring the results of science and experience. Under his guidance, Marxism-Leninism became very malleable and was employed to mobilise the population. To be effective, it had to hold out the hope of a better tomorrow. Whereas Stalin concerned himself with the here and now, Khrushchev was willing to peer into the future. He was full of boundless enthusiasm and optimism and this permeated his interpretation of Marxism-Leninism. It is fair to say that he had a very inadequate grasp of fundamental Marxism. He was unable to think through any ideological problem, and so Marxism-Leninism during his years in office tended to be confused and confusing but, nevertheless, innovative. Some of this survived him.

If the Khrushchev period saw a 'leap into communism', the Brezhnev era was characterised by 'mature, developed socialism'.

Full communism in the Soviet Union was conceived as evolving through three phases: i) a transitional phase ending in the victory of socialism; ii) a phase which begins with the construction of the bases of socialism and leads to the appearance of a developed socialist society; and iii) a phase of developed socialism which grows into full communism. Developed socialism can be found in the first or lower phase of communism, and contains classes and other social differences. The second, or higher, phase of communism emerges from developed socialism, although this will be a 'long, gradual process' and will be related to economic growth.

The key elements of developed socialism are: the further expansion of the material-technical base of socialism in the form of contemporary, major, socialised production; electrification of the whole country and the extension of automation to the whole economy and in distribution and exchange as well as production; the gradual creation of an optimal branch structure in the economy; the socio-political and ideological unity of all social groups and nations; the transformation of a state of the dictatorship of the proletariat into an all-people's state; the raising of the cultural level of the whole population, and the gradual elimination of discrepancies between town and country and between mental and physical labour; the emergence of a common, socialist way of life and social consciousness. These elements would come into existence over a protracted period, but not simultaneously.

Class structure under developed socialism would diminish in significance but social structure – professional role, the type of housing and level of consumption – would grow more complex, only attaining homogeneity under full communism. Social structure would become more complex in the short run due to the demands of the scientific-technical revolution. The intelligentsia would expand rapidly under developed socialism, and this stratum would dominate social and economic planning. The party's role was to increase during the whole period of developed socialism. This was due to the need to provide overall guidance of economic and social development. The party would evolve into a party of the whole people, and it would continue to exist long after the state had withered away. Nevertheless, under developed socialism the party was to retain its 'class essence' as the party of the working class. Despite the new name, the policy of restricting recruitment to a small proportion of the population would continue.

The state of the whole people passed from the scene with Khrushchev but was resurrected as an important part of developed socialism. Under Brezhnev emphasis swung from the transient nature of the state of the whole people to underlining its significance and role during the whole period of developed socialism. The growing significance of the state was linked to the construction of the material base of communism which involved the state playing an increasingly active role in planning and in the direction of economic and social development. Democracy, especially at the local soviet level, was stressed, but unlike the Khrushchev period, the development of public self-administration was very slow.

During the late 1970s and early 1980s the dominant theme of the current stage was declared to be the further perfection (*sovershenstvovanie*) of socialist institutions and not the transformation of socialist into communist relations. This makes clear that the possibilities of progress during the first phase of communism are 'far from exhausted'. The laws which govern change at present are still those peculiar to socialism.

Leninism can be seen as primarily a revolutionary strategy and Stalinism as forced modernisation of a backward country. The structures which evolved fitted the vast, multi-national Soviet Union but were found wanting elsewhere. The founding of the *Cominform* in September 1947 was the signal for all communist parties to imitate closely the CPSU, and this involved the subordination of the regions to Moscow. Yugoslavia refused, and this led to the expulsion of the Communist Party of Yugoslavia from the Cominform in June 1948. Stalin thought that he could overthrow Josip Broz Tito and ensure the election of a Yugoslav party leadership which would follow his lead. He miscalculated, and *Titoism* was born. Titoism and Yugoslav communism are synonymous and stand for the equality of all communist parties and states – this involves the recognition of the notion that there are separate roads to socialism and communism; the dismantling of the centralised bureaucratic planning system and its replacement by workers' self-management; decollectivisation, if the peasants so wish; the party ceases to dictate to society and its chief role is to educate and inspire the people on the road to communism; the state has already begun to wither away; socialist realism and *partiinost* are no longer the guiding principles of art and literature. In foreign policy Yugoslavia refuses to side with either the USA or the USSR and is unaligned; it is also dedicated to the struggle against national chauvinism. Khrushchev came to Yugoslavia in 1955 to heal the breach, but this was only achieved after the denunciation of Stalin in 1956. Khrushchev then spoke of peaceful coexistence being the dominant force of Soviet foreign policy; Yugoslavia practised active coexistence. Socialist legality was stressed in the USSR and was welcomed by Tito. From the orthodox Soviet point of view, Titoism was revisionism, and the conservative element in the Soviet leadership opposed the rapprochement with Tito. Khrushchev's anti-Stalin speech opened the floodgates of criticism of Stalin's handling of the world communist movement. Togliatti, the Italian leader, spoke of polycentrism and maintained that it was no longer obligatory to follow the Soviet model: national considerations had to be given their due weight. Most Western European parties called for a more penetrating analysis of the circumstances which had permitted Stalinism to flourish in the Soviet Union. Lukacs, the Hungarian philosopher, advocated humane socialism and a dialogue with opponents of Marxism-Leninism. Havemann, in the German Democratic Republic, wanted a free ranging debate about the mistakes committed and the type of society desired, and in Poland voices were critical of the subordination of the party to Moscow and the degeneration of the Polish party under Stalin. In Hungary, Imre Nagy, Prime Minister between 1953 and 1955, tried to introduce wide-ranging reforms but was unsuccessful. After his dismissal he continued to avocate a socialism which was strictly based on socialist legality, and warned against personal dictatorship buttressed by control of the instruments of coercion. The Petöfi circle was active in spreading reformist ideas. The Polish October and the Hungarian revolution saw a return to orthodoxy – in the latter case by the use of Soviet military might. Economic problems, however, could not be solved by force. In the German Democratic Republic economists such as Behrens and Benary advocated fundamental reforms of the centrally planned economy inherited from the USSR. Their market socialist ideas were rejected but, in 1963, Ulbricht, the party leader, was prepared to adopt some of them. The relationship between the Soviet and Yugoslav parties was never easy and the new Yugoslav party programme of 1958 caused considerable friction. The Soviets attacked revisionism and national communism with the Yugoslavs in mind. The Soviet party programme of 1961, which looked forward to communism, was welcomed in Belgrade, but the advent of developed socialism under Brezhnev cooled the atmosphere. Economic failure played a major role in unseating Novotny in Czechoslovakia and his successor, Dubcek, presided over the 'Prague Spring' of 1968 when 'socialism with a human face' was in vogue. This development was an indirect result of the 1961 party programme, with its stress on economic growth (hence the need for economic reform) and development of social self-government inherent in the theory of the 'state of the whole people'. The Czechoslovak goal was to replace party dictatorship by socialist democracy while holding on to the achievements of socialism – in other words, socialism by consent, not coercion. Brezhnev and his associates decided in August that the Czechoslovak party had lost control and so the Warsaw Pact invaded. This underlined the fact that socialist states, apart from the Soviet Union, enjoy limited sovereignty. Moscow arrogated to itself the right to intervene if it considered that socialist orthodoxy was in danger. Romania and Yugoslavia condemned the invasion and refused to recognise the Brezhnev doctrine of limited sovereignty. Various reform ideas surfaced in the 1970s, the most cogent being from Rudolf Bahro in the GDR. He condemned 'politbureaucracy' and advocated the abolition of the planned economy and bureaucratic party apparatus and a return to Marx's free association. Bahro was imprisoned and later moved to West Germany. 'Real, existing socialism' continued to dominate the GDR and indeed all Warsaw Pact states. This is doctrinally indistinguishable from developed socialism but includes the belief that the Soviet Union is ahead on the road to communism. The greatest threat to a ruling party since 1968 appeared in Poland in August 1980. Again, the source was economic failure and a free trade union, *Solidarity*, became a centre of legitimacy in the state along with the Roman Catholic Church. A 'state of war' was declared in December 1981, underlining the gulf which existed between the working class and the Polish United Workers' Party.

In Asia, the 'great thought of Mao Zedong', Maoism, is based on the revolutionary potential of the peasantry – 'the village is the revolutionary base'. Proletarian consciousness is breathed into the peasantry and they can then achieve revolution. Given the fact that there was practically no Chinese proletariat before the revolution, Mao's stress on the rural dweller is understandable. Another aspect of prime significance in Maoism is the military – 'power comes from the barrel of a gun'. Until the mid 1950's Mao was an orthodox Stalinist when it came to building socialism. He then reacted against the growth of the communist party, its bureaucratisation and inflexibility, and the emergence of managerial and technocratic élites. These were accepted by other communist parties as natural concomitants of industrialisation, but not by Mao. The *Great Leap Forward* of 1958-59 – in reality it was a small hop – was a vain attempt to circumvent these phenomena. The conflict between China and Soviet Union was exacerbated by the personalities of the two leaders. They were really pursuing different goals. Whereas Khrushchev wanted to build up Soviet power and minimise the risk of thermo-nuclear war, so as to demonstrate the superiority of the Soviet system worldwide and to exploit the weak spots of the non-communist world without going to war, Mao sought the elimination of the Kuomintang (see KUOMINTANG) regime in Taiwan and needed huge Soviet military and economic aid to overcome China's backwardness. He favoured revolutionary action and saw the United States as a paper tiger which would retreat if challenged sufficiently strongly. Soviet and East European technicians were withdrawn in 1958 and thereafter relations worsened. The Chinese accused the Soviets of falling down on their obligations to the international communist movement, of abandoning the revolutionary banner of Marxism-Leninism and of being 'great power chauvinists'. A full-scale restoration of capitalism took place in the Soviet Union in 1963, according to the Chinese, and the Soviet leaders thus became members of a ruling class and as such class exploiters. The Soviets countered by declaring that the Mao clique had taken over the communist party and the country and had abandoned Marxism-Leninism. The cultural revolution (1966-76) was designed to eliminate bourgeois elements – élites and bureaucrats – and to galvanise the population to greater revolutionary feats. Mao believed in uninterrupted revolution, continuous conflict, since it would be beneficial in the long run. He also held, however, that history could destroy everything that history had created. This appears to be connected with Mao's views of the Marxist dialectic. He reduced the three laws to one: the unity and struggle of opposites. In 1964 he stated he did not believe in the other two laws: the negation of the negation and the transformation of quantity into quality. Hence he tended to view historical progress as ambiguous and imprecise.

The peasant's lack of sophistication was viewed as a source of strength. Maoism stresses the power of primitivism – the power of subjective forces over apparently objective economic forces and relations. Economic growth is achieved by mass struggle and not by élites. The collective will of the people is constantly being pitted against the dictates of economics in order to keep the revolution in motion. Mao's death in 1976 signalled the end of full-blown Maoism. Since then the 'Gang of Four', the pure Maoists, have been imprisoned and Deng Xaioping has embarked on a pragmatic course of modernisation. The pursuit of economic growth has replaced the purity of ideology as the chief goal.

The Sino-Soviet split forced communist parties everywhere to consider their position *vis-à-vis* Moscow and Peking but it has had the greatest impact on Asia. Vietnam was involved in a war with the United States until 1975 and remained neutral since she needed economic and military aid from both powers. In 1978 Vietnam opted for Moscow and has repudiated her Chinese connections. During the war against the French (1946–54) Chinese guerrilla tactics were used. Vietnamese invasions of Laos and Kampuchea aroused Chinese anger as the *Khmer Rouge* in Kampuchea were seen as allies. Their primitivism and their anti-urban and anti-cash bias were probably influenced by Chinese experience. The economic policies adopted by the Communist Party of Vietnam since 1975 have been a failure and this led to a crisis within the party and the expulsion of a third of its membership for corruption by 1983. Without Soviet support the party would have lost control. The Japan Communist Party parted company with the CPSU in 1964 over the partial nuclear test ban treaty, but there was a rapprochement in 1979. This cost the Japan Communist Party twelve seats in the June 1980 national elections. The party now sees itself as independent and relations with both the CPSU and the Communist Party of China are strained. There are splinter groups in Japan which are pro-Chinese. In India the *Communist Party of India* (Marxist) is the strongest of the three communist parties, but is equidistant between the CPSU and the communist party of China. The communist party of India is pro-Soviet. Another party which refuses to side with either the Soviet or the Chinese party is the ruling *Worker's Party* in North Korea. In Sri Lanka the communist party is resolutely pro-Soviet and holds that the Soviet invasion of Afghanistan was 'completely justified'. The communist parties of Burma and Thailand are pro-Chinese; in the Philippines one communist party is pro-Soviet and the other becoming pro-Chinese; there is a pro-Soviet and a pro-Chinese party in Nepal; the communist party of Malaya is pro-Chinese and the communist party of Australia is Eurocommunist but there is also a pro-Chinese communist party; in New Zealand the Socialist Unity Party, the strongest numerically, is pro-Soviet but there are two pro-Chinese parties. Hence the Sino-Soviet rift has led to splits in many communist parties. Fear of Vietnamese expansionism has benefited the Chinese.

In Cuba, Fidel Castro links José Martí, the nation's most respected poet and humanist, and Lenin as the sources of revolutionary legitimacy. The Cuban leader, however, has over the last twenty-five years gradually become a more and more orthodox communist – from Moscow's point of view. A formative development on Cuban development during the 1960s was exercised by Che Guevara. He stressed moral incentives and thought that the goal of egalitarianism could be retained during the transition period when socialism was being built. Indeed Cuba attempted a non-monetary egalitarian approach to modernisation. The new socialist man and woman, however, did not emerge. Guevara left for Bolivia when he again regarded the peasantry as the vanguard of the revolution. Guevara's contribution to the Cuban revolution is mainly moral and his ideas were clearly influenced by Chinese practice. Until 1968 Castro was quite independent in foreign policy, but the continued hostility of the USA and the economic chaos forced him to seek closer links with Moscow and Eastern Europe. The first congress of the Communist Party of Cuba was not held until 1975 when the appalling state of the economy was highlighted. The Cubans intervened in Africa and played a decisive role in the victory of the MPLA in Angola. At the second congress of the Communist Party of Cuba in 1980 the economy was again the major topic. Basic wages were raised and differentials stressed. Cuba's reliance on the Soviet Union is clearly greater than ever and Soviet advisers can insist that their counsel be heeded. The Soviet invasion of Afghanistan in December 1979, which Cuba defended, cost her much international support in the non-aligned world. The pro-Cuban *New Jewel Movement* in Grenada lost power after US intervention in October 1983.

The communist parties of Latin America are pro-Soviet, but Bolivia, Brazil, Columbia, the Dominican Republic and Honduras have pro-Chinese communist parties or groups as well. The *Sandinistas,* a pro-Soviet grouping, are now in power in Nicaragua. In Peru, the Sendero movement has waxed since 1980. It draws much of its inspiration from Mao's teachings on warfare: the first stage is the creation and consolidation of base areas, the strategic defensive; the second is the expansion of the base areas, stalemate is reached against the enemy; and the third stage is the strategic offensive, in which the enemy's army is defeated. The gulf between the urban and rural areas in Peru favours the Sendero who have 'liberated' some parts. The Sendero leader, Abimael Guzman, has developed ideas reminiscent of Pol Pot's *Khmer Rouge* and is equally intolerant of dissent and ruthless in his elimination of opponents.

The Soviet Union's first embassies in Africa were established in 1958 in Guinea and Ghana when high hopes were placed in black 'revolutionary democratic' leaders. It was held to be possible for such leaders to proceed directly to socialism without going through the capitalist phase. These hopes were soon dashed with defeat in the Congo (Zaire): a bitter lesson. A richer harvest was reaped in the 1970s when the Soviet Union sided with the victorious national liberation movement in Angola and Mozambique. Ethiopia also has a Marxist-Leninist ruling party.

Eurocommunism is a movement which owes its origins to the effects of the Twentieth CPSU congress, de-Stalinisation, the Hungarian and Polish events, the Sino-Soviet conflict and the rise of *detente* in international politics. The term itself was coined by a Yugoslav journalist in June 1975 to describe the views of the leaders of the Spanish party (PCE). In November 1975 the French (PCF) and the Italian (PCI) parties issued a joint statement. These three parties formed the core of the Eurocommunist movement until 1980. Eurocommunism was also a response to the need of communist parties to appeal to a wider constituency than the working class. The 'road to socialism' was to be peaceful and democratic. Democraticisation of party life and the abandonment of democratic centralism led to a rejection of Soviet hegemony over the world communist movement. Eurocommunism involves a tactical alliance with other parties so as first to share power and set in train far reaching democratic reforms. This will facilitate the transition to socialism. The PCF, seeking a tactical alliance with the socialists, abandoned its commitment to the Soviet model and the dictatorship

65

of the proletariat in 1976.

The hopes of the Eurocommunists had faded by the early 1980s. The PCI failed to sustain the impetus it had generated and gained little from its tactical alliance with the Christian Democrats. In 1981 it reverted to favouring a 'union of the left' with the Italian socialists. It condemned the invasion of Afghanistan and the imposition of the 'state of war' in Poland, however, and regarded the progressive energies of the October Revolution as 'exhausted'. The PCE lost much ground to the new Social Democratic party in Spain. A fundamental weakness of the PCE was the continual fighting.

The PCF was disappointed by the success of Mitterrand and the French socialists in 1977 and thereupon discarded its Eurocommunist clothes. It became again strongly pro-Soviet and hostile to social democracy in an effort to halt the advance of the socialists. The 1980s have seen a further decline in its fortunes.

Eurocommunism as the third way between Soviet communism and social democracy was in crisis in the mid-1980s. The PCE and the PCF fell victim to resurgent social democracy. A major reason for this was the unwillingness of the leadership to permit a full-blown democratisation of the communist parties. Only in Italy did Eurocommunism survive in its orginal garb, but even there the PCI was a long way from power.

Further reading

THE ORIGINS OF SOVIET COMMUNISM
Isaiah Berlin, *Karl Marx*.
R. N. Carew-Hunt, *The Theory and Practice of Communism*.
D. McLellan, *Karl Marx, His Life and Thought*.
D. Lane, *Leninism: A Sociological Interpretation*.
G. & H. Weber, *Lenin, Life and Works*.
STALINISM
M. McCauley, *Stalin and Stalinism*.
A. Nove, *Stalinism and After*.
L. Schapiro, *The Communist Party of the Soviet Union*.
R. Tucker (ed.), *Stalinism Essays in Historical Interpretation*.
THE WORLD MOVEMENT UP TO STALIN'S DEATH
Z. B. Brzezinski, *The Soviet Bloc: Unity and Conflict*.
M. McCauley (ed.), *Communist Power in Europe 1944-1949*.
DEVELOPMENTS SINCE STALIN
R. Medvedev, *Khrushchev*.
A. Brown and M. Kaser (eds.), *The Soviet Union since the Fall of Khrushchev*.
S. Schram, *The Political Thought of Mao Tse-tung*.
M. Tatu, *Power in the Kremlin from Khrushchev to Kosygin*.
GENERAL
G. F. Hudson, *Fifty Years of Communism Theory and Practice 1917-1967*.
D. McLellan, *Marxism after Marx*

Conservatism

Conservatism is not clearly embodied in a set of doctrines; it is a political attitude rather than a philosophy or a movement. The term implies fear of sudden and violent change, respect for established institutions and rulers, support for elites and hierarchies and a general mistrust of theory as opposed to empirical deductions. Conservatism, strictly speaking, enshrines this spirit in a definite political standpoint, although there have of course been many examples of 'conservatively-minded' Liberals (see LIBERALISM), Soviet bureaucrats and socialist trade unionists. Conservatism has found many different forms of expression according to country and period. The belief that there is no universal political system applicable to all nations is, indeed, fundamental to a conservative viewpoint.

It is misleading, however, to describe as 'conservative' anyone on the 'right wing' of a political spectrum, though that is how the phrase is often used in the USA and France for example. 'The right wing' in a country may well consist of strongly conflicting elements – *laisser-faire liberals, anti-Communists, authoritarians, monarchists, jingoes. Fascism* (see FASCISM) is certainly a 'right wing' political creed: but it has nothing to do with any brand of conservatism, involving as it does a sense of social and national grievance, devotion to the state, an appetite for violence, the cult of a leader, and the subjeection of politics, morality and the whole culture of a nation to the fascist party. It does not involve continuity with past institutions and relationships – as does conservatism – but a 'new order'. Neither are all 'reactionaries' conservative. The *Islamic* overthrow of the Shah of Iran in 1979 was inspired by a conservative aim – the restoration of an older moral and cultural order – but the means used were revolutionary.

One of the most important forms of conservatism has prevailed in England. It was also the standpoint of the Founding Fathers of the American Constitution and of the shortlived *Federalist* party in the USA which collapsed in the early nineteenth century. It has been influential on the Continent. This tradition has stressed the achievements of the past while allowing for gradual change. It has been closely bound up with a support for representative institutions.

It is normal to date modern conservatism in Britain from the end of the eighteenth century. At that period the following of Prime Minister William Pitt joined forces with another Whig group, that of Lord Portland, to pursue a policy in reaction to the antimonarchist, reformist and anti-religious influence of the French Revolution. After 1812 this alliance was generally known as the 'Tory' party. It took its name from the 'Tories' of the later seventeenth century who were ancestral in spirit, though not in organisation. At that time, the 'Cavalier' landowning interest had defended royal prerogatives, the divine hereditary right of kings, and the supreme authority of the Anglican Church

67

in politics and society, as against the aspirations of the 'Whig' party – who were supported by protestant dissenters, new landed and commercial wealth and latitudinarian and rationalist elements. The Whig and Tory parties of the seventeenth century had evolved as a result of issues arising from the Commonwealth period (over land ownership, monarchical power and religion) and in particular over the Exclusion Bill crisis of 1679 when the Whigs sought to prevent James the Duke of York's inheritance of the English throne, on the grounds of his Roman Catholicism – the Tories taking up his cause. The term 'Tory', originally one of abuse, implied 'traitorous Irish Catholic Outlaw', while 'Whig', also perjorative, meant 'bigoted horse-thieving Scots Covenanter'. The succession and religious questions kept the party feud alive, but, after the death of Queen Anne in 1714, when the succession issue had been decisively settled and the Whigs had triumphed over their opponents, the Tories disappeared as an organised party. The term 'Tory', however, continued to be used loosely during the eighteenth century for the defenders of royal power: for example, it was applied to George III, Lord Bute and their followers and, in North America, to colonists faithful to the crown during the Revolution.

After 1830, the revived Tory Party in England was also called 'the Conservative Party' and to this day the same organisation bears these two alternative names. The word 'toryism' has sometimes been used specifically to designate an ultra-traditional type of English Conservatism, a 'High Tory' politician of the nineteenth and early twentieth century, for example, meaning one who made a strong stand for the House of Lords and the Anglican Establishment. Today 'tory' can be used to indicate an emphasis on traditional hierarchies and customs – more frequently a rural rather than an urban phenomenon – but there is nothing to distinguish toryism fundamentally from the mainstream of English conservatism.

The writings of Edmund Burke gave Pitt's new 'Tory' grouping its ablest apologist and most important inspiration. Burke's fears that ancient liberties were under threat led him to attack violent radical change in his *Reflections on the Revolution in France* (October 1790). Liberty, he argued, could only exist through the traditional structure of society, with its protective laws and customs. Man must be guarded from his fallen nature if he was to reach his full civilised potential: in England, this involved the acceptance of the governing authority of both as hereditary monarchy and aristocracy and the Anglican church over his moral and political outlook. Co-operation, duty, loyalty and reverence were necessary to prevent society breaking up. Burke's idea of the constitution was contractual but organic. The contract's nature was such that it could not suddenly be put aside. 'As the ends of such a partnership cannot be obtained in many generations, it becomes a partnership not only between those who are living, but between those who are living, those who are dead and those who are to be born.' He greatly stressed the importance of the British constitution's adaptability: 'A society that is without the means of some change is without the means of its conservation'. Passionately devoted to Parliament,

Burke regarded its happy development as the result of that flexible spirit. He believed that new 'ideal' constitutions, created by revolutionaries from scratch out of 'natural rights', were too rigid to survive.

Burke was highly influential on the Continent as well as in Britain. In France, for example, Alexis de Tocqueville owed much to his thought; in Germany, Leopold von Ranke. Even the Austrian Chancellor, Prince Metternich – the leading political reactionary in Europe from 1815 to 1848 – was affected by it He appointed as his secretary Friedrich von Gentz, the translator of Burke's *Reflections*: like Burke, Metternich viewed constitutions as the products of national character, gradually and variously developed – they could not be suddenly created. Like Burke, he too did not deny the possibility of change; he accepted the French Revolution as a fact – unlike the French Legitimists – and that the old Europe was coming to an end. He tried, however, to secure the 'natural development' of the new Europe by preventing further revolutionary outbreaks in his own country and abroad. He quoted, with approval, Burke's dictum about a man having an interest in putting out the flames when his neighbour's house was on fire. In practice, his actions involved suppression of those liberties which showed an authoritarian spirit: for example, by the Carlsbad Decrees (1819) he drastically curtailed the freedom of the universities and the press throughout the German Confederation.   In Britain, following Burke's view that *some* change must from time to time be admitted, Sir Robert Peel later accepted – as leader of the Conservative party – the *fait accompli* of the 1832 Act introducing parliamentary reform, which his party had largely been formed to resist. The Conservatives continued to stress the traditional importance of the Church, monarchy and aristocracy, and under Benjamin Disraeli, Prime Minister from 1874–80, this was linked to a claim that the party stood for 'the elevation of the condition of the people' – a reassertion of the unifying role of the Conservatives in the nation. Disraeli was confident that the further extension of the franchise in 1867 would not endanger the position of the aristocracy as the country's natural rulers. His successor, Salisbury, more accurately foresaw and feared the 'distant but rising storm of democratic spoliation', but though Salisbury continually argued against constitutional change on empirical grounds he, too, recognised that it could not be indefinitely resisted. He had written in the *Quarterly Review* (October 1867): 'It is the duty of every Englishman, and of every English party, to accept a political defeat cordially, and to lend their best endeavours to secure the success, or to neutralise the evil, of the principles to which they have been forced to succumb.'

In the twentieth century, until recently, the British Conservative party favoured a policy of cautious accommodation to social change. This enabled it, while opposing *socialism*, to accept a large measure of state control, though in the 1980's under Margaret Thatcher there has been an effort to reverse that trend.

Conservative parties on the continent after the Second World War have shown characteristics similar to those of their equivalent in Britain. The names of two of these, however, the Italian *Democrazia Cristiana* and the German *Christlisch-Demokratische Union* (see CHRISTIAN DEMOCRACY), indicate a further important conservative influence – the Roman Catholic Church. The nineteenth-century resistance of the Papacy to *Liberalism* (see LIBERALISM) the ideas of the French revolutionaries and the Church's emphasis on tradition and hierarchy meant that on the Continent loyalty to Catholicism was linked inseparably with conservatism. This link has contributed to the existence of another reactionary and *Authoritarian Conservative* tradition quite different in character from that in England. The leading ultra-loyalist writers in France in the years after the Revolution were ardent Catholics. Joseph de Maistre in *Du Pape*, the charter of *Ultramontanism* (see ULTRAMONTANISM) set forth the doctrine of Papal Supremacy. To such men, the revolutionary terror was God's chastisement of France for straying from the path of truth. It was her duty to repent, and return to submission to the ancient political and moral authorities – an absolute monarchy closely bound up with an infallible Papacy. The French Revolution had been an historical aberration, and nothing could be gained from it but spiritual improvement through suffering. The theme of national atonement for godlessness recurred among French Conservatives after the Franco-Prussian War. Bonapartism (see BONAPARTISM), the legacy of Napoleon Bonaparte's rule (1799-1815), has also contributed to the authoritarian tendency in France.

There are many standpoints, systems and policies which have often been associated with conservatism but are not in themselves conservative. For example, though there are many capitalists who are conservative, capitalism and conservatism should not be too closely identified: they are really opposed in spirit. Capitalism involves the continual destruction of the old to make room for the new – because many old trades and ways of life cease to be economically viable. In practice, however, there has been a tendency for Conservative parties in Western Europe – and Japan – to take on the role of the nineteenth-century Liberals in being the opponents of state control, high tax and public expenditure and in stressing individualism, as against uniformity. In twentieth-century England, the increased influence of the commercial interest in the Conservative party's ranks and the decline of the Liberal party after the First World War, have contributed to this development – very markedly since 1979. But all this does not invalidate the claims of these parties to be Conservative, rooted as they ultimately are in reverence for historic political and religious institutions.

In America, however, where there is no Conservative party as such, the term is too often used inaccurately to describe Republicans like President William Howard Taft ('Rural Toryism') and President Ronald Reagan, who have stood for *laisser-faire* capitalist individualism ('libertarianism') in domestic affairs. Moreover, though a conservative is bound to be anti-communist, in the USA the conservative label has often been applied carelessly to any offensive against Communism. In fact, the witch-hunting campaign of Senator Joseph McCarthy in the early 1950's was untraditional, demagogic and disruptive. Nor can the term be rightly applied to America's Vietnam policy: 'The belief that one's own nation had to defend justice in any other nation, no matter what that nation thought of the matter, is not conservative or liberal so much as lunatic. It is extravagant, and radical, and anti-historical' (Gary Wills, *Confessions of a Conservative*, 1979).

Chauvinism – extreme and aggressive patriotism (see NATIONALISM) – though it is not in itself 'conservative' and is by no means the exclusive province of the 'right wing', has been a powerful motive force among many conservative groups – for example in ultra patriotic organisations like those for ex-servicemen in America, France and Germany, with their emphasis on authority and past military glory. In France, Bonapartism, *Action Francaise* and *Gaullism* (see GAULLISM) have also represented ardent nationalist manifestations of conservatism. In Britain, the Conservative party became, from Disraeli's time as leader, preeminently the party of Imperialism – i.e. of a 'greater patriotism'. Yet even at the height of imperial expansion the Conservative leader, Salisbury, could deplore *jingoism* – mindless national self-assertion – and put peaceful relations before total diplomatic victory.

Racialism and Conservatism are not necessarily linked, though distrust of aliens is an element of instinctive 'natural' conservatism which has been widely exploited by right-wing parties. In the United States a Conservative tradition has been closely bound up with the race question. America's foremost conservative philosopher, John C. Calhoun (1782-1850), was also her leading defender of slavery. He arrived at this position through concern to preserve the traditional way of life of the rural south against the domination of a growing northern industrial interest. He concluded that the rights of individual states and numerical minority interests must be defended against the tyranny of the majority in a democracy. This was a genuinely conservative view. The stand on states' rights as against federally imposed safeguards to the civil and political rights of blacks continued up to the late 1960's and early 1970's, though much of the agitation – such as George Wallace's independent campaign at that time – has had a radical populist (see POPULISM) colour and cannot be strictly described as conservative.

The American slave holders were actually supporters of *Free Trade*; however – and this demonstrates the complications involved in an explanation of this kind – *Protectionism* is another movement which has come to be associated with conservative parties. The Conservatives in England, before 1846, resisted the removal of duties which protected British corn growing landowners. In the later nineteenth century the pressure for the erection of tariff barriers throughout Europe and North America came from conservative elements which included the farming Junkers of Prussia as well as industrialists. In the United States, the Republicans were the party of the protective tariff, despite being opposed generally to state intervention in the home economy. The Conservative Party of Canada was traditionally protectionist. Nonetheless, although its opposite, *Free Trade*, was fundamental to *Liberalism* (see LIBERALISM), protectionism is not a doctrine central to Conservatism, and has more to do with the growth

71

of capitalism. It is significant that the man who persuaded the English Conservatives to accept tariff reform as part of their programme in the early years of the twentieth century was a radical ex-liberal, Joseph Chamberlain. He dreamt of a British Empire free trade area, its industries defended from outside competition by tariff walls, prosperous and unified by close economic ties. This dream faded with time and as ceased to be a hallmark of British Conservative policy – thus providing evidence of the non-doctrinaire nature of Conservatism. Protective trade barriers have at times been advocated by adherents of other political faiths – by *Socialists* (see SOCIALISM) like Anthony Wedgwood Benn and *Fascists* (see FASCISM) like Oswald Mosley – in such cases because of fears aboute employment and national self-sufficiency.

The chief objection always levelled at Conservatism is that it is essentially uncreative – that it tends not to favour experimentation in any form, or to provide the theory for constructive social reform. Against this can be set the argument that the Conservative spirit, with its emphasis on common roots, tradition and experience provides the soundest foundation for stable political development and liberty.

Further reading

IN BRITAIN

Alan Beattie, *English Party Politics, 1660-1906*
  English Party Politics, 1906-1970
Robert Blake, *The Conservative Party from Peel to Thatcher*
Philip Buck, *How Conservatives Think*
Edmund Burke, *Reflections on the Revolution in France*
Lord Butler, *The Conservatives*
Maurice Cowling ed., *Conservative Essays*
Lord Hugh Cecil, *Conservatism*
J. A. S. Grenville, *Salisbury and Foreign Policy*
Noel O'Sullivan, *Conservatism*
Michael Pinto-Duchinsky, *The Political Thought of Lord Salisbury 1854-1868*
Roger Scruton, *The Meaning of Conservatism*
Alan Sykes, *Tariff Reform in British Politics 1903-1913*

IN NORTH AMERICA

William F. Buckley, Jr., *Up from Liberalism*
Jack Kemp, *An American Renaissance: A Strategy for the 1980s*
O. J. MacDiarmid, *Commercial Policy in the Canadian Economy*
Stephen L. Newman, *Liberalism at Wit's End: The Libertarian Revolt against the Modern State*
Vernon Parrington, *Main Currents in American Thought: The Colonial Mind 1620-1800*
  The Romantic Revolution in America 1800-1860
Rod Preece, 'The Anglo-Saxon Conservative Tradition', *Canadian Journal of Political Science*, XIII, March 1980.
Gary Wills, *Confessions of a Conservative*

IN EUROPE AND GENERAL

Isiah Berlin, *Against the Current*
W. H. Dawson, *Protection in Germany*

M. P. Fogarty, *Christian Democracy in Western Europe*
Russell Kirk, *The Conservative Mind from Burke to Eliot*
René Rémond, *The Right Wing in France from 1815 to de Gaulle* (tr. James Laux)
Nathaniel B. Thayer, *How the Conservatives Rule Japan*
F. L. Woodward, *Three Studies in European Conservatism*

Ecumenism

The belief that the Christian church is one and universal has been championed from the beginning of Christian history, not least by those who contributed most by their writings to the great divisions between East and West, and, within the West, between Catholics and Protestants. There has also been a long-standing tradition of eirenic literature in almost all the divided communities, aimed at overcoming the profound theological differences which, at one level at least, were the original causes of conflict and schism. This concern to find theological solutions to theological disputes has undoubtedly been one major influence in the modern history of ecumenism, leading on the one hand to numerous 'Conversations' between divided churches, and on the other, to the formation of such organisations as the *World Conference on Faith and Order* (initiated at Lausanne in 1927 and later absorbed into the World Council of Churches). More rarely it has led to successful unions between churches, as for example in the Church of South India, inaugurated in 1947 by churches representing the Anglican, Congregational, Methodist and Presbyterian traditions.

The main roots of modern ecumenism, however, lie in the confrontation between Christian leaders of all denominations and the non-Christian world, whether on the mission field or in secularised Western society, and in a widespread and by no means uncomplicated desire to make a 'Christian' contribution to the search for social justice and the international peace movement. The first major international, interconfessional conference of non-Catholic churchmen in the present century was the World Mission Conference at Edinburgh in 1910. From this emerged the International Missionary Council, which was subsequently absorbed into the World Council of Churches. The preoccupation with contemporary social problems prompted functional co-operation between different churches at national level in the nineteenth and early twentieth centuries e.g. *Innere Mission* in Germany and the Federal council of Churches in the United States) and found expression at international level in the Universal Christian Council for Life and Work which grew out of a conference at Stockholm in 1925. The influence of the search for international peace, which was also evident in the growth of *Life and Work*, was even more pronounced in the pre-First World War development of a number of Christian peace organisations, including notably The Associated Councils of Churches in the British and

German Empires for fostering friendly relations between the two peoples, which were set up in 1910. Representatives of this and other organisations met in Constance on August 2, 1914, a meeting, which though broken short by the outbreak of the war, led amongst other things to the formation of the *World Alliance for Promoting International Friendship* through the Churches and a number of unofficial attempts to mediate between the belligerents.

Practical concern with contemporary social, political and international problems has also been a major influence on the development of co-operation between the Catholic and non–Catholic churches. Historically, a major impetus was given by the Second World War, where the confrontation with National Socialism and the ideals of the Resistance helped to make denomination seem irrelevant to those who participated in the conflict and made those who did not less anxious to flaunt their parochialism. The fundamental theological issues, including the question of the authoriity of the papacy, continue to divide the churches, but, since the Second World War, increasing secularisation and dechristianisation, and, by no means least, the emergence of a new generation of Catholic leaders (especially Pope John XXIII), helped to bring about more cordial and fruitful relations between Catholics and Protestants than had existed before. Nonetheless, in certain parts of Europe, notably in Western Germany, the hierarchy has fought strongly for the maintenance of denominational schooling, while in Rome itself, the liberal 'dawn' associated with the early days of the Second Vatican Council has proved to be more limited than appeared likely to enthusiastic commentators at the time.

The Enlightenment

In some respects it is difficult to envisage the Enlightenment as an age of ideologies at all. There were in the eighteenth century no widespread parties or mass movements formed around the political ideas of leading thinkers, and the major wars of the European powers were then fought over colonies and territories rather than secular or religious doctrines. Following the devastating schisms of sixteenth-century Christendom and the constitutional upheavals of seventeenth-century England, but preceding the nationalist revolutions and class struggles of the nineteenth century, Enlightenment political theories may appear to have lacked the popular impact of the ideologies of both earlier and later epochs. The eighteenth century was, nevertheless, a period of great ideological ferment and confrontation, whose advocates and critics alike saw their cause as promoting, or threatening, a new order of politics and society.

Three main reasons above all account for this. Firstly, political thinkers of the Enlightenment were more concerned than those of any previous age with the application of principles in the world of public affairs, and with the institutional links between social theory and practice. Opponents came to hold this point against them by charging that their seditious doctrines had given rise to the French Revolution, but investigations of the means by which ideals might be realised in practice comprise a central feature of those doctrines in themselves. Secondly, the proponents of Enlightenment advanced most of the political theories around which the ideological movements, parties, and factions of the nineteenth century were formed. Some of the major ideologies of the next epoch have antecedents which long predate the eighteenth century, but it is in their Enlightenment formulations that such doctrines acquired the characteristic terminology, flavour, and connotations by which we understand them now. Thirdly, political thinkers of the eighteenth century recognised themselves as forming an intellectual party engaged in a common cause of constitutional or social reform. They did not always agree – in fact they were often in bitter conflict – about the nature of the problems faced by their societies, and about the remedies needed to solve them. But through their publicity campaigns and their alliances with politicians, they sought to influence government policies on a scale which men of letters had never before attempted. However small their popular following, the leaders of the Enlightenment, known collectively as *philosophes*, made up the first European intelligentsia and the earliest ideological vanguard of a kind which came to steer the fortunes of most of the radical movements of the nineteenth century.

The Enlightenment is often described as an Age of Reason, but not all its major thinkers were rationalists, and many expressed serious doubts about the role of speculative reason as a guide to the conduct of practical life. The description is apt, however, in so far as it portrays the Enlightenment as an intellectual movement opposed to ignorance, mysticism, superstition, and irrationalism in general. These forces of darkness were the enemies of Enlightenment everywhere, and it was in 'reason's light' that the *philosophes* sought to dispel the shadows in which their adversaries lurked. Voltaire, d'Alembert, Condorcet and many others argued that the whole of human history was in reality a struggle between the friends and enemies of Enlightenment, between nefarious tyrants, priests, and barbarians, on the one hand, and civilized, educated, liberated men of science and letters, on the other. Sometimes, as in ancient Mesopotamia or in medieval Europe, the mysticism of priests and oppression of barbarians predominated; sometimes, as in classical Greece and Rome or in the Europe of the Renaissance, it was the party of humanity and culture that was stronger. In the contemporary world, the *philosophes* maintained, the conflict was essentially between their own Enlightenment fraternity and those insidious purveyors of gloom and despondency, the established churches of orthodox Christianity. They perceived Christianity mainly as it was reflected in Revelation and Scripture; as the inheritor of an Old Testament theology of mysteries, miracles, torments, and tribulations, constructed round the dogma of original sin and the messianic vision of an other-worldly redemption. Yet so far from being inherently sinful, mankind, they believed, has a natural capacity for virtue, or

75

a faculty of perfectibility, as Rousseau termed it. Only blind faith, credulity, and resignation in the face of spurious supernatural powers prevented most of us from acquiring a knowledge of the good and a desire to practise it. In contrast with the Christian conception of a penitential history of struggle against vice, many Enlightenment thinkers – though not Rousseau himself – adopted the idea of perfectibility to show that our history was marked by an irregular progress in the arts, sciences, culture, and politics, of which the eighteenth century formed the most advanced stage yet attained. Some of the *philosophes*, to be sure, were rather more sceptical about the past. They agreed with Gibbon that history was a record of the 'crimes, follies, and misfortunes of mankind', or even with Rousseau, that it was the account of the growing decrepitude of our species. Nearly all, however, upheld an optimistic view of our moral potentialities, and most supposed that our actual or prospective improvement should be understood with reference to the secularisation of politics and the humanisation of society.

Not only was blind obedience incompatible with rational conduct and the pursuit of virtue; it was also the corollary of bigotry, oppression, persecution and malice. For the *philosophes*, the greatest evils we had suffered were those we inflicted upon one another in pursuit of Christian salvation. The Crusades, the Inquisition, and the fanaticism of religious wars were the real monuments of Christian morals, and to oppose such crimes they rallied round Voltaire's battlecry, 'Ecrasez l'infâme!' In his assaults upon the injustice of ecclesiastical courts, the abuses of wealth and privilege by the Catholic hierarchy and the philistine intolerance characteristic of the Calvinist ministry, Voltaire did much to fan the secularism and anticlericalism of Enlightenment thought as a whole, of which the confiscation of Church properties and the Civil Constitution of the clergy during the French Revolution were to prove the crowning achievements.

Yet not all the *philosophes* were unbelievers. La Mettrie and d'Holbach may have been atheists, but some, like Condillac and Mably, were trained for the priesthood and made at least nominal bows to the tenets of their faith. Montesquieu and Lessing were deists who believed God's work was manifest in Nature and not superimposed mysteriously above it, while Rousseau and Kant held to still more traditional Catholic or Protestant creeds. But Enlightenment thinkers were almost unanimously opposed to theocratic government and to all forms of blind obedience to mystical powers. Such religions as they did respect needed to be rational in doctrine and tolerant in practice, and the *philosophes* saw themselves as the publicists of a dawn which would release mankind from the cruelty, idolatry, and superstition which led most Christians to despair of the attainment of any worldly happiness.

In addition to rejecting what they saw as the dogmatism of Christian theology, the leading thinkers of the Enlightenment also criticized the speculative tradition of philosophy which had culminated in the great metaphysical systems of the seventeenth century. The cosmologies of Descartes, Leibniz, Spinoza and Malebranche were in the Enlightenment esteemed for their breadth but at the same time challenged for their abstractness, infused as they were by what d'Alembert described as the 'spirit of system' rather than the 'systematic spirit' of his own enlightened age. The difference between these methodologies is of striking importance, if not always clear. Enlightenment thinkers generally believed that it was necessary to adopt an empirical approach to the study of human nature and behaviour, and they lavished praise upon the seminal contributions to European thought made by such figures as Bacon, Locke and Newton, who had seen the need to collect facts and make inferences from observable data, and who had applied their genius to the practice or groundwork of experimental science. But they found the doctrines of those eminent thinkers of the preceding age which were based upon abstract principles, occult qualities, Divine Will, and even natural law, less congenial. In political theory, in particular, they frequently objected to the philosophies of Bodin, Grotius, Hobbes, Filmer, and Bossuet, in part because they judged these theorists lacking in a clearly defined scientific outlook, despite statements to the contrary such as Hobbes himself had made. The *philosophes* acknowledged a substantial debt to the triumphs of seventeenth- and early eighteenth-century natural science, but they believed the social sciences to be still in their infancy, and they looked to the analysis of the human mind, and to the disciplines of psychology and linguistics, for the proper foundation of the study of man, rather than to the postulated commands of God, or the *Corpus juris* of Rome, or the cosmic laws of matter and motion.

They were also disappointed with the neglect of an historical and cultural dimension in the doctrines of their predecessors, who – like the illustrious Pufendorf they otherwise so much admired – had wrongly supposed that men were everywhere and at all times governed by the same passions, vices, tendencies or laws. Figures like Montesquieu and Ferguson addressed themselves instead to the anomalies of climate and soil in diverse countries, and to the peculiar manners and customs of distinct peoples, as they sought to discover and interpret the local and specific qualities of various cultures in different parts of the world and in different epochs. Even if men could not change their nature they could change their situations, observed Hume, and it was with the evolution of such changes rather than the immutability of nature that the Enlightenment was most centrally concerned.

Above all, the *philosophes* believed that their metaphysical precursors had focused too much attention on the first principles of government, and not enough on government's ends, aims, functions and purposes. Seventeenth-century thinkers had been preoccupied with the problem of sovereignty and its origin, whether it should be absolute or limited, whether a gift of God or an achievement of the social compact, and they had failed to place due emphasis upon the popular interests which sovereigns were intended to serve. In their rejection of the doctrine of man's original sin, most Enlightenment theorists instead shared the view of Hutcheson and the philosophers of moral sense in

77

Scotland who followed him that man was a creature of benevolence and that benevolence was the principal source of human virtue. And by extending the idea of benevolence from the individual to the community, they came to address themselves more than did their precursors to the humane and beneficent policies which governments ought to pursue.

Their criticisms of Christian dogma and speculative philosophy, then, were informed by their interest in how political principles should be applied, both in general and in particular cases. It would perhaps be an exaggeration to say that they condemned Christianity as an oppressive practice and metaphysical politics as hollow theory, but their concern with such matters made Enlightenment thinkers especially sensitive to what later came to be termed the unity of theory and practice. They believed religion ought to be rational and philosophy practical, and in their doctrines they characteristically turned to the question of how theory and practice might be joined through a science of legislation for the public welfare.

This regard for the rational administration of government on behalf of the public interest lies at the root of all descriptions of the eighteenth century as an age of Enlightened Despotism, however elusive has been the meaning of that idea in the history of political thought. The first use of the terms 'enlightened despotism' in accounts of the period dates only from the mid-nineteenth century and is most generally applied to the policies of Frederick II of Prussia, Catherine II of Russia, and Joseph II of Austria. It should of course be understood that these policies were at least as much the offspring of the centralising autocratic régimes that preceded them in each case as of the philosophical principles borrowed from the international Republic of Letters. The *philosophes* themselves characteristically believed 'despotism' to mean absolute and arbitrary rule, as Jaucourt defined it in his article on the subject in the *Encyclopédie*, and such unholy alliances as were formed between Voltaire and Frederick, or between Diderot and Catherine, for instance, more often than not expressed a desire for patronage, on the one hand, and for intellectual approbation, on the other, rather than a real marriage of theory and practice.

Nevertheless, it remains true that in the eighteenth century philosophy and kingship came together in a manner and on a scale which both Plato in the ancient world and his humanist followers in the Renaissance had so often held to be necessary, but hardly dreamt possible. In the Enlightenment, the *philosophes* and their allies served as ministers in the courts of Maria Theresa, Joseph II, Leopold II, George III, Louis XVI and other European rulers. Sometimes, as in the case of Condillac and the Duke of Parma, they tutored their sons. Kings, in turn, corresponded with *philosophes*, sought their company, and solicited their advice. They established scientific and literary academies over which distinguished *philosophes* presided, they wrote treatises and occasional essays in defence of philosophical politics, and, through Grimm's *Correspondance littéraire* and other journals, they subscribed to a news service provided by *philosophes* to keep them informed of the latest fashion in ideas circulating in the cosmopolitan capitals of their day.

Among the fashionable doctrines that inspired them was *Utilitarianism*, whose leading exponents in the eighteenth century were Helvétius, Beccaria, Bentham, and, in certain respects, Hume. Utilitarians argued that pain and pleasure constituted the sole measure of what was right and wrong for each individual and that governments should encourage the greatest possible amount of happiness and the least pain among their subjects, thus promoting public welfare and utility overall. Because of their hostility to institutions and practices which thwarted the realisation of their programmes, most utilitarians were also opposed to those estates, privileged classes and clerical orders, customary laws and precedents, which abounded in Christian and feudal Europe. And though it was mainly the defects of criminal justice that attracted their interest in the eighteenth century, the rhetoric and substance of their campaigns on behalf of uniform and impartial codes of law also bore fruit in the civil and constitutional reforms of Joseph, Catherine, and the French revolutionaries, even before their still greater triumphs of the nineteenth century.

Another noteworthy source of the ideology of Enlightened Despotism was the Physiocratic philosophy of such figures as Quesnay, Le Mercier de la Rivière and Dupont de Nemours. Like the Utilitarians, the Physiocrats believed that political administration should be founded on scientific principles, and they also regarded Christian dogma and its ministers as largely unsuited to the secular management of public affairs. But in their focus upon the rational organization of policy they dealt more with commerce, trade, and economics in general, than with criminal law. They advocated currency reform, the elimination of tariff barriers to trade and industry, and, perhaps above all, the rational planning of agricultural production. While hostile to the militarist politics of some of the European régimes, they were generally well disposed to monarchy, provided its rule was made efficient. They believed constitutional principles were of less consequence than the manner in which laws were administered, and Le Mercier de la Rivière even endorsed what he termed 'legal despotism' to encapsulate their concern with actual policy and their disregard for the mere form of government.

In Austria and Germany, Sonnenfels, Justi, Moser and other publicists of the doctrine of Cameralism pressed for more benevolent statesmanship by monarchs well-informed of the needs of their subjects and by ministers able to implement standardised policies throughout their kingdoms. They adhered, as Sonnenfels remarked, to the principle that the chief foundation of government was 'the promotion of general happiness', and they did much to encourage the growth of bureaucracy in late eighteenth-century Europe. Less liberal and more paternalist than the Utilitarians or Physiocrats, Cameralists nonetheless exercised a greater influence in their own day upon those régimes of which they were occasionally advisers and ministers, and they did much to foster the belief of radical reformers of the nineteenth century that in an enlightened age all varieties of oppressive political control over men would be supplanted by the rational administration or supervision of things.

Of course the links between each of these doctrines and the practices of monarchical rule in the eighteenth century are indirect, complex, and invariably obscure. But in the great ideological brew of Enlightened Despotism such theoretical potions were important constituents, and Frederick's prohibition of torture, Joseph's abolition of serfdom, Catherine's zealous commitment to the improvement of Russian culture, and above all the constitutional reforms and legal codes introduced by these and other rulers, were distilled through and impregnated with the flavour of those doctrines. In the next century they were to be embraced once more, and to take new shape, in the ideologies and movements of both Philosophic Radicalism (see RADICALISM) and Saint-Simonian socialism (see SOCIALISM).

In contrast with the Utilitarians, Physiocrats, and Cameralists, many Enlightenment thinkers maintained that the beneficiaries of wise legislation should also be its agents. Diderot, d'Holbach, and Kant, among others, argued that for the State to serve the needs of its subjects it must not only act on their behalf but also ensure that their voices be heard, largely through parliamentary assemblies or other representative institutions. Occasionally, such figures invoked a property qualification to differentiate fully active from merely passive citizenship – a thesis which, elaborated by Sieyes and promulgated in the French Constitution of 1791, came to form a doctrinal barrier to the political self-expression of the *sans-culottes* during the Revolution. Yet the distinction between active and passive citizenship was more generally upheld in the Enlightenment for precisely the opposite reason: not in order to exclude the masses from state control but to ensure that legislators had earned sufficient means to be the masters of their own wills. Eighteenth-century defences of representative government were essentially doctrines in favour of the political exercise of liberty against paternalist rule, as supported by the advocates of Enlightened Despotism. Kant in particular stressed the importance of this view of liberty. 'No one can compel me to be happy in accordance with his conception of the welfare of others', he insisted in an essay on the subject of theory and practice, and he extended his account of representation for the purpose of protecting individual freedom to international assemblies designed to preserve the independence of states. Such an approach to world peace had already been anticipated earlier in the eighteenth century in the writings of the abbé de Saint-Pierre and was developed further in the nineteenth century, especially by Saint-Simon.

The leading Enlightenment advocate of popular participation, however, was Rousseau, and his view of liberty, though it greatly influenced Kant's perspective, precluded legislative representation altogether. Rousseau insisted that the only legitimate form of sovereignty was self-rule or direct democracy, and he differed from most other thinkers of his day in condemning English parliamentary practice, whereby electors, he argued, did not so much depute their authority as relinquish their freedom. Inspired by images of ancient Sparta and the Roman Republic, he believed, like Machiavelli, that citizens should exercise vigilance to protect their liberty from danger, and among major eighteenth-century thinkers he was the most anxious to preserve the place of individual liberty in public affairs. He distinguished the general will, or the politically concerted voice of independent citizens, from the will of all, which was his phrase for the sum of the interests of particular factions, and he described the true freedom or autonomy of subjects in terms of obedience to common rules and the pursuit of collective goals which paternalist or delegated forms of authority were unable to promote. Consolidated action in accordance with the general will was, Rousseau supposed, more likely in small states, enjoying popular assemblies, simple economies, and face-to-face public relations, than in the impersonal complex networks devoted to self-aggrandisement so prevalent in the larger and more advanced European societies of his time. Although his pessimistic view of the decadence of our institutions set him apart from those of his contemporaries who believed in the actual progress of civilization, he was in theory just as optimistic as any thinker of his day about the potentialities for virtue arising from the fundamental goodness of human nature.

Rousseau's uncompromising commitment to the sovereignty of the people fired the imagination of many radical critics of the Ancien Régime, and during the Revolution no figure of the Enlightenment was more eulogised and venerated than 'le bon Jean-Jacques'. Rousseauism then came to represent especially, if not exclusively, the most lofty principles of Liberalism and Egalitarianism, a natural simplicity of manners and customs, a purging of both the spirit and State from moral corruption, as well as patriotic service on behalf of the national interest, opposition to patronage, and religious devotion fuelled by civic enthusiasm rather than priestly theology. In the Cult of the Supreme Being and the hymns and festivals of the Revolution, in the political clubs, corresponding societies, and above all in the Jacobin movement of that period, his political doctrines acquired the force and trappings of a popular creed whose moment of historical realization had arrived. The most impassioned practical expression of his philosophy, moreover, can be found in the political career of the Incorruptible Robespierre, champion of the poorer classes, and herald and guardian of the Republic of Virtue. It was largely because of this association with Robespierre that the real legacy of Rousseauism was later held to be the sour fruit propagated by the policies of the Committee of Public Safety and the Reign of Terror under its dictatorship.

A number of predominantly French Enlightenment thinkers stressed the importance of economic equality rather than political liberty as the fundamental goal to which states should aspire. Rousseau had claimed there was an unbreakable bond between the two, and he attributed the lack of liberty in most states to the inegalitarian distribution of property which had marked their origin and whose preservation remained the dominant function of their governments now. But he also recognised that some policies might encourage equality to the detriment of liberty, and he believed that legislation should only seek to remedy those inequalities of wealth which tended to make the majority of individuals dependent on the will of the few. Nowhere did he encourage a uniform distribution for all persons, and nowhere did he advocate the collective ownership of property as a matter of public interest. Enlightenment socialists such as Dom Deschamps, Morelly and Mably, however, characteristically argued that the state should regulate property so as to ensure that no one enjoyed more than the necessities of life. In order to overcome the vices of avarice and indolence, they contended that there must be public authorities to organize the allocation of goods and services, to enforce strict sumptuary laws, and, in some cases – so as to foster the right frame of mind in the young – to control education. Morelly in particular anticipated the famous dictum of Marx, 'From each according to his ability, to each according to his needs', and in the course of the Revolution itself such figures as Babeuf and Sylvain Maréchal proclaimed that true equality could only be achieved if the iniquitous institution of private property were abolished altogether.

Other thinkers stressed the importance of liberty at the expense of equality, along lines almost diametrically opposed to those pursued by the Socialists. Turgot maintained that the unequal distribution of property everywhere was as desirable as it was inevitable, since otherwise there would be no incentive for enterprising individuals to cultivate the surplus yield from their land, upon which the creation of wealth ultimately depended. The Italians Genovesi and Palmieri each maintained that the fundamental task of the state was not to impose the heavy hand of equality upon all subjects, but rather to lay the delicate foundations for the exercise of individual liberty and initiative, which alone could give their country a prospect of development out of its state of economic backwardness and stagnation. In England and Scotland, Mandeville, Addison and Smith asserted that the public interest was best achieved by encouraging each individual to pursue his own separate gain in competition with others. This, they believed, would naturally result in common benefit for all, while, on the other hand, there was little to be expected, and much to be feared, from a concentration of powers designed to promote the general welfare. Smith in particular argued that governments should be 'discharged from. . . the duty of superintending the industry of private people', since with the elimination of tariffs, entails, duties and monopolies, persons would exercise their liberty to their own best advantage, which, in turn, would lead to the production of commodities and distribution of resources most needed by everyone. He thus agreed with those Physiocrats who had proclaimed 'Laissez faire, laissez aller', and, although Smith himself expressed certain doubts about the social implications of such policies, it was ideas of this sort that gave rise to the principles of free market enterprise so central to nineteenth- and twentieth-century Liberalism.

Another quite distinct ideological perspective in the Enlightenment was the so-called doctrine of the separation of powers elaborated by Montesquieu. Like Smith and other liberals, Montesquieu opposed the institution of absolute power, even for the sake of facilitating egalitarian ends. In its place, however, he put the case for political liberty which he identified far more closely than natural liberty with responsibility, obligation, and law. For Montesquieu, it was a triumph of the English Constitution that it had promoted such liberty more than any other nation, through the division of legislative, executive, and judicial powers, and the accountability of each branch of government under the scrutiny of the others. This was a novel conception of the proper exercise of power, significantly different from the views of Aristotle, Locke, or Bolingbroke to which it is often compared, and however inaccurate Montesquieu's opinions about English politics may have been, his ideas came to exercise an immense influence upon the formation of the 1787 Constitution of the United States and its defence by Hamilton and Madison in their *Federalist Papers*.

In his day, Montesquieu was regarded as the most important of all Enlightenment social theorists, and his European admirers drew their main inspiration from further aspects of his doctrine. Hume shared, and indeed conceived independently, the same respect for the rule of law and the excellence of an English Constitution whose mixed and balanced nature protected liberty best. Other philosophers of the Scottish Enlightenment, like Ferguson and Millar, were especially impressed by his account of the spirit of the laws and the need to accommodate particular forms of goverment to suit the established customs, manners, and mores of distinct peoples. Following this general concern with the social context and background of political institutions, moreover, Ferguson stressed the function of conflict and hostility between groups, which he believed promoted cohesion within them as well as the evolution from one epoch of civilisation to the next. Both Montesquieu's and Ferguson's perspectives, together and separately, were to have a profound bearing upon the development of nineteenth-century sociology, through the writings of Comte, Durkheim, and Marx.

It was also from Montesquieu that so many Romantic thinkers, like Möser, Herder, Schlegel, and Schelling, could draw their initial conceptions of cultural Pluralism. That idea is today often regarded as a doctrine of the German counter-Enlightenment, designed to repudiate the view of an invariable and unchanging human nature upheld by eighteenth-century rationalists in France. But, as well as Montesquieu, such figures of the Enlightenment as Prévost, Raynal, Rousseau, and Diderot were deeply interested in the diversity of institutions throughout the world, and in the peculiarities of local habits, the multiplicity of moral values, and the richness of variety. Massive collections of travel literature about exotic civilisations were printed in the period, and no earlier age had been better informed about how mankind lived beyond the shores of Europe. Nor had any writer before ever achieved more success than Montesquieu in showing how a comparative study of cultures might illuminate the defects of one's own.

Political thinkers of the eighteenth century thus differed markedly about the nature and policies of government most conducive to the public welfare, but at the same time they were drawn together by their common endeavour to promote ideological and social reform. The Enlightenment, if not the outstanding age of speculative philosophers, was the foremost age in our history of practical *philosophes* – that is, of men whose enthusiasm for the arts and sciences, and whose passion for learning in general and applied wisdom in particular, were matched by their desire to disseminate knowledge as widely as possible so as to make it useful for the management of ordinary affairs. This is why the eighteenth century was so much an age of encyclopedias, dictionaries, lexicons, guides, manuals, and handbooks for specialized or popular instruction. This is why it was also an age of of newspapers, gazettes, scientific periodicals, gossip sheets, and moral journals, such as, in England, the *Tatler, Spectator* and *Gentleman's Magazine.* Eighteenth-century thinkers sought to publicize their ideas and bring enlightenment to fruition through their separate and collective literary ventures. They wrote topical essays and *pièces fugitives*; they exchanged ideas in the salons which they frequented and in the clubs, institutes, and academies of which they were members; and they aimed at direct influence on public policy in their association with the rulers of European states as tutors, secretaries, ministers, and advisers.

The intellectual movement orchestrated by the *philosophes* had its centre in Paris, but it also drew upon provincial custom and ancient culture imbibed during the 'Grand Tour' they often made of Europe, and it was significantly inspired by what they perceived to be the virtues of civic life in England. Nearly every major figure of that period, with the notable exception of Rousseau, was deeply impressed by England. It was there that the spirit of empirical science and scepticism was seen to prevail, and the mixed constitution reigned; there that religious toleration and political liberty reinforced one another and animated the bustle of commercial enterprise, so that, as Voltaire put it, the only infidels are those who go bankrupt. The term 'Anglomania' was devised in the eighteenth-century to characterize, and sometimes caricature, those Frenchmen who loved England with excessive zeal, and no figure of the French Enlightenment loved England more than Voltaire. He was the most eloquent exponent on behalf of the genius of such English sages as Locke and Newton, as well as of the economic pragmatism of English people in general, and his vision of that country as a whole nation of *philosophes* won wide appeal and approval among many of his contemporaries in France and elsewhere in Europe.

Enlightenment thinkers held disparate views about the merits of particular programmes, but they were in almost unanimous accord about one policy which should be shunned: Revolution. Despite their contempt for the Church, their opposition to privilege and tyranny, and their criticisms of the abuse of power under the Ancien Régime, they were all anxious to avoid violent political upheaval, which they regarded as a remedy worse than the disease. After 1789 a few of the small band of surviving *philosophes* did join revolutionary parties, though even then the caution and prudence they counselled sometimes lost them their heads. None had helped to form revolutionary parties before. On the contrary, most progressive figures of the period thought that the best safeguard against revolution lay in the adoption, by governments, of the doctrines advanced by the *philosophes,* while the pessimists among them, like Rousseau, believed even constitutional reform could no longer protect the monarchies of Europe from destruction. As he stated in his portentous words of 1762, 'We are now on the threshhold of the century of revolutions'.

It is one of history's many ironies that when that century of revolutions *did* come, its battles were fought largely round the doctrines which the *philosophes* had conceived in order to avert it. While their ideas had not been put forward with revolutionary intent, they were, nonetheless, regarded as having revolutionary implications, and it was through them that the political conflicts and movements of the next age were articulated and expressed.

The eighteenth-century doctrine of Utilitarianism came to underlie the campaigns of the Philosophic Radicals and their allies which culminated in the great Reform Bills of the British parliament in the next century. The individualism and Laissez-Faire economic principles of other *philosophes* have come to be the watchwords of European Liberalism ever since. From the secularism and anti-clericalism of the Enlightenment we have inherited Materialism, Humanism, and many of our present justifications of the separation of Church from State. From the cultural Pluralism and historical focus of certain eighteenth-century perspectives were developed the doctrines of Nationalism and Conservativism, first by Romantic, and, later by Fascist, thinkers, sometimes to discredit that period of our intellectual history as a whole. And from Enlightenment accounts of the morally corrupt and economically ruinous institutions of private property and arbitrary government have stemmed some of the most striking elements of the Communist and Socialist ideologies of the next epoch. We may not yet have achieved the Enlightenment's ideal of a unified political theory and practice, but the real legacy of that age lies in the conflicting ideologies to which we adhere, or by which we are ruled, in the contemporary world.

Further reading

Matthew S. Anderson, *Historians and Eighteenth-Century Europe, 1715-1789*
Stuart Andrews, *Enlightened Absolutism*
Keith M. Baker, *Condorcet: From Natural Philosophy to Social Mathematics*
Timothy Blanning, *Joseph II and Enlightened Despotism*
Stuart C. Brown (ed.), *Philosophers of the Enlightenment*
Marilyn S. Butler (ed.), *Burke, Paine, Godwin and the Revolution Controversy*
Ernst Cassirer, *Rousseau, Kant and Goethe*
Henry S. Commager, *The Empire of Reason: How Europe imagined and America realized the Enlightenment*
Cecil P. Courtney, *Montesquieu and Burke*
Lester G. Crocker, *An Age of Crisis: Man and World in Eighteenth-Century French Thought*
Lester G. Crocker, *Nature and Culture: Ethical Thought in the French Enlightenment*
Lester G. Crocker (ed.), *The Age of Enlightenment*
Peter Gay, *Voltaire's Politics: The Poet as Realist*
Peter Gay, *The Party of Humanity: Studies in the French Enlightenment*
Peter Gay, *The Enlightenment: An Interpretation* (2 vols.)

Knud Haakonssen, *The Science of a Legislator: The Natural Jurisprudence of David Hume and Adam Smith*
Norman Hampson, *The Enlightenment*
Istvan Hont and Michael Ignatieff (eds.), *Wealth and Virtue: The Shaping of Political Economy in the Scottish Enlightenment*
Nannerl Keohane, *Philosophy and the State in France: The Renaissance to the Enlightenment*
Leonard Krieger, *An Essay on the Theory of Enlightened Despotism*
J. Q. C. Mackrell, *The Attack on 'Feudalism' in Eighteenth-Century France*
Isabel de Madariaga, *Russia in the Age of Catherine the Great*
Kingsley Martin, *French Liberal Thought in the Eighteenth Century*
David Miller, *Philosophy and Ideology in Hume's Political Thought*
James Miller, *Rousseau: Dreamer of Democracy*
R. R. Palmer, *The Age of the Democratic Revolution* (2 vols.)
Harry C. Payne, *The Philosophes and the People*
Roy S. Porter and Mikulas Teich (eds.), *The Enlightenment in National Context*
Louis Schneider (ed.), *The Scottish Moralists on Human Nature and Society*
Anthony Strugnell, *Diderot's Politics*
Franco Venturi, *Utopia and Reform in the Enlightenment*
Franco Venturi, *Italy and the Enlightenment: Studies in a Cosmopolitan Century*
Donald Winch, *Adam Smith's Politics: An Essay in Historiographic Revision*

European Integration

The term 'European Integration' may refer to either a process, a presumption, or a prescription. As a process, it stems from the growing interdependence of European society, and is reflected in a complex network of laws, conventions, institutions and alliances designed to cope with the consequences of complex interdependence. As a presumption, the awareness that, despite the existence of separate sovereign states, European society was in certain senses one and interdependent, was arguably an important, though often unspoken, element in the conceptual equipment of European statesmen long before the breakdown of European society in the modern period helped to transform this unspoken assumption into an overt prescription for Europe's ills. As a prescription, it embraces a wide range of political strategies and ideologies, each concerned in one way or another to advance the goal of European unity as an alternative or supplement to a European system founded on the sovereignty of national states. Alternatively hardly less frequently, it was to provide the cloak of legitimacy for the transformation of that system in the interests of a particularly powerful, hegemonous state or group of states.

The idea of European unity, of a common cultural and political identity which encompasses all the peoples of Europe, whatever their political affiliation or nationality, was a persistent theme in the political theory of the Middle Ages, invoked and abused by apologists for both Church and Empire. Even after the emergence of modern, sovereign states in France, England and elsewhere, the sense that Europe was, as Gibbon wrote in 1781, 'a great republic' distinguished above the rest of mankind by a 'system of arts and laws and manners' and 'a general state of happiness', upheld by the balance of power and the 'politeness and cultivation of its inhabitants', persisted as a spoken or unspoken assumption of and constraint on the great majority of those who governed European society before the First World War. The idea was underpinned by the existence of a highly integrated European élite, whose members moved and married across national frontiers and shared a considerable stock of ideals and prejudices regardless of their particular national origins. Even those most identified with the struggles for national independence (see NATIONALISM) in the nineteenth century, such as Mazzini, thought within and spoke of a European dimension, within which free nations could and ought to exist at peace.

There is only a fine line between the conviction that the unity of Europe has already been achieved, and that it serves as a constraint on those who govern different parts of it, and the belief that it needs to be deliberately created – or recreated. In the sixteenth to eighteenth centuries there were always some who advocated a deliberate programme of European unification, Grotius being a notable example, but they wrote against the background of an international system in which the states, both national and dynastic, had neither the means nor, in most cases, the will to cause more than local and limited damage to European society in pursuit of their ambitions. The theme of European Integration, however, became more insistent in the latter half of the nineteenth century as expanding international communications brought increased independence and as the capacity for mutual destruction in modern warfare became more apparent. The belief that, in this type of world, a system based on the absolute sovereignty of nation states was totally inadequate and that some form of European unity was essential was, however, by no means confined to idealists in the international peace movements and elsewhere. It was a working assumption of a significant number of politicians, soldiers and officials in the mainstream of European affairs. It is essential, when attempting to explain what has happened since the Second World War, to recognise that , however diverse their motives, there is a significant family likeness between the political strategies of Bethmann-Hollweg, whose memorandum of the German peace aims of September 1914 envisaged a new European order founded upon a Berlin-Vienna axis: of Jean Monnet and Arthur Salter who saw in the machinery of the wartime alliance the seeds of a new political system in which, under force of circumstances, national resources were pooled for the common good: of Coudenhove-Kalergie, founder of the Pan-European movement and of French and German businessmen who, particularly after the Ruhr-crises of 1923, advocated Franco-German co-operation as an alternative to semi-permanent conflict. These and other plans from the first three decades of the present century did not take root, but the problems posed by the process of integration continued to haunt even those who most vehemently advocated national or imperialist strategies. The National Socialist 'New Order' was not merely a propaganda device dreamt

87

up by Goebbels, but a set of plans, many of them half-baked and mutually incompatible, for a new European political system which allowed for and encouraged integration, albeit on German terms. The contradictions between and within these strategies and Hitler's commitment to aims whose pursuit was incompatible with the systematic construction of a New Order, meant that the latter was never more than a superficial and fragmented reality, but it still remains important in the history of European Integration.

The Second World War was still more important, however, because it created the conditions for a new and more durable series of experiments in co-operation and integration, particularly in Western Europe: The emergence, as a reaction to the world crisis (which was military, economic, political and moral in character) of a widespread consensus, both within and outside occupied Europe, that many of the most fundamental problems of modern industrialised societies could only be solved through international co-operation; the development of complex machinery for intergovernmental co-operation within the wartime alliance, particularly amongst the Western powers, which provided a whole generation of Western European leaders (e.g. Monnet, Spaak, Pleven, Gutt, Beyen etc.) with practical experience of the management of interdependence and in certain cases created the foundations of postwar institutions; the destruction of Germany, the only European nation state remotely capable of matching the non-European superpowers, the Soviet Union and the United States: the emergence of the latter as the dominant world powers and the destruction of what remained of European hegemony in the world at large. These conditions provided the background to a significant number of proposals for and experiments in European integration and co-operation both during and after the war. Plans for a new European order based on the wartime alliance were a feature of Allied discussions during the Anglo-French period, 1939-40, and subsequently during the years of the Grand Alliance. These wartime plans and experiments already revealed a wide diversity of assumptions about the optimum types of institutional structures and the geographical extent of European Union. Advocates of federal, confederal and functional strategies and of a Pan-European Union and a Western Block jostled together under the general banner of European Integration. The division of Europe between East and West, already anticipated during the war itself and consolidated in the Cold War, provided a harsh solution to at least some of these questions, and from 1947 onwards, plans for European Integration tended increasingly to be confined to one or other of the regional blocks in Western and Eastern Europe. Differences of opinion about the types of constitution which would be most appropriate in the new regional groups were still numerous and significant, however. Hopes of creating a full-blown Federation, which were high in certain parts of continental Europe, particularly in 1947-49, received a severe set-back in the failure of the Council of Europe to develop in the sense that many of its advocates had intended, but federalist ideology and hopes lived on to complicate the debate about and development of the European Coal and Steel Community,

Euratom, and the European Economic Community, even though these latter drew their immediate inspiration from Jean Monnet whose functional supra-nationalism was in many ways quite different from the strategies of the federalists. In the course of time, the three communities themselves have acquired more and more the characteristics of intergovernmental institutions, and it is quite impossible now to define the political system of Western Europe in terms of any of the classical categories (federation, confederation etc.) which exercised and continue to exercise a powerful influence on those engaged in creating the system. The emergence of a European Council in the later 1970's as the highest organ of intergovernmental co-operation, coupled with the establishment of a European Parliament whose members are directly elected, may provide the basis for what will in due course be a European Confederation, but at present the European policy is an untidy amalgam of political strategies and *ad hoc* institutional devices intended to cope with the problems of complex interdependence.

Fascism

At the height of its power, Fascism seemed to be an ideology capable of conquering the entire globe. 'Germany today, tomorrow the whole world', proclaimed the chorus of a Nazi marching song. By the mid-1930's there was virtually no European country without a Fascist party. The Fascists stressed the univeral applicability of their doctrines. These would create the foundations for a new type of state, which would supercede decadent liberal parliamentarianism and satisfy the demands of the socially disadvantaged classes and groups, thereby destroying the appeal of Jewish-dominated (see ANTI-SEMITISM) and anti-national Bolshevism (see COMMUNISM). The twentieth century, proclaimed Mussolini, would be a 'Fascist century. . . Fascism as an idea, a doctrine, a realisation is universal. . . Never before have the people thirsted for authority, direction, order as they do now. If each age has its doctrine, innumerable symptoms indicate that the doctrine of our age is the Fascist one'. In a speech to the Fascist party in 1926 he announced that Fascism was to be 'a new principle in the world, the clear final and categorical antithesis of Democracy, Plutocracy, Freemasonry and the eternal principle of 1789'.

The Fascists were able to make such elevated claims on their own behalf – claims which seemed entirely capable of being realised — yet by 1945 both Hitler and Mussolini were dead. Their regimes and those of almost all their allies and satellites had collapsed, leaving their states in ruins. Fascism disappeared after a brief period in power, leaving little behind in the way of positive achievements.

There is still no scholarly consensus as to the nature of the principle fascist

89

régimes in Europe and the term 'fascist' has become frequently little more than a term of abuse. Yet, in spite of all the disagreement, almost all explanations of Fascism can be divided into two groups. The first sees Fascism above all as a reactionary movement, a secondary product of the class struggle (see SOCIALISM). It argues that fascism was an attempt by the *grande bourgeoisie* to defeat a revolutionary challenge to its position. This point of view was given its classical formulation by the Comintern in December 1935 (see COMMUNISM). It asserted 'Fascism is the unconcealed terrorist dictatorship of the most reactionary chauvinistic and imperialistic elements of finance capital'.

The second set of explanations sees Fascism as a revolutionary movement. It succeeded in gaining support from all sections of the community, even though it obtained its backing above all from the middle and lower-middle classes. Its hostility to Liberalism (see LIBERALISM) was derived from the belief that parliamentary government had allowed special groups – Jews, Masons and capitalists – to manipulate the political system to their advantage. In its place they advocated a national revolution, which would create a sense of national community and win the support of those classes oppressed and neglected by the liberal establishment. To gain power an alliance with traditional conservative (see CONSERVATISM) forces was necessary, but in fact this alliance was purely tactical since landowners, industrialists and the churches were likely to prove major obstacles to the revolutionary transformation of society desired by Fascists. Far from being the tools of the big industrialists, the Fascists sought goals incompatible with the interests of *laisser-faire* capitalism. Unlimited economic growth was seen by them as a distruptive force and they sought rather to stabilise society in a period in which the gross national product could no longer be expected to rise indefinitely. The claims of national solidarity and the ruthless pursuit of national interest in foreign affairs (see NATIONALISM) would enable class conflict to be transcended while special protection would be provided for those groups – small businessmen, traders, artisans and peasants – threatened with extinction by big capital.

Neither of these explanations is wholly convincing. It is certainly true that the alliance of Fascists and traditional conservatives was one of convenience and that once in power, the Fascists attempted — with varying success — to establish for themselves a dominant position in the relationship. Yet this was not generally pursued in order to achieve the pursuit of revolutionary objectives. On the contrary, the principal goal of the major Fascist regimes was foreign expansion. This dictated a measure of compromise with the conservatives whose co-operation was essential if this aim was to be successfully pursued. The imperatives of imperial expansion thus led to the postponement of cherished Fascist objectives such as the protection of small businessman and artisans, the creation of a stable caste of peasant proprietors or the reduction of the number of women in factories. Whether these goals would have been pursued after a Fascist victory, as Hitler sometimes claimed in his table talk, remains very much open to doubt.

Fascism emerged as an effective political force as a consequence of the First World War. Yet it had its roots in an intellectual revolution which took place in Europe between 1890 and 1914. It was in these years that thinkers like Nietzsche, Sorel, Maurras and Marinetti set out all the basic concepts which were to constitute the ideology of fascism. The revolt of the 1890's took many forms but it was above all a rejection of the dominant ideology of Liberalism, based as it was on a belief in progress, free trade, international co-operation and a society composed of rational individuals each seeking his own interest, which, by the providential operation of Adam Smith's 'hidden hand', would lead to the general benefit of all. With Liberalism, democratic political principles were particularly virulently criticised. In the words of Edward Berth, one of Sorel's pupils, 'Democracy was the greatest error of the nineteenth century. . . in economics and politics [it] permitted the establishment of the capitalist regime which destroys in the State that which democratic ideas dissolve in the spirit, namely the nation, the family, morals, by substituting the law of gold for the laws of blood.'

The fascists were well aware of their indebtedness to the new intellectual climate which developed at the turn of the century. As Rosenberg told Hitler in 1934, 'You, *mein Führer* have rescued from oblivion the works of Nietzsche, Wagner, Lagarde and Dühring, works which foretold the doom of the old culture'.

The attack on Liberalism and democracy took many forms. Social Darwinism had already caused a devaluation of liberal political principles. The liberal ideal of a society of rational and co-operating individuals was an illusion and unceasing struggle was the law of all animal life, leading to the survival of the fittest. Élitism was thus given a new justification. The Italian sociologist, Pareto, put forward the thesis that all societies were characterised by an 'iron law of oligarchy'. History was characterised not by class struggle but by a conflict between rising and falling élites and the principal function of political institutions was to perpetuate a successfully functioning élite.

Social Darwinism also led to a new interest in racial differences (see NATIONALISM). The idea that there was a hierarchy of superior and inferior races, with the pinnacle of human achievement represented by Germanic Aryans was given wide publicity in Houston Stuart Chamberlain's *Foundations of the Nineteenth Century*. He even asserted that Jesus could not have been a Jew but was Canaanite Aryan. Certainly one of the consequences of the new racialism was a heightened anti-semitism (see ANTI-SEMITISM). Hostility to the Jews was now justified not on religious or social but on racial grounds. In the words of Wilhelm Marr: 'There must be no question of parading religious prejudices when it is a question of race, and when the difference lies in the "blood"'.

A further effect of the acceptance of Social Darwinism was a growing rejection of the liberal ideals of international co-operation and free trade. Calls for the singleminded assertion of a narrowly conceived national interest were widely expressed in France, where right-wing ideologues often argued that France's decline and defeat by Prussia in 1870 was the result of the negative effects of revolutionary liberal ideas. Charles Maurras, the leading figure in *Action Francaise*, asserted that: 'Those people who are governed by their men of action and their military leaders win out over those peoples who are governed by their lawyers and professors.'

Views of this sort were also widely held in Italy, whose national pretensions never matched up to the reality of the weak and divided kingdom. Enrico Corradini, an Italian nationalist ideologue who ended up as a strong supporter of Mussolini, called for an Italian 'National Socialism'. Italy, he claimed, was a 'proletarian nation':

> Just as socialism taught the proletariat the value of the class struggle, so we must teach Italy the value of the international struggle.
> But international struggle means war.
> Well let it be war! And let nationalism arouse in Italy the will to win a war.

This glorification of war and violence was a major characteristic of the intellectual climate of the end of the nineteenth century. The rigid and often stifling conventions of bourgeois society provoked a desire to break out of its trammels and led to a fascination with violence as a liberating force. The view that social life in advanced industrial societies stultified and deformed human nature was most clearly articulated by Frederick Nietzsche, whose works were widely read and distributed after his death in 1889. Nietzsche, a subtle and enigmatic thinker, was a penetrating critic of late nineteenth-century values and is far from being a cruel advocate of the 'blond beast', for which he is sometimes attacked. He called for a new morality, a rethinking of all values, which would make it possible for mankind to control the blind forces which drove it to its destiny. For this to be accomplished, all the false values of society would have to be destroyed by a new race of 'supermen' who would not be restrained by sentimental inhibitions, but would be prepared to use violence without scruple to create a new and better world. The radical right seized above all on Nietzsche's hostility to 'liberal sentimentalism', his belief in the hollowness of material progress and his faith in the purifying virtue of violence.

Another crucial figure of the period was Georges Sorel, the French supporter of anarcho-syndicalism (see ANARCHISM) who at the end of his life gave his support to both Lenin and Mussolini. Sorel stressed the significance of 'myths', emotional symbols for which one could be induced to die and which were to be assessed not by whether they were true or false, but by their effect in mobilising masses of men. He too saw violence as a purifying force and was strongly anti-intellectual.

This dissatisfaction with the effects of modern life led different thinkers to contradictory conclusions. In Germany, calls for a reassertion of traditional moral values and a return to a pre-industrial society were most widespread. In Germany, Wilhelm Moeller von der Bruck stressed the decadence of modern society and the need to return to the ordered and hierarchical life of the middle ages in a significantly-named *Third Reich*. Similar ideas were expressed by Julius Langbehn, who claimed that the decline of German culture would only be ended by a return to the land and the rejection of rational in favour of instinctive values: 'The nearer the culture of the spirit and the soil are to each other, the better for both; and and people, body and soul, belong to each other'.

Hostility to modern civilisation could also lead to a cult of the machine as a violent force which could rise out of the fake values of democracy. This was the view of the Italian Futurists, led by Giacomo Marinetti who remained a faithful supporter of Mussolini right until the end of his rule. In their manifesto of 1909, the Futurists asserted 'We want to glorify war, the only cure for mankind, and militarism, patriotism, the destructive gesture of the anarchists, the beautiful ideas which kill and contempt for woman. . . We want to demolish museums and libraries, fight morality and feminism and all opportunist and utilitarian cowardice.'

The aversion to the emancipation of women expressed by Marinetti was a common feature of the new right-wing ideologists. Acccording to Nietzsche:

Wherever the spirit of industry has triumphed over the military and aristo-cratic spirit, woman now aspires to the status of clerk. As she thus seizes new rights, looks to become master. . . the reverse is happening with dread-ful clarity; *woman is retrogressing*. . . to seek with virtuous assurance to destroy man's belief that a fundamentally difference concept is involved in *Woman*, what does all this mean if not a crumbling of the feminine instinct, a defeminising.

These ideas led to the creation of a number of political groups before 1914. Among them perhaps the most significant was the *Action Française* founded by Charles Maurras in the aftermath of the defeat of the French right in the Dreyfus affair. It combined, in a not wholly consistent fashion, proto-fascist ideas, such as the belief in a Jewish world conspiracy (see ANTI-SEMITISM), with traditionally conservative views – above all, the belief in the need to restore the monarchy and the rejection of the French revolution and all its works. The weakness of France which had caused the defeat of 1870 was the result, the movement claimed of, the destructive effects of the revolutionary tradition. Unlike the true essence of France, which was Royalist and Catholic, the revolution was an alien movements, inspired by Jews, Protestants and Freemasons, who were referred to by Maurras as the embodiments of 'Anti-France'. Right radical and proto-fascist groups also emerged in a number of other European countries. They included the various pan-German and anti-semitic parties in Austria-Hungary and Germany, the *Union of Russian Men* and the *Union of the Russian People* in the Tsarist Empire and the Italian Nationalists led by Enrico Corradini. They all shared certain characteristics, rejecting liberalism and parliamentary government in favour of an authoritarian system. Nationalism and expansionism were regarded as vital to the health of the state, which was seen as threatened by anti-national elements (see NATIONALISM), socialists, Freemasons and – except in Italy – Jews. Yet nowhere were these groups able to mount a serious assault on the *status quo*.

The war gave them a new lease of life. Everywhere the war was welcomed by the radical right which revelled in the patriotic outbursts it called forth. The union of all classes and groups which they had so long called for now seemed to be achieved. The war was indeed supported by the majority of socialist parties (see SOCIALISM) and many who had long scorned patriotism as a bourgeois illusion, like Benito Mussolini, the leader of the revolutionary faction of the Italian socialist part of Gustave Hervé (the French pacifist), became enthusiastic protagonists of their countries' war efforts. In Italy, nationalist pressure groups known as interventionists even succeeded in forcing the country into the war on the allied side in April 1915, thereby demonstrating how a determined and aggressive minority could succeed in imposing itself on the government in the name of its conception of the national interest.

The war created a new set of myths. It strengthened the right radical belief that parliamentary government was merely a screen behind which sinister forces – Jews, Freemasons, capitalists – pursued their private and sectional interests. The fighting had been done in appalling conditions in the trenches, while the politicians had merely remained in the capital and talked. Everywhere in Europe the right extolled the solidarity of the fighting front. Its hardships entitled the survivors to play a special role in politics. Organisations of front-line soldiers were a common feature of post-war Europe and were often linked with the rising fascist groups. Certainly many Fascist leaders served at the front, among them Hitler and Rohm, Mussolini and de Bono, Szalasi in Hungary and Codreanu in Romania. The claim of the returning soldiers was vociferously asserted by Mussolini. 'We who have survived,' he claimed in March 1919, 'we who are returning demand the right to rule Italy. . . We alone have the right to the succession because we were the men who forced the country into the war and won the victory.' Widespread use of frontline symbols was made by the fascists, above all the dagger of the *Arditi*, the élite shock troops of the Italian army.

Defeat, after the patriotic exaltation of the war, came as a bitter shock in Germany, and resentment at the post-war situation was intensified by the fact that the German surrender had occurred before any allied troops had occupied German territory. This gave rise to a potent myth that the country had been on the verge of victory when a disloyal clique of socialists and Jews had stabbed it in the back. As a result the Treaty of Versailles, under the terms of which Germany lost all her colonies, thirteen per cent of her territory in Europe and was obliged to pay large but unspecified reparations, was never accepted by large sections of the population. This discontent was exploited by the radical right and meant that the new republic lacked legitimacy in the eyes of many of its citizens.

Similarly in Italy, victory turned very quickly to disillusionment as it became apparent that the country was going to acquire rather less in the way of territory than she had been promised by the allies and in the Treaty of London of 1915, and much less than what Italian nationalists (who wished to acquire a dominant position for their country in the Adriatic) regarded as their due (see NATIONALISM). The 'mutilated peace' was accordingly widely attacked as insufficient recompense for the role Italy had played in the allied victory. Elsewhere too, particularly in Hungary, Bulgaria and Finland, dissatisfaction with the peace settlement and irredentist sentiment lent considerable strength to anti-democratic and right radical forces.

Political stability was further undermined by the economic and social dislocation which followed the war. The prosperity of the pre-war world could not be re-established and Europe's economic system was plagued by the twin evils of inflation and unemployment. In the early 1920s runaway inflation occurred in Germany, Austria, Hungary and Poland. In Italy, too, the cost of living increased fourfold between 1913 and 1919. The results of inflation were everywhere the same. The savings of the middle class were largely wiped out and its members became much more prone to political extremism. Speculators were moreover quick to benefit from inflation and stories, often exaggerated, of their windfall profits strengthened opposition to parliamentary democracy which was held responsible for the inflation and also contributed to the growing climate of anti-semitism.

From 1924 to 1929 a degree of prosperity was re-established, but the crisis returned in 1929 when the impact of the US slump was felt in Europe. This time the main manifestation was unemployment, which rose to unheard-of levels. In Germany in 1932, for instance, six million people, or a quarter of the labour force, were out of work. Liberal democracy and capitalism seemed to be incapable of running the economy and calls for a new political system, whether of the right or left, became widespread.

Certainly the war had been followed by a wave of revolutionary upheavals (see SOCIALISM; COMMUNISM). The class truce of 1914 had not been accepted by all socialists and a minority, led by Rosa Luxemburg, Karl Liebknecht and Lenin, had argued rather that the working class should seize the opportunity caused by the severe hardship it imposed to convert the war into a civil conflict. Russia was the first to crack and by 1921, after winning a civil war and repelling foreign attempts to overthrow them, Lenin and the Bolsheviks had established themselves securely in power.

Their success in overthrowing one of the principal strongholds of European reaction led to many attempts at emulation. In Italy, the return of over two million soldiers from the front led to a major social crisis, marked by strikes and the occupation of factories. The years 1919 and 1920 have been referred to as the _biennio rosso_ (the red two years), although the socialist party, soon to split into socialist and communist groups, was in fact, too weak to take power. In Germany, the estabishment of the republic in November 1918 was followed by an ill-fated and bloodily suppressed insurrection of the left-wing _spartakists_ led by Luxemburg and Liebknecht. Short-lived soviet republics were also established in Bavaria, Hungary and Slovakia.

These upheavels caused a wave of panic among the upper and middle classes in Europe. The *status quo* appeared seriously threatened and democratic institutions seemed incapable of resisting revolution. Demands for a more authoritarian political system became widespread. The revolutionary wave also led to an intensification of anti-semitism, already fanned by the influx of less Germanised Jews into Germany and Austria during the war. There had been many people of Jewish origin among the revolutionary leaders, including Trotsky, Karmenev and Zinoviev in Russia, Bela Kun in Hungary and Kurt Eisner in Bavaria. The equation of Jew with Bolshevik now became a commonplace on the radical right (see ANTI-SEMITISM). In the words of the leader of the Romanian fascist Iron Guard, 'Every Jew, whether he is a trader, intellectual or banker is a conscious agent of communist ideas directed at the Romanian people.'

The fascists took power in three waves. The first of these came in the 1920s. The immediate post-war crisis in Italy gave Mussolini the opportunity to compel the Italian political establishment to make him Prime Minister in October 1922 and by the end of 1925, the fascist dictatorship was securely established. In Hungary, the short-lived Soviet republic was followed by the estalishment of a regime which was a somewhat incongruous coalition of traditional conservatives and the right-radicals who had provided the bulk of the Hungarian counter-revolutionary armies. Neither of these groups had much respect for the other, and, in the relatively prosperous conditions of the twenties, the conservatives were able increasingly to dominate the political system at the expense of their fascist allies. In Germany an unsuccessful attempt was made by Hitler and his National Socialist Party to seize power in November 1923 in Bavaria, already a stronghold of right-radical opponents of the new republic.

The late 1920s saw a measure of political stability re-established, but with the severe impact in Europe of the Great Depression, the atmosphere of crisis reasserted itself and led to a general revival of fascist groups and parties. The second wave came when Hitler was appointed chancellor of Germany in January 1933 as head of a coalition of Nazis and Nationalists. He rapidly consolidated his power, banning all parties other than the Nazis in the summer of 1933, and by mid 1934 his power was virtually unassailable. In Austria, Englebert Dollfuss, leader of the Christian Social Party, unwilling to enlist the support of the Social Democrats and alarmed by the growing strength of the Austrian Nazis, decided in March 1933 to dispense with parliament. He set up a single party, the 'Fatherland Front', and, after crushing the socialists in a brief but bloody civil war in February 1934, introduced a new constitution in May. This was corporative and authoritarian in character and claimed that its clerico-fascist principles were based on the views enunciated in the papal encyclical *Quadragesimo Anno* of 1931 which sought through industrial syndicates to mitigate class conflict and reconcile the workers with capitalism. In April 1933, Portugal, which had been a right-wing dictatorship since April 1926, adopted a similar constitution in the form of the *Estado Novo* of the austere Catholic economist, Antonio Salazar. In Spain, the first impact of the depression had been to cause the collapse in 1931 of the dictatorship of Primo Rivera. It was succeeded soon after by a republic, whose ambitious plans for reform soon provoked violent right-wing resistance. This culminated in a military revolt and the victory in 1939 of the forces of General Franco, an ill-assorted alliance of traditional conservatives and right radicals. The *Falange* (founded by Primo de Rivera's son, Jose Antonio) the principal Spanish fascist group was a constituent part of the anti-republic coalition, but its influence over the essentially cautious and old-fashioned Franco was always rather limited. In Hungary, fascist ideas and personalities gained ground at the expense of conservatives like the Regent, Admiral Horthy.

The German foreign policy successes from September 1938 made possible the third fascist wave. Germany invaded the Czechoslovak republic in March 1939 and facilitated the setting up of a nationalist state with a clerical-fascist character in Slovakia. The defeat of Yugoslavia in April 1941 saw the setting up of a similar state in Croatia. In Western Europe, German conquest saw the creation of fascist collaborationist regimes headed by the local fascists in Norway and Holland. In Belgium, though no actual pro-German regime was set up, the Flemish fascists, the extreme wing of the Flemish national movement and Leon Degrelle's *Rexist* party welcomed the establishment of the German dominated 'New Order'. Degrelle, a disciple of Maurras, even formed a unit to fight alongside the Germans in Russia.

In France, the regime set up in Vichy in 1940 was made up of two groups: Pétain and his followers who wanted to establish an old-fashioned authoritarian and clerical state, and opportunists like Pierre Laval, whose sole concern was to mitigate as far as possible the consequences of France's defeat. Alongside the Vichy authorities, the Germans encouraged out-and-out Fascist groups, particularly in Paris, and these were used as an additional means of keeping the Vichy authorities in line. In Romania, the abdication of the King in 1940 led to the setting up of a government which was an uneasy coalition of fascist Iron Guard and old-style conservatives, such as General Antonescu. Invariably, their co-operatives did not prove easy and in November 1940, Antonescu, with German support, crushed the Iron Guard. In Hungary, events moved in the opposite direction. The Germans occupied the country in March 1944 and in October, after an unsuccessful attempt by the government to reach a separate peace with the allies, a radical fascist regime was set up with German help under Ferenc Szálasi. Everywhere else in axis-occupied Europe, fascist groups and individuals were prominent among those who hoped by collaboration to find for themselves some place in the German 'New Order'.

The processes by which the fascists established themselves in power had many similarities, above all in the two most important fascist states, Italy and Germany. In the first place, the emergence of the fascists as a major political force was only made possible by the collapse of the existing political system.

97

Table 1   *Results of the 1913 elections in Italy*

		Votes	Seats in parliament
1	Giolittian coalition	3,392,000	
	a) Liberals, nationalists and democrats		310
	b) Radicals		73
	c) Reformists		27
2	Catholics	302,000	29
3	Republicans/Independents	437,000	17
4	Socialists	883,000	52
	Total	5,014,000	508

Table 2   *Results of the November 1919 elections in Italy*

		Votes	Seats in parliament
1	Giolittian coalition	1,779,000	
	a) Liberals and nationalists		23
	d) Democrats		91
	c) Radicals		57
	d) Reformists		22
2	War veterans	320,000	33
3	Popolari	1,167,000	100
4	Republicans/Independents	581,000	26
5	Socialists	1,835,000	156
	Total	5,682,000	508

Source: G. Salvemini, *The Origins of Fascism in Italy*, revised (New York, 1973).

In Italy, the introduction of universal suffrage with a secret ballot and proportional representation in the elections of November 1919 destroyed the dominance long enjoyed in parliament by the liberals (see Tables 1 & 2). The largest parliamentary groups were now the Socialists, torn between reform and revolution, and the *Popolari*, a radical Catholic party. The Liberals, men like Giolitti and Nitti, did not believe that these groups could be integrated into the political system and were correspondingly more willing to reach an accommodation with the fascists.

In Germany, too, the new republic established in 1918 was confronted with at least two serious right-wing attempts to overthrow it. In addition, in order to defeat the threat from the left, the government had found itself compelled to enlist the support of the army. Any attempt to purge the officer corps was therefore abandoned and the army was able to claim a special role for itself in political life. In the words of its commander General von Seeckt, 'The army serves the state, the state alone, for it is the state!'.

A measure of political stability returned in the late 1920s under the chancellorship of Gustav Stresemann. Yet the anti-republican forces remained powerful and already in 1925 were able to have their candidate, former Field-marshal Hindenburg, elected to the powerful office of President. Stresemann's death and the impact of the Depression caused the collapse of his coalition. Politics was now dominated by the backstair intrigues of various groups in the German conservative establishment, all of whom hoped to enlist Hitler's backing to acquire popular support for an authoritarian transformation of German politics in the form either of military dictatorship or a return to the pre-1914 political system.

What were the principal sources of fascist support? Almost all fascist groups aimed in the first instance at winning the working class away from Marxism by a combination of socialism and nationalism. In Italy, this was clearly expressed by Mussolini's choice of the title *fasci di combattimento* for his political movement. *Fascio* means 'fist ' or 'bundle' and in Italian political life the terms had long been imbued with overwhelmingly left-wing and insurrectionary implications. To resort to a *fascio* was to take extra-parliamentary action out of despair at the failure of parliament. Yet, in spite of the radicalism of the original *fasci di combattimento* programme, Mussolini's attempt to acquire left-wing support proved almost entirely unsuccessful. It was only when the fascists began to attack the socialists that they were able to emerge as a mass movement. The breakthrough occurred in the rich agricultural provinces of the Po valley. Socialist agitation among agricultural labourers had aroused strong opposition from local landowners here, and they quickly rallied to the strike-breaking activities of the fascists. The professional and trading classes of the towns were also soon won over. With their financial support and the tacit acquiescence of the bulk of the police, army and judiciary the fascists were soon a mass anti-revolutionary force organising punitive anti-socialist 'expeditions' throughout northern Italy.

The Nazis, too, initially attempted with not much success to win working class support. From about 1928, however, they began rather to look for backing in new areas, principally from small businessmen, artisans and tradesmen, the German *Mittelstand*, as well as from the peasantry. It was the referendum on the Young plan on reparations in July 1929 which enabled the Nazis to emerge as a major political force. They were able to shed their working-class image and associate with such impeccably conservative forces as the ex-servicemen's association, the *Stahlhelm* and the German nationalists.

The new respectability of the Nazis bore dividends in the elections of September 1930 and July 1932. In this second election, the Nazis won thirty seven per cent of the vote and became the largest group. The typical Nazi voter was now 'a middle-class self-employed protestant who lived either on a farm or in a small community and also had previously voted for a centrist or regionalist political party strongly opposed to the power of and influence of big business and by labour'. Indeed, by 1932, the Nazis dominated the entire North German

99

plain, largely rural and protestant, with the exception of a few large cities like Berlin and Hamburg. By now, they had become much more than an anti-democratic protest group. They could with some justification claim to be a national movement which would unite all the different groups and classes in Germany in a way which the democratic parties had signally failed to do. As Hitler put it during the electoral campaign of July 1932:

> We National-Socialists are not to be compared to any of the other thirty political parties (in Germany). We fight as the greatest People's Movement Germany has produced and we will not abandon our struggle after the elections. . . Millions of people in Germany in the past days have found themselves united who previously were split up into thirty parties which fought and made war on each other. What is this, if not a German National Revival?

The fascists' rise to power was also aided by their skilful exploitation of violence while simultaneously proclaiming their loyalty to constitutional legality. Violence was a feature of Italian fascist political activity from the very inception of the movement. Yet Mussolini frequently expressed his desire to reach a compromise with the political establishment. In the tense period before October 1922 he continued throughout to negotiate with the liberal parliamentarians even suggesting a coalition headed by Giolitti. Yet all the while he was planning an insurrection which finally took the form of the march on Rome. Since he had so often compromised before, his revolutionary preparations were not taken seriously and his path to power was accordingly considerably easier. Indeed, once he had been handed it, Mussolini had to reassure his blackshirt followers by stressing quite falsely that he had seized power in a revolution.

The Nazis were even more adept at the exploitation of violence. After the catastrophic collapse of the Munich *Putsch* Hitler became aware that a frontal assault on the Weimar republic could only end in failure. Yet the Nazis' resort to constitutional methods did not involve an abandonment of revolutionary goals. As Goebbels put it in 1928, 'We go into the *Reichstag* in order the acquire the weapons of democracy from its arsenal. We become *Reichstag* deputies to paralyse democracy with its own assistance.' The use of street violence, precipitated by the SA and SS was a favourite Nazi tactic, which served very effectively both to terrorise their opponents and to intensify the growing belief in the collapse of existing political institutions. The cult of violence also attracted to the movement some of the most desperate and dedicated activists, and was linked with a stress on the 'manly comradeship' of the SA.

Violence also played a significant part in the rapid Nazi consolidation of their hold on power and in the collapse of opposition. Action by the brown-shirted SA against the left after January 1933 was partly spontaneous, but it was also made use of by the Nazi leadership to establish control over provincial governments still in the hands of their opponents. The SA did not limit itself to sporadic attacks on leftist parties and trade unions but even established its own 'unofficial' concentration camps.

Fascists held themselves to be the vanguard of a revolutionary nationalist upsurge. Yet, in order to achieve power, they were everywhere compelled to co-operate with the traditional conservative forces in their societies. Since each side was primarily concerned to exploit the other to its own advantage, their co-operation was, largely, half-hearted. Indeed the tug of war between the traditional conservatives (see CONSERVATISM) and radicals fascists was a constant element in the political life of all fascist states and its outcome was by no means uniform. In Italy, Mussolini, having secured his grip on power attempted to co-operate with the political establishment, stressed his respect for the monarchy and parliament. What pushed him to adopt a more authoritarian system was the political crisis caused by the murder by fascist zealots of the socialist deputy Giacomo Matteotti who had exposed fascist frauds in the parliamentary elections of 1924. This crisis even led Mussolini to contemplate resigning. Instead he gave way to pressure from his hard-line fascist lieutenants, and between January 1925 and the middle of 1926 proceeded to lay the basis for a totalitarian state.

In his bid for power, Hitler, too, sought the backing of the established elements in Germany. For their part, the principal conservative forces – the army, the industrialists, the landed aristocracy – were not particularly enthusiastic about the Nazis, who appeared to them to be lower-class demagogues. Equally, none of them felt strongly opposed to the Nazis being given a share in government. On the contrary, they believed that the Nazis could be used to provide popular support for the authoritarian transformation of German politics which they desired. Blindly confident in their long standing 'right' to rule Germany, they consistently underestimated Hitler and the Nazis, whom they believed they could 'tame' and with whom they shared expansionist goals. They were soon to be disillusioned.

The suppression of the SA in June 1934 was intended by Hitler to bring the Nazi rank and file under control. By replacing the spontaneous and dedicated activists of the SA by the bureaucrats of the SS, Hitler hoped to convince the conservatives that he could be trusted so that they would acquiesce in his hoped-for union of the offices of Chancellor and President, which occured in 1935 and laid the basis for his 'leadership state'. This did not mean that Hitler had given in to the conservatives. Rather terror was institutionalised and bureaucratised and the integration of the conservatives into the new Germany took place almost entirely on Hitler's terms.

A charismatic leader stood at the head of every fascist regime. He was to embody the nation's will and aspirations and was subject to the most extreme adulation. According to Rudolf Hess,

My *Führer*. . . You are Germany. When you act, the Nation acts. When you pass judgements, it is the German people that passes judgement. Our thank offering is our vow to stand by you for better and for worse, come what may! . . . The party is Hitler; Hitler however is Germany, just as Germany is Hitler.

The *Duce* was the subject of similar praise:

> His name was Benito Mussolini, but in fact he was Alexander the Great and Caesar, Socrates and Plato, Virgil and Lucretius, Horace and Tacitus, Kant and Nietzsche, Marx and Sorel, Machiavelli and Napoleon, Garibaldi and the unknown soldier (Ottavio Dinale).

The authority of the leader was to be unquestioned and absolute. The fascist credo in Italy ran: 'Obey! Believe! Fight!', while in Germany the formula was, 'Authority from above; Obedience from below'. At the same time the Fascist state claimed that in the masses would obtain a more satisfactory means for expressing their views, which would no longer be distorted by sectional and divisive political parties as in a liberal state.

In Italy, this was to be made possible through corporativism, which would mean that people would be represented not as individuals, but through corporations or syndicates which embraced all those who pursued a particular occupation. These syndicates in turn would send representatives to the Fascist Grand Council. However this ambitious political programme provoked strong opposition both within the fascist party and from the established groups in Italian society, the Church, the Monarchy and the industrialists. Its principles were first breached by the *Concordat* with the Vatican of February 1929. This greatly strengthened the political stability of the regime, but at the cost both of concessions which the liberals before 1922 had not been prepared to consider and of any pretensions to totalitarianism. In the same way, from 1926 onwards a series of concessions were made to the representatives of heavy industry which ended any illusions that the fascist state intended to play the role of arbitrator between labour service. The consequence was that by 1932 the corporate state had become largely a meaningless façade and that the regime was little more than a personal dictatorship, with a sedulously fostered cult of the *Duce*. As a result, when the political situation worsened Mussolini found himself with very little support. The King and army became a focus for opposition, as did the fascist Grand Council, which was in fact responsible for Mussolini's dismissal in early 1943.

In Nazi Germany, the function of integrating force in the new society was designated not to the state, but to the party. In Hitler's words, it was to be the 'giant marching column of the united nation, which will lead together the people which has been divided and torn asunder in the past. In accordance with *Völkisch* ideas, the party was seen as a spontaneous growth from the masses and was to be 'the elite of the nation.' Reality, invariably, was less impressive. The party was never able to acquire for itself a role similar to that of the Communist Party in the Soviet Union. The old governmental apparatus continued to function side-by-side with the new and it was only in a very few cases that the party was able to assert its primary role. Indeed, one of the most typical features of the Nazi state was the emergence of parallel and rival authorities, an arrangement which resulted both from Hitler's aversion to the practical tasks of administration and from his conviction that a system of competing bureaucracies would enable him more easily to assert his will. He was, however, much more successful than other fascist regimes in subordinating to his control the traditional conservative forces in society, the army, the industrialists and both Catholic and Protestant churches.

The fascist regimes also placed great emphasis on their ability to provide for the interests of special groups in society such as workers, farmers, women and youth. In Italy, the dignity of labour was constantly stressed and the _Dopolavoro_ organisation set up to provide cultural amenities for workers. This process went still further in Germany. In order to retain the support of the army and big business, which was necessary for his expansionist aspiration, Hitler sacrificed the anti-capitalist aspects of his programme. Yet he continued to assert the need to create a national _Volksgemeinschaft_ by winning the support of the workers. This was primarily to be achieved through the _Kraft durch Freude_ and labour service organisations which would underline the dignity of labour and integrate the working class into the wider community. Agricultural work was similarly glorified, although in both Italy and Germany the attempt to stem the flight from the land proved in vain. A similar fate met the attempt to make child-bearing and rearing the main task of women, for labour shortages, especially in Germany, led rather to an increase in factory employment for them. More successful was the mobilisation of young people. This was a major feature of fascist regimes, which had always seen themselves as embodying youthful values of vigour and strength. It took above all the form of the encouragement of youth movements whose task was to prepare the nation for war. None of these integrative appeals involved any significant change in the political balance of power, yet they were very successful in gaining adherents and mobilising society. It was only in the face of defeat that, both in Italy and Germany, the radical social aspirations of fascism were again revived.

These were not the only means employed to achieve national consolidation. A major role was also played by the repression of political dissidence and non-conformist views. This took relatively mild forms in Italy but was on a much larger scale in Nazi Germany. The unofficial concentration camps of the SA were soon taken over by the _Gestapo_ (the Prussian Secret Police) and were employed to imprison and terrorise opponents of the regime. The judicial system was subjected to Nazi control and special courts were also set up to try offences against the State. No legal control was established over the activities of the Gestapo, whose power was further increased when it was combined with the SS under Himmler's control in June 1936. The war saw a further intensification of political repression and the introduction of the death penalty for a wide range of political offences.

While out of power, the Fascists had attacked capitalism as responsible both for the oppression of the workers and for the destruction of the small trader and artisan. Once in power, however, these anti-capitalist aspirations were sacrificed to the need to co-operate with big business and to the goal of territorial expansion, which needed a flourishing economic base. Economic growth thus became the main priority. This was fairly effectively pursued, partly through an enormous expansion of public works programmes, many of which had been started before the Fascists took power. Rearmament also contributed to the growth of the economy and the reduction of unemployment, while the ending of free collective bargaining kept wage levels low. These policies were very much to the taste of the great industrialists, although they became increasingly uneasy about the inflationary consequences of the growing interventionism of the state in both Italy and Germany and the determination to pursue rearmament at whatever cost.

The ruthless quest for economic growth forced the abandonment, at best postponement, of other fascist economic policies. In agriculture, for instance, it proved impossible to halt the shift of workers from the countryside, which was accelerated by the needs of industry for labour. Some success was achieved in achieving agricultural self-sufficiency. The interests of small businessmen and artisans were also rather neglected. Indeed, in their economic policies, the fascist regimes acted neither as the tools of monopoly capitalism nor the embodiment of the anti-modernist feelings of the threatened lower middle class. Rather, in the economic field, these regimes subordinated all policy to the drive to national self-assertion and temporial expansion.

Anti-semitism and racialism were a central feature of the Nazi *Weltanschanung*. Belief in the Jewish conspiracy (see ANTI-SEMITISM) to destroy the German people provided the Nazis with a unifying explanation which brought together the disparate strands of Nazi ideology. Of the sincerity of Hitler's hatred of the Jews there can be no doubt. It formed the central core of his political convictions from the moment he first became aware of the Jewish question in pre-1914 Vienna until his suicide in May 1945. Having achieved power, however, the Nazis were not at all sure how to deal with the 'Jewish problem'. The boycott of Jewish shops, for instance, which was never total anyway, was introduced primarily to put an end to the spontaneous anti-Jewish violence of the SA. Though he gave subsidies to a number of anti-semitic groups in Eastern Europe, Hitler claimed that his anti-semitism was not for export and that his aim was to end Jewish assimilation and persuade Jews to leave Gemany. The Nuremberg laws of September 1935 accordingly prohibited intermarriage and barred Jews from the professions and the civil service.

Nazi policy towards the Jews began to harden in 1938. The incorporation of Austria and the Czech lands had enormously increased the size of the Jewish population under German control and pressure to emigrate was now intensified. The assassination of a German diplomat by a desperate Jewish youth was used by the Nazis to unleash a ferocious pogrom in November 1938. The conquest of Poland, with its large Jewish population, was followed by the first Nazi massacres, which were committed both by SS men and front-line troops. the decision to provide a 'final solution' of the Jewish problem through mass murder was one of a number of measures taken in conjunction with the invasion of the USSR in June 1941. Mobile murder squads for killing Jews were now set up and when these could not function sufficiently quickly, Jews were collected in camps and killed by gassing.

Racialism (see NATIONALISM) at first played very little part in the ideology and practice of Italian fascism. The adoption by Mussolini of a policy of racial anti-semitism in 1938 has generally been attributed to the tightening links between Italy and Germany. It was also intimately connected with the goal of a colonial Empire and with efforts to emulate the racial consciousness of older colonial powers. Italian propaganda thus presented the Ethiopians as barbaric savages and inter-racial marriages were forbidden.

Everywhere that the Fascists took power in the wake of German victories, racial laws modelled on those of Germany were introduced. Though the degree of collaboration with the 'final solution' was not uniform, the end result was the murder of between five and a half and six million Jews, two-thirds of those in Europe and two-fifths of those in the whole world.

A major role in the rise of fascist groups was played by feelings of national humiliation and the desire for national self-assertion (see NATIONALISM). Once in power, the Fascists glorified war and sought successes in foreign policy to legitimise their role and make possible the establishment of new empires. The *Duce* embarked on an expansionist course from about 1931 and Hitler's coming to power merely increased his eagerness to act. The area he chose was Ethiopia, long desired by Italy and adjacent to her East African colonies. The rapid conquest of the country between October 1935 and May 1936 was a major triumph which enormously increased the prestige of the fascist regime.

Mussolini's intervention in the Spanish Civil War, which was dictated both by his hope of acquiring naval and air bases in the Balearic islands and his desire to prevent a left-wing victory, was much less successful. Relations with the western powers became still worse while Italy became increasingly dependent on Nazi Germany, with which an agreement setting up a 'Rome-Berlin Axis' was signed in October 1936. In view of the enormous disparity in power and industrial resources of the two countries, their relationship was inevitably an unequal one and Mussolini proved incapable and possibly unwilling to halt the Italic slide into dependence. Italy, poorly prepared and equipped, only entered the war on Germany's side in June 1940 and was soon in severe difficulties. In 1943 Mussolini was overthrown and the country entered the war on the Allied side. Though he was rescued by the Germans and set up in power in North Italy, he was now little more than a German puppet, whose hopes of empire had vanished

Expansion was always central to Nazi policy. In *Mein Kampf*, Hitler had made clear his desire to pursue a policy alongside which the plans of his conservative allies paled into insignificance. His ultimate goal was a victorious war against Bolshevism which would destroy forever the threat which communism (see COMMUNISM) posed to Europe while at the same time striking a mortal blow at world Jewry which, it was claimed, had achieved a dominating position in Moscow. It would also provide territory for colonisation which would make it possible to create a continuous German land empire with a population of two hundred million.

The pursuit of these objectives was central to Hitler, as is clearly shown by the grandiose building plans of the Third *Reich*, most of which were on the drawing board before the outbreak of war in 1939 and certainly before the invasion of the USSR. At their centre was a scheme intended to make Berlin the administrative heart of a great empire, a city which, according to Hitler, would be imbued with 'the enchanted and magical atmosphere that surrounds a Mecca or Rome'.

Hitler's initial foreign policy successes – the remilitarisation of the Rhineland, the annexation of Austria, the break up of Czechoslovakia and the conquest of Poland, Norway, the Low Countries and France – greatly strengthened the domestic popularity of his regime. The Nazis had, it seemed, at little cost, reversed the verdict of the First World War and gained for Germany the dominant position in Europe. Indeed the summer of 1940 marked the high point of Hitler's successes. Hitler's decision to invade the USSR in June 1941 seems primarily to have been taken because of his belief that only if the Soviet Union were destroyed as a potential ally could Britain be induced to make peace. Yet it was also the logical realisation of his deepest goals. In the event, the Soviet regime did not collapse and Hitler found himself involved in a war of attrition – something he had always dreaded. He had finally taken on too much, and the collapse of his empire, and of almost all the other fascist regimes, was merely a matter of time.

Could fascism recur? In Western Europe, the experience of the war and the sustained economic growth between 1945 and 1973 has strengthened democratic institutions enormously. The threat of revolution has receded with prosperity and the communist parties of Italy, Spain and France have become reconciled to many apsects of the liberal democratic State. The Soviet Union looks even less like the centre of a world revolutinary movement and has come to seem merely a conventional expansionist great power. Even the increase in unemployment and slowing of economic growth since 1973 has not yet undermined stability, above all because social welfare policies in Western Europe have cushioned most of the population from the worst effects of these developments. Under these circumstances, the small neo-fascist groups there have been little more than irritants, unable to mount a serious challenge to the political *status quo*.

Paradoxically, it has been in the 'Third World' that the combination of nationalism and social radicalism so characteristic of fascism has made its greatest impact since 1945. Regimes like that of Gadafi in Libya or Sukarno in Indonesia displayed many similarities to the social transformation sought by fascist groups like the Romanian Iron Guard. It has been in the developing world too that antagonism to ethnically distinct minorities -- like the Indians in East Africa and Burma, the Chinese in South East Asia and the Tamils in Sri Lanka -- have sparked off demands for the creation of ethnically cohesive states which have often seemed like an eerie echo of pre-war fascist demands. It could be argued that the most characteristic political institution of the twentieth century is the one-party modernising dictatorship, and this probably derives far more from fascist experience than from attempts to emulate the political experience of the USSR, as is usually claimed by its sponsors.

Federalism

Federalism is best regarded as one expression of pluralism (see PLURALISM) in so far as the latter is concerned with the structuring and articulation of interests in society. It follows that the assumptions and arguments of pluralism are largely reflected in federalism and are given an institutional form in the structure of the state. Federalism can be defined as a constitutional device for securing the decentralisation of authority within a state by regulating the distribution of power on a territorial basis.

Federalism differs from other techniques of territorial decentralisation (such as local and provincial government, regionalism, and home rule) in that the terms of the regulation are embodied in the fundamental constitutional form of the state and are therefore not amenable to change by unilateral action on the part of the central authority of the federation. The traditions of federalism are part of the larger doctrine of _constitutionalism_ and the theory of constitutional 'checks and balances'. Federalism has come to be particularly associated with the constitutional structure of the United States as the historical archetype of the federal 'model', in which, according to Wheare, 'the general and regional governments are each, within a sphere, co-ordinate and independent'. This 'co-ordinate' view of the distribution of powers within a federal state, giving the constituent parts guaranteed and independent areas of action is, however, only one version. Another is a 'developmental' approach, outlined by Sawer, in which co-ordinate federalism represents a 'strong' type, thence moving to a 'co-operative' form where the member states maintain 'bargaining powers' in relation to the federal government, ultimately shading off to an 'organic' type in which the states virtually become the administrative agents of the federal authorities. This scheme may represent an actual course of development, and applies in part to the United States, but alternatively a federal state may begin life at any one stage: the present Austrian Republic as 'organic', the Federal German Republic as 'co-operative'.

107

There are objections to assuming that only the co-ordinate type represents 'real' federalism. Thus in the West German case, the states (*Länder*), although lacking important independent functions, nevertheless have considerable financial resources, *direct* governmental representation in the federal legislature, strong protection from the constitutional court, and in addition have a wide administrative competence. Hence, it is not so much the 'original' constitutional powers that are of significance, but the provisions which enable the constituent states to maintain their position in the face of changing social, economic and political circumstances.

The spectrum covered by federal states, alterations within that spectrum, and the growth of methods aimed at securing a territorial dispersion of power short of federalism, reduce the value of the term as a unified concept. It is probably more useful to speak of a 'federal situation', and a number of tests could be devised to determine the nature and extent of 'federal' ingredients. Such tests would be of particular relevance to situations of 'façade federalism', ones where the formal constitutional structure of a federal state is largely contradicted by the reality of unified political control. Thus the extent of federalism in the USSR is sharply limited by the power vested in the Communist Party of the Soviet Union. That conclusion could be expected to follow from the association of federalism with the doctrine of pluralism.

Federal arrangements are principally concerned with the preservation of areas of local autonomy and are therefore geared to maintaining sub-national, often ethnic, differences. Consequently on one level they act in a non-integrative fashion. However, a successful federal system also serves to promote national integration, and so the degree of success of federalism in any country may be judged by its increasing redundancy: the federal structure may remain intact but become subordinate to the actual distribution of power, typically contained in the national political parties and resulting in a form of 'party federalism'. This rendering accords with the developmental view of federalism.

In this connection a distinction should be made between the 'old' federal states, chiefly Australia, Canada, Switzerland and the United States, and the new ones, largely those having achieved independence since 1945. Whilst the long-established federal states do show a pattern of increasing integration, with the notable exception of Canada in recent years, the experience of the newer federal systems has been less satisfactory; in Africa, Asia, the Caribbean and Latin America. In countries such as Nigeria the federal implantation succeeded mainly in exacerbating existing ethnic and other differences by giving them a fixed territorial expression, leading in turn to the assertion of regional dominance and to attempted separatism. It can be seen that the imperatives of modern nation-building may easily conflict with the principles of constitutionalism, and the discarding of federal structures by states soon after gaining independence has often been accompanied by a rejection of other aspects of pluralism.

The failures should not detract from other examples, such as India, where federal institutions have worked reasonably well, nor should the importance of quasi-federal solutions be left out of account. Many of the advanced, unitary states, especially those of Western Europe, have had to face claims by sub-national, minority groups for varying degrees of regional autonomy. In the United Kingdom such movements have not yet produced a substantial modification of the unitary state. On the other hand, a large measure of decentralisation has occurred in Italy and Spain; and in Belgium the need to accommodate the competing claims of the Francophone and Flemish-speaking sections of the population has led to a substantial amendment of the unitary constitution.

It appears that, as a general rule, when countries have had a long experience of government based on constitutionalist checks and balances they will show themselves to be more amenable to later federal-type adaptations, albeit of a partial nature. The same tendency is also evident in the development of supra-national organisations, especially in the drive towards European integration and the emergence of the European Community. This organisation has yet to acquire the full range of powers of a political community and in several ways still resembles more a confederation of essentially independent states, but a federal form of association could ultimately emerge. It may be reasonable to conclude that the concept of federalism, even though defective if treated as single, model form, does have a continuing relevance to the problem of dispersing political power and it is not necessarily restricted in application by the nature of historical precedent.

Further reading

K. Banting (ed.), *The Politics of Constitutional Change*
H. Burgess (ed.), *Federalism and Federation in Western Europe*
C. J. Friedrich, *Limited Government: A Comparison*
A. Hamilton, J. Madison & J. Jay, *The Federalist Papers*
U. K. Hicks, *Federalism: Failure and Success*
W. S. Livingston, *Federalism and Constitutional Change*
W. H. Riker, *Federalism: Origin, Operation, Significance*
W. H. Riker, 'Federalism', in F. Greenstein and N. Polsby (eds.) *Handbook of Political Science*
G. F. Sawer, *Modern Federalism*
H. G. Thorburn, *Pluralism and Federalism*, special issue of *International Political Science Review* volume 5, No.4, 1984.
K. C. Wheare, *Federal Government*

Feminism

Feminism is too diffuse a body of changing ideas to be termed an ideology; rather, it is a response generated by a sense of injustice on the part of women who resent the conferring of certain rights on men simply because they are men, and the withholding of rights from women because they are women. This response has provided the driving force behind movements to secure for women equal rights and equality of opportunity with men in the legal, educational, economic, political and moral order of society. There have been two major periods of feminist activity, in the later nineteenth and earlier twentieth centuries, from c. 1870 to c. 1920, and then, after some forty years in decline, in the 1960's and 1970's. Particularly in the earlier period, feminist activity was strongest in the United States, predominantly Protestant European countries, and Britain and her 'white' Empire, that is, in the economically and industrially more advanced areas of the world. While these have again been the areas most affected by the new feminism of the 1960's and 1970's, other countries, including predominantly Roman Catholic ones and some in the Third World, have also experienced the rise of feminist movements.

It is to some degree misleading to call the movements for women's rights in these two distinct periods by the same name, since there are marked differences between them. The feminists of the earlier period, the 'classical' feminists, had on the whole a number of clear and limited objectives which varied slightly from group to group, according to local conditions, and which underwent only relatively minor changes. The new feminists, by contrast, as adherents of the Women's Liberation Movement, have aims which are much less programmatic and are, in effect, limitless. Both groups owe their outlook to a prevailing political philosophy of their time, in the earlier case to liberalism (see LIBERALISM), and in the latter to the ideas of the New Left. The earlier feminists pursued their aims within the existing social and political structure of capitalism and the Christian family, seeking to win a place that was politically, legally and professionally equal to that of men within it. As middle-class liberals, they accepted and indeed upheld the existing class system. By contrast, the new feminists demand a complete restructuring of society as the precondition of achieving equality between the sexes. Nothing short of revolution, they say, will achieve this, since the present order of society is, as the product of centuries of male domination, axiomatically incapable of providing the basis for a truly egalitarian society in which no preconceived roles and functions are attributed because of a person's gender. This new society, free from discrimination against currently disadvantaged groups, will be classless in structure.

Although the term 'feminism' did not gain currency until the late nineteenth century, the ideas which it came to represent derived from those introduced by the writers of the Enlightenment (see THE ENLIGHTENMENT) and briefly in vogue during the French Revolution. Within this context, Mary Wollstonecraft wrote *A Vindication of the Rights of Woman* (1792), in which she attacked the dependence of women on men as the product of long-term social conditioning and as the excuse used by men to justify the denial of equal rights to women. Her ideas had little influence on feminist thought in the nineteenth century, but have, slightly incongruously, become more fashionable among the new feminists of the later twentieth century because of their emphasis on equality and role distribution without reference to gender. By contrast, the liberal theories of the mid-nineteenth century, with their emphasis on the autonomous development of the individual, created the intellectual and political climate in which feminist aims could be formulated and pursued at the time, but are now totally rejected by the new feminists. Nevertheless, the influence of John Stuart Mill's essay on *The Subjection of Women* (1869) was considerable in moulding the attitudes and aspirations of the liberal feminists of the later nineteenth century. His argument that women would be emancipated when all laws discriminating specifically against them were revoked, thus allowing them the freedom – already enjoyed by men – to realise their full potential, became the guiding principle of middle-class, liberal feminist movements in many advanced countries (although not, on the whole, in strongly Catholic ones) in the latter part of the nineteenth century. The extent of Mill's influence ensured that the feminists would concentrate their campaigns on legal equality, access to educational and professional opportunities, and property rights, matters which were predominantly of interest to middle-class women, and of little relevance to the condition of working-class women. Contrary to the worst fears of its conservative opponents, liberal feminism was a reforming, not a revolutionary, creed.

The far-reaching changes wrought in society and the economy by the industrial revolution and its concomitant urbanisation removed a number of women's traditional functions in the family and in economic life, while providing middle-class men with increasing opportunities in business, the professions, education, politics and property ownership. A middle-class woman could enjoy her family's new prosperity and property only as the dependant of a father or a husband. She was not permitted to hold property in her own right, nor to open a bank account or start a business. She was denied admission to academic senior schools, to universities, to the professions. She was required to obey her father in all matters on which he pronounced, until, on marriage, this authority passed to a husband. She had no rights over her children – including illegitimate children – and no hope of ending an unhappy marriage, although, in Protestant countries at least, a husband could divorce his wife without difficulty if he chose. In most countries, women were forbidden to participate in political activity of any kind, and although by 1900 agitation was growing for the extension of the franchise to women, the first feminists did not, on the whole, seek the vote. In general, their demands were modest, even negative, since what they chiefly sought was the removal of barriers to their aspirations and an end to their total dependence on their menfolk.

The disabilities imposed on middle-class women were in direct contrast with the increasing extension of civil rights to formerly disadvantaged groups such as working-class and Jewish men. This was underlined by the institution of universal adult male suffrage in France, the German Empire and Switzerland from the 1870's with other countries following suit. This apparent alignment of the male sex as a whole in a legally superior position to the female sex helped to radicalise feminist movements in two ways: by 1900, most feminists were convinced that the only way for women to secure equality of opportunity was by first winning the vote; and for a time there was an attempt to create unified feminist movements which cut across class barriers. The insistence of middle-class women on retaining the leadership and deciding the policy of the movements led those working-class women who had been mobilised increasingly to feel that liberal feminism had little to offer them as a solution to their distinctive problems – as low-paid workers in factories, 'sweated' trades, domestic service, and as wives and mothers struggling against poverty – and they began to turn to the new socialist parties (see SOCIALISM) to promote their interests. The major campaigns of the middle-class feminists concerned opportunities in higher education and property rights; they were prepared to campaign for working-class women's interests, as they saw them, only to the extent of launching moral reform crusades against state-regulated prostitution and in favour of temperance. Thus they restricted the constituency to which they could appeal, while the working-class women who left feminist movements for socialist parties came to accept the Marxist view that the liberation of women would follow logically from the liberation of the entire working class, when the revolution came; increasingly from the 1890's, and certainly by the time of the First World War, it was clear that the allegiance of working-class women – in so far as they were organised – was to be to the class struggle and not to a campaign for women's rights.

The growing demand by feminists for women's suffrage by the end of the nineteenth century led to the formation in many countries of suffrage unions; British and American feminists were decades ahead of the rest in their demands for the vote from the 1860's. But while a number of barriers to women's aspirations were removed, in terms of admission to higher education, the right to engage in trade, and the right to own property, some liberal as well as most conservative men were very reluctant to extend the franchise to women, even on a selected basis, for example one involving a property qualification. Success in winning the vote in some countries, for example in New Zealand, some states in both Australia and the United States, and Finland and Norway before the First World War, only encouraged feminists elsewhere to campaign more forcefully, nowhere more so than in Britain. Disillusionment with the Liberal Party and liberal methods led to an alliance of feminist suffragists with the Labour Party in the 1906 election campaign, and this disillusionment combined with frustration at the failure to achieve the vote after decades of campaigning to produce a militant suffrage movement in Britain in the early years of the twentieth century whose most extreme wing, the Pankhursts' Women's Social and Political Union (founded in 1903), engaged in acts of increasing violence to draw attention to its cause.

The term adopted to describe violent militant feminists who demanded the vote, 'suffragette', derived from the title of one of the Union's newspapers, and was used at the time by opponents of women's rights generally as a pejorative one to cover feminists of all kinds, not only in Britain but also elsewhere. Suffragettism implied rowdy mass demonstrations, assaults on policemen, campaigns of window breaking, and other kinds of violent behaviour used to try to frighten or bludgeon authorities into granting extreme demands. Suffragettism was disowned and condemned by many liberal feminists who found the suffragettes' tactics distasteful and believed them to be counter-productive; it is probably the one element of the earlier feminism which is regarded favourably by the new feminists and from which they are prepared to claim heritage.

While suffragettes and more moderate suffragists alike claimed the credit for the significant successes achieved by the end of the First World War in winning for women more rights including the franchise, granted at last in the United States as a whole, in Germany and in Britain in 1918, the reason for this was not least men's realisation that the mass of women were inclined to be conservative in outlook. This was why French socialists opposed women's suffrage and blocked it until 1945. Now, at the end of the First World War, with the general admission of women to higher education and the professions and with their enfranchisement, the death knell of liberal feminism sounded. While radical minority groups in a number of countries still aimed for surer guarantees of genuine equality for women, the mainstream feminist movements, true to their liberal origins, decided that with the removal of the legal prohibitions which had prevented women from realising their potential their limited objectives had been achieved; with the opportunities provided, it was up to women to take advantage of them and thus gain full equality with men as individuals, through their own effort. In addition, by the 1920's liberal feminists had gained in their respective countries the kind of recognition which made them respectable and their leaders part of the establishment, largely because of their patriotic contributions to the war effort. The feminists had fought their battles and won, it seemed.

But disillusionment set in when it quickly became clear that women were either unable — because of prejudice — or unwilling to avail themselves of the new opportunities, in education particularly. In reality, the feminists had always been a minority interest group, and the rights which they helped to win appealed immediately only to a small minority; they themselves had not fully realised this. A combination of their disillusionment and the reaction against feminism which developed during the world economic crisis contingent on the Wall Street Crash in the autumn of 1929 – as men and women competed bitterly for jobs and lower-paid women often won – led to the decline of feminism in the 1930's;

113

this was facilitated by the growth of right-wing governments in many countries and by the ascendancy of Fascism (see FASCISM) in some others, although the United States, too, experienced it in full measure. Until the major crises of the economy, a world war, post-war austerity and the Cold War had receded, feminism remained the insignificant fringe interest into which it had declined after the legal and political achievements of the First World War era.

The reaction against feminism was partly a reaction against the Bolshevik Revolution (see COMMUNISM) which emancipated Russian women from their degraded status in Tsarist times. With the Revolution there occurred a split between communists and social democrats in most countries, with radical socialist women, like Rosa Luxemburg and Clara Zetkin in Germany, joining the communists' ranks. Socialist parties were left to pursue a gradualist policy of slow, long-term endeavours to dissipate working-class and, particularly, trade-union prejudice against increased opportunities for women, especially at work. By contrast, in Russia from 1917 Lenin's policies gave women full equality as spouses and parents, in education and employment, and indeed in all aspects of life, until Stalinist reaction set in the 1930s. The extent to which equality for women was introduced, on paper at least, and the introduction of measures such as legal abortion within this context, in the Soviet Union's earliest years, frightened liberals and conservatives alike, helped to discredit feminism in capitalist countries, and contributed to its decline in the 1920s and 1930s.

Nevertheless, it was out of left-wing political ferment that the new feminism of the 1960s and 1970s developed. The new feminists of the Women's Liberation Movement owed only one debt to the classical feminists: they were the products of the higher education system, the winning of access to which had been the subject of major campaigns by the liberal feminists. While the earliest stirrings of radical feminist activity were manifested in the United States in the early 1960s, it was the emergence of the New Left, particularly in universities, in the later 1960s which provided the impetus for new women's movements. The young men and women who joined together in radical socialist groups, and, in the United States particularly, in civil rights groups, rejected both capitalism and communism as practised in eastern Europe. They demanded a revolution in society to produce a system in which all people, regardless of race, colour, creed or sex, would be treated as absolutely equal and given fully equal opportunities – if necessary, by discriminating 'positively', that is, in their favour, to counteract any existing in-built disadvantages. Campaigning for the emancipation of a variety of disadvantaged groups at first produced co-operation between the men and women involved, and provided the women with some of the theoretical constructs and language they would use in specifically feminist campaigns. The experience convinced some women, however, that even politically sympathetic men did not and could not comprehend their problems as members of a disadvantaged group.

Disillusioned by men who agreed intellectually with their analysis and objectives but who also behaved – in social and sexual relationships – much the same

114

as men who were indifferent or hostile towards them, the articulate, well-educated feminists of the 1960's abandoned them as allies. Their campaign centred increasingly on the disparity between legal and theoretical equality of opportunity – and even, in the professions, for which their education had prepared them, equal pay – and the prevailing informal, non-institutional prejudice and discrimination which dogged them in certain kinds of job and in large areas of social life. These were, it seemed, the product not of laws but of custom and ingrained attitudes, and therefore could not be removed by legislation alone. Following J. S. Mill, the liberal feminists had assumed that the removal of barriers could of itself promote equality between the sexes; for many reasons, this had proved illusory, and now Mary Wollstonecraft's strictures about the social conditioning of men and women to accept distinctive roles in life from time immemorial seemed to provide a more penetrating analysis.

The attitudes stemming from this conditioning came to be described by the new feminists as sexist, deriving from the tendency of people to regard gender as the most important characteristic of individuals and the one which determines their abilities and functions to an overwhelming extent. Sexism has become a pejorative term used to describe every attempt to differentiate between men and women on the grounds of their sex alone, and is generally seen as an unconscious response, the product of centuries of conditioning. As such, sexism is not to be equated with anti-feminism or misogyny; rather, it is condemned not so much for undervaluing women but for valuing them only in certain roles or for the wrong reasons – appearance or alleged feminity, for example, rather than genuine ability which can be measured in precisely the same terms as a man's.

If sexism has been under attack as a set of unconscious attitudes which are accepted by men and women alike, male chauvinism is under attack as the conscious expression of sexist attitudes and also, increasingly, as a defensive response by men who discern that their long-held superiority over women is under threat. To this extent, male chauvinism is partly to be equated with anti-feminism, but it is essentially a more positive assertion of the differences between the sexes, the superiority of male characteristics and abilities over female – mainly in terms of physical strength, but also in terms of male 'rationality' as opposed to female 'emotionalism'. Male chauvinist attitudes are epitomised by the tendency of men to gravitate towards exclusively male institutions, in colleges, clubs and pubs, and to relegate women to responsibility for home and family. Recognition of this gave rise to a determined but genteel campaign to desegregate professional, social and familial roles after the publication in 1963 of Betty Friedan's pioneering work *The Feminine Mystique*. The moderate views and tactics of Mrs Friedan's supporters in the United States in the mid-1960's were soon superseded, towards the end of the decade, by a much more radical approach, epitomised in the explicitly sexual detail of Germaine Greer's *The Female Eunuch* (1970). Above all, the new feminists, with their awareness of the freedom which reliable contraceptives now give women,

115

have attacked marriage as a device for enslaving women; they reject it as a social institution because of its role as the linch-pin of patriarchal society.

The entire range of social and sexual mores had been scrutinised and criticised by the new feminists for assuming and reinforcing the alleged superiority of the male as male, and the dependence of the female on the male for status. Whereas the classical feminists wanted nothing more than to achieve equality of opportunity with men, on the assumption that men were in the optimum position, the new feminists demand a revolution to sweep away 'traditional' attitudes and assumptions and to create a society based on the fully equal division of labour, in the home and at work, with education geared to a child's aptitudes and the elimination of the attribution of specific roles to children according to gender in school courses and literature. But there remains the problem of the present generations of women and girls who have been brought up to accept sexist attitudes implicitly.

The aim is to bring them into a wide-ranging women's movement which will represent the interests of women as a whole, cutting across class barriers in a way in which the liberal feminists failed to do, and drawing attention particularly to the discrimination suffered by the least articulate, especially in the manual working class. The process of educating the women themselves to reject sexist attitudes is to take place in group therapy sessions. The pooling of experiences in women's groups, with a view to making women aware of the extent to which they are discriminated against purely because of their gender and to giving them greater self-confidence *vis-à-vis* men, is called consciousness-raising, and is a technique borrowed directly from the Black Power movement (SEE BLACK CONSCIOUSNESS). The women are to analyse their own experience and to try to learn from others in a process of mutual self-help; above all, they are to learn to reject current notions that women's inescapable function as the child-bearers of the species renders them incapable of exercising rights and duties that are fully equal with those of men, both in and outside the home.

The proponents of Women's Liberation have come to adopt the term feminism as a description of their motive force, although there was for a time a marked reluctance to do so. This was no doubt because it has been so closely associated with the kind of limited objectives for which liberal feminists campaigned, with significant success, before 1918. There are, however, enough features common to both the new feminism and classical feminism to justify the application of the same term in both the earlier and the later periods. In both, the activists have tended to be a small minority of largely middle-class women, who have found a sympathetic response among large areas of the population for their more moderate demands. In recognition of this, these demands have been either wholly or partially met by governments. Feminist movements in both periods have, then, enjoyed some success, in objective terms as well as by their own estimation. But limited success has satisfied the activists' supporters in the population at large, and been a direct cause of a decline in support for feminist movements at the very time when the activists, encouraged by their support and success, have aimed to promote more radical objectives which have attracted very limited approval from the wider circle of their sympathisers – for example, legal abortion in the earlier period, the abolition of the family in the later one. To some extent, then, the success of feminist movements can be measured only once they have gone into decline.

Further reading

Mary Wollstonecraft, *A Vindication of the Rights of Woman*
J. S. Mill, *The Subjection of Women*
August Bebel, *Women under Socialism*
Richard J. Evans, *The Feminists*
Renate Bridenthal & Claudia Koonz (ed.), *Becoming Visible: Women in European History*
W. L. O'Neill, *The Woman Movement: Feminism in the United States and England*
Constance Rover, *Women's Suffrage and Party Politics in Britain, 1866-1914*
Eleanor Flexner, *Century of Struggle: The Women's Rights Movement in the United States*
Fannina Halle, *Women in Soviet Russia*
Hilda Scott, *Women and Socialism*
Gail W. Lapidus, *Women in Soviet Society*
Elisabeth Croll, *Chinese Women since Mao*
Richard J. Evans, *The Feminist Movement in Germany 1894-1933*
Jill Stephenson, *Women in Nazi Society*
J. F. McMillan, *Housewife or Harlot: the Woman Question in France under the Third Republic*
Alva Myrdal & Viola Klein, *Women's Two Roles*
Juliet Mitchell, *Woman's Estate*
Sheila Rowbotham, *Woman's Consciousness, Man's World*
Berenice A. Carroll (ed.), *Liberating Women's History: Theoretical and Critical Essays*
Janet Radcliffe Richards, *The Sceptical Feminist*
Jessie Bernard, *The Female World*
Liz Stanley & Sue Wise, *Breaking Out: Feminist consciousness and feminist research*
John Charret, *Feminism*

Free Soil

In the United States, this was the doctrine that the expansion of chattel slavery into the nation's western territories should be prohibited.

Free Soil is a doctrine as old as the American republic. The Northwest Ordinance, adopted by Congress in 1787, prohibited slavery in the Northwest Territory, a region which would subsequently encompass the states of Ohio, Indiana, Illinois, Michigan and Wisconsin. The idea was also incorporated in the Missouri Compromise of 1820, which barred slavery in most of the territory acquired by the Louisiana Purchase of 1803.

Free Soil, however, did not become a major political issue until the 1840s. One stimulus was the rise of militant abolitionism, demanding the immediate emancipation of slaves in the American South. At the same time, the acquisition of new lands as a result of the Mexican War (1846-48) raised anew the question of the expansion of slavery.

Free Soil was thrust to the centre stage of politics in 1846, when Congressman David Wilmot of Pennsylvania introduced a resolution – the famous 'Wilmot Proviso' – requiring that slavery be prohibited in all territory acquired from Mexico. Its language copied from the Northwest Ordinance, the Proviso passed the House of Representatives, where northern states possessed a majority, but failed in the Senate. The result demonstrated the political potency of the free soil issue, and sent political leaders searching for a way of compromising the question of the expansion of slavery.

Free Soil quickly became the most prominent expression of anti-slavery sentiment in the North, the lowest common denominator of hostility to slavery and the 'Slave Power' of the South. It attracted the support of millions who deemed outright abolition too radical a doctrine. While direct action against slavery in the Southern states was impossible under the Constitution, free soil was a time-honoured and perfectly legal means of expressing hostility to slavery. (During the 1840s, however, Southern spokesmen, in response to rising free soil sentiment, articulated the view that any interference with the right to hold slave property in the territories violated the South's constitutional rights.)

Free Soil, in addition, appealed to those Northerners who resented what they perceived as the excessive political power wielded by the South, a power resting on slavery because three-fifths of the South's black population were counted for purposes of representation in Congress. The expansion of slavery would create more slave states, whose representatives, it was feared, would prevent the enactment of such measures desired by many northerners as a protective tariff and government aid to canals and railroads. On the Southern side, free soil raised the spectre of a permanent minority status within the Union, if the expansion of slavery were blocked.

As a political stance, free soil was acceptable to many abolitionists, because it did raise the question of slavery itself, if only indirectly. It was widely believed that because of soil exhaustion, slavery, once confined to existing areas, would decline economically. Free soil could thus be seen as a first step towards abolition. Simultaneously, free soil appealed to many Northerners who opposed abolitionism because of racial prejudice. Many who hoped to settle in the West objected to the presence of blacks, whether slave or free. Wilmot called his measure the 'White Man's Proviso', and free soil, by appealing to the racial prejudices of the North, was able to mobilise far wider support than egalitarian abolitionism ever could.

Most fundamentally, free soil raised the question of the future course of American development. Its proponents believed a fundamental struggle was under way between two antagonistic societies, one based on slave labour, the other free. The ultimate status of the West would determine which system of labour would dominate America's future. Free soil thus combined hostility to slavery and southern power, racism, and a belief in the superiority of free labour, in a powerful ideology which would soon become the dominant political force in the nation.

The first organised political expression of free soilism was the Free Soil Party, founded in 1848 by dissident Democrats and Whigs who believed their parties were dominated by the South. The platform endorsed the Wilmot Proviso, and incorporated a call for a Homestead law, under which the federal government would provide public land free of charge to settlers in the West. The homestead not only added a new dimension to the idea of 'free' soil, but attracted considerable support from Northern farmers who desired to settle in the West but did not wish to compete with slave plantations. Simultaneously, the Free Soil platform omitted any reference to the political and legal rights of Northern blacks, a major concern of previous anti-slavery organisations. In the election of 1848 the Free Soil candidate, former President Martin Van Buren, polled nearly 300,000 votes, approximately ten per cent of the total.

The Compromise of 1850, which left the question of slavery to the actual settlers of each territory acquired from Mexico (a solution known as 'popular sovereignty'), appeared for a time to resolve the slavery controversy. The Free Soil party saw its vote halved in the election of 1852. But in 1854, Congress enacted the Kansas-Nebraska Act, applying 'popular sovereignty' to the Louisiana Purchase territory from which slavery had been barred by the Missouri Compromise. This, in effect, opened to slavery a vast fertile area west of the Mississippi River, and provoked a reaction of outrage in the North. The result was the disintegration of the Whig party and the rise of the Republicans, organised around the principle of free soil. In 1860 the Republicans elected Abraham Lincoln the sixteenth President, on a platform pledged to prohibit the further extension of slavery. In response, a majority of the Southern states seceded from the Union, viewing Lincoln's election as a direct threat to the institution of slavery.

Once Civil War had begun, Congress enacted the free soil principle, barring slavery from all territories, and soon thereafter, the Homestead Law was enacted, offering 160 acres to settlers. Having played so crucial a role in the disruption of the Union, free soil was, however, quickly superceded, for on 1 January 1863, Lincoln's Emancipation Proclamation decreed the freedom of slaves not simply in the territories, but in all rebellious areas of the South.

Further Reading

Eric Foner, *Free Soil, Free Labour, Free Men: The Ideology of the Republican Party Before the Civil War*

Frederick J. Blue, *The Free Soilers*

Richard H. Sewell, *Ballots for Freedom: Anti-Slavery Politics in the United States 1837-1860*

Gaullism

Like Bonapartism (see BONAPARTISM), Gaullism takes its name from its founder, and, like its predecessor, it seems to reveal latent tendencies in modern French political thought – the desire for national prestige, and a strong government with a democratic base which will provide political stability and economic progress. But there are important differences, because French society had altered considerably in the years between 1870 and 1958, when de Gaulle finally achieved power, due to social and political development, as well as the experience of the catastrophe of 1940 and the ensuing occupation.

Significantly, de Gaulle never claimed to be the heir of either the First or the Second Empire, but stressed his legitimate descent from the Third Republic, which he claimed to have inherited in 1940 when he established his government in exile as the 'true' government of France. Furthermore, Gaullism was not dynastic in its outlook and no one seriously suggested de Gaulle should be followed by his son as President of the Republic. However, one point is common to both ideologies: they stress the unity of France as a nation and her national interests which transcend those of any political party or economic group. Gaullism was therefore never an appeal to 'party', but was rather a *rassemblement:* a drawing together of the French people in an effort to work for the common good. Paradoxically, this has not prevented the emergence of 'Right' and 'Left' Gaullists – just as there had been 'Right' and 'Left' Bonapartists.

The Constitution of the Fifth Republic reflects this search for unity and stability, in that it is authoritarian in a way in which neither the Third nor the Fourth Republics were. The election of the President by direct universal suffrage gives him considerable personal power as the *Nation's* representative.

The nature of Gaullism is explained partly by aspects of de Gaulle's political thinking, based on his dislike of the divisive and stultifying nature of French party politics, but also by the events of 1958 which brought about the collapse of the Fourth Republic. The danger of a civil war resulting from the crisis over Algeria meant that a strong, stable government was essential – and de Gaulle was the only one with sufficient prestige to be able to provide this.

Once established, Gaullism under the General provided the impetus for the development of France's economic and commercial growth and for her assertion of her place in the European community. De Gaulle aimed for an efficient 'technocratic' government, as well as pledging to 'modernise' France, and his success can be measured not only by the economic development of France, but by the survival of the political institutions he founded.

Imperialism
(including Jingoism and Chauvinism)

Imperialism is an ideology more formulated by its opponents than by its advocates; it is also a comparatively late description of an historical process that operated well before that formulation. *Empire* is a concept with a long and complex history, as has the process of a state acquiring strength and wealth from overseas trade and possessions (thalassocracy and mercantilism are older terms for this). Imperialism entered the English language as a term describing the political attitude of the France of Napoleon III (1851-1870), and it was only after Queen Victoria had been created Empress of India (1876) that the shift to its present meaning began. Britain was given a status equal to the Continental Empires by the dependent Empire she acquired in the nineteenth century and this dignity's formal proclamation led to the new usage. However, British advocates of Imperial Unity, Imperial Federation and imperial strength called themselves Imperialists, those who put the Empire first, rather than the proponents of any *-ism* or ideology. Morover, though the means were sometimes economic – Imperial (Tariff) Preference for example – their motivation was usually political or military. Merchants trading overseas often saw the assumption of British political control as meaning higher taxes and restriction and advocated informal influence, what later historians have dubbed 'the imperialism of free trade'. It was the opponents of Imperialism, notably Hobson and Lenin (see COMMUNISM), whose analysis argued that its motive power was economic, indeed economic exploitation. The unfortunate consequences of the nineteenth-century world-wide extension of the European economy were criticised as resulting from an ideology, i.e. Imperialism. Some, like E. D. Morel, were outraged by what they saw in Africa; some, like Lenin, wanted to explain why Marx's prognosis of imminent European revolution had not happened – the population of the imperialist state derived economic benefits from the imperial position and so one now had exploited and exploiting peoples throughout the world rather than classes within a state.

Imperialism became a party-political slogan and issue in late nineteenth-century Britain: the Liberals were charged with being *little-Englanders* and favouring 'a policy of scuttle' overseas; while Gladstone portrayed the late 1878 British invasion of Afganistan as resulting from the Tories having drunk deeply 'of the intoxicating beverage of the new Imperialism'. The national strength increased through overseas expansion could also be used in Europe: Disraeli (then Earl of Beaconsfield) brought seven thousand troops to Malta in May 1878 as a move in a Balkan crisis. Imperialism appears to require an Emperor;

so, as a country's expansion need not necessarily be overseas, that of Russia or the Hapsburg Empire (Dual Monarchy) are probably within its scope. There is another mid-nineteenth century word for the ideology of extending one's country's frontiers across seas – *colonialism* (the usual word in French as France was not an Empire after 1870). Colonialism has overtones of settlement, while Imperialism rather has those of the power motive and the desire to impose one's will and culture on a subjugated people. In this sense Imperialism is close to two nineteenth-century terms for extreme patriotism, the 'my country right or wrong' attitude, implying bellicosity or at least readiness to go to war. Chauvin, a Napoleonic veteran in Cogniard's *Cocarde Tricolore* (published 1831), gave his name to *Chauvinism,* an insistence that for France all things must be done. In England it tended to mean the swaggering bombastic patriotism of any foreigners and as such it is doubly pejorative. Jingoism was a British coinage for a similar emotion in Englishmen. In 1878 a popular song supported Disraeli's threatening the Russians with war over a Balkan crisis: it ran "we don't want to fight, but by Jingo if we do, we've got the ships, got the men, and we've got the money too". The subsequent usage is again pejorative: a liberal or radical would refer to a Jingo or Jingoism in attacking a stance of unreasoning bellicosity in dealing with foreigners. Both Chauvinism and Jingoism imply that the degree of patriotism shown is excessive; the more neutral or favourable term for the concept is often Nationalism (see NATIONALISM). However, what they share with Imperialism is the implication that the fervour or interest is to be carried outside the boundaries of the state concerned and pays little or no regard to the nationality of those who are to be subjugated or contended with.

The Imperialist professed concern for his own country's strength and for law, order and good government throughout the world; he assumed unique virtue in his own culture and was uncomprehending of others. His beliefs included the universal establishment of trading conditions suitable to European mercantile norms. However, in general before 1914 the initial expenditure was far greater than the return and the purely cash profit was not as directly nor as quickly sought or expected as the critics argued. After the First World War the Versailles Settlement was hostile to this form of expansion and the main opposition to the settlement came from Fascism (see FASCISM). The democratic rhetoric was now in favour of eventual colonial self-rule, although progress towards this was virtually nonexistent before 1945. Between the wars, however, the colonial Empires were defending their existing holdings rather than seeking new acquisitions (see ANTI-COLONIALISM). In the wake of the eventual (post 1945) retreat there remains a form of neo-imperialism based on indirect control by the use of economic power, which is much closer to Lenin's original Marxist critique than was the late nineteenth-century exercise of the power of European states to subjugate the 'lesser breeds without the law' whose opponents attacked it under the name of Imperialism.

Internationalism

The early nineteenth century opponents of Absolutism assumed that Liberalism and Nationalism were natural allies in this struggle and had no conflict of interest – an assumption especially notable in the works of Giuseppe Mazzini (1805-1872) (see NATIONALISM). The events of 1848 to 1871 led to this compatability being questioned on the progressive side of politics. Nationalism came to be seen as a force which prevented the perception of common class interests across linguistic boundaries and fomented destructive and unproductive wars. In socialist criticisms of nationalism the emphasis was on the former element, in liberal ones on the latter.

The words *Internationalist* and *Internationalism* were first used in English to mean supporters of the International Working Men's Association founded in 1864. Shortly afterwards the term came to be used for those who wanted to extend international law from being something that protected the commerical interests of individuals into a force that would regulate relations between state governments, and of the writings of those, such as Alfred Nobel and Andrew Carnegie, who advocated co-operation between people despite their differing nationalities. 1889, the year of the founding of the Inter-Parliamentary Union and the first Pan-American Conference, was when this form of Internationalism first made a significant impact. The attempt to negotiate armament reduction by international agreement became associated with the term after Tsar Nicholas II's imperial rescript of 24 August 1898. The results of the consequent Hague Conferences (1899 and 1907) were meagre, but the agreed codification of some of the laws of war was seen as a first step in fostering Internationalism.

During the First World War, whose cause was blamed by many on narrow nationalism, there arose a demand that the peace settlement should include an international organisation empowered to adjudicate conflicts and prevent any future wars. This demand was articulated by US President Woodrow Wilson and it was point number fourteen of his 'Fourteen Points' on the basis of which Germany agreed to surrender in 1918. The League of Nations created by the Versailles Settlement was an inadequate expression of that desire and the inter-war period saw Isolationism, Appeasement and "internationals" organising the rival ideologies the *Comintern* or Third Socialist International (see COMMUNISM) and the "Green" peasants international. The League was the 1930s version of collective security and the outbreak of the Second World War marked its collapse.

The United Nations Organisation, created after the Second World War, had more limited hopes invested in it. It has played a useful role in the problems caused by decolonisation and the cold war, but support for the U.N. has hardly been a predominant or well-articulated ideology. The rules of international law are often disputed and lack an enforcement agency. Today many people would reject Nationalism or patriotism as a sufficient justification for automatically supporting one's own country; to assert, however, that the whole world should be one united state normally requires another more specific ideology in addition to Internationalism to make that unity even seem feasible. Socialist internationalism (see SOCIALISM) has been dealt with elsewhere, the internationalism of supranational organisation and world federation are part of the tradition of most Liberal parties and the rhetoric of international agencies.

A newer form of Internationalism, based on people's common distrust of all governments, may well be in the process of being born – the *Live Aid* concert of 13 July 1985 is an example of this emotion. It is not very ideological, however, although theoretically this position will lead to a form of anarchism (see ANARCHISM).

Islamic Fundamentalism

The term 'Islamic Fundamentalism' is usually applied to those movements in the Islamic World which aim, overtly or covertly, at the establishment of an Islamic state in which some Islamic laws or customs will be enforced. Although these movements vary considerably from one region to another, the areas of Islamic law they would like to see enforced generally include 'modest' dress for women, sexual segregation, financial and economic measures such as the banning of *riba* or interest on bank loans and the institution of *zakat*, the compulsory charity or tithe, as well as the imposition of Quranic penalties for certain crimes, including robbery and sexual relations outside marriage. It should be stressed that these measures do not really amount to a comprehensive restoration of Islamic Law as it was applied in medieval or pre-modern times. They involve, rather, the adoption of particular Islamic laws, or customs perceived as Islamic, which have been selected for their symbolic value as a way of demonstrating opposition to Western culture and to governments, such as that of the Pahlavi dynasty in Iran (1923-1979), considered excessively pro-Western. For this and other reasons, the term 'fundamentalism', borrowed from American Protestantism, is, strictly speaking, inaccurate. Nearly all believing Muslims are 'fundamentalist' in that they consider the *Qur'an* to be the literal and final revelation of God, as dictated to the Prophet Muhammad (*c*.570-632 AD). 'Fundamentalists' differ from other Muslims not in their belief in the inerrancy of scripture, but rather in the importance they attach to certain aspects of the law derived from scripture and their insistence that it should be imposed on Muslim society, whether by consent or by revolutionary means. The terms 'Islamist' or, in some cases, 'neo-traditionalist' are more appropriate.

Unlike Christianity, which only became the state religion of a highly developed polity (the Roman Empire) after a long gestation as an opposition or underground cult, Islam began its career as a state. The Prophet Muhammad, as well as revealing what he believed to be the Divine Word in the *Qur'an*, was the leader of a tribal commonwealth, based on Medina in Northern Arabia. After the Prophet's death in 632 this state expanded to include most of North Africa and the Middle East, with new capitals in Damascus and, later, Baghdad. Although the original empire of the Prophet's successors, the Caliphs, disintegrated within a few generations into a welter of competing successor-states, the Sultans and *mirs* ('authorities' and 'commanders') who inherited caliphal power held certain things in common – most notably that their legitimacy depended on being seen to uphold the Divine Law or *Shari'a* – in the Quranic phrase, 'to enjoin the good and forbid the evil'. This law, derived from the *Qur'an* and the *Sunna* (the Prophet's precepts, as reported by tradition), was elaborated by scholars in the eighth and ninth centuries into a comprehensive system of *fiqh* or jurisprudence which covered every aspect of a Muslim's life, from religious duties to the details of personal hygiene, from the conduct of politics to the regulation of financial and commercial dealing. Although this system was never applied comprehensively – the *Shari'a* was supplemented or sometimes replaced by the decrees of rulers in substantial areas of commerce, taxation, public and criminal law – the impression was maintained that Islam was a 'total way of life' which made no distinction between private and public behaviour, religion and politics. Changes in social patterns, for example in relations between the sexes, in modes of dress, could be represented as deviating from the *Shari'a* and its divinely-sanctioned way of life.

Throughout Islamic history there have been movements led by Islamic reformers who aimed to purge society of alien or non-Islamic accretions and restore Islam in its orignal pristine form. This aim was explicit in the original movement of Muhammad, who claimed not to be inaugurating a new dispensation, but to be restoring an old one, the original faith of Abraham. The leaders of such movements – like Muhammad himself – often succeeded in creating tribal confederations which led, by conquest, to the founding of new dynasties. Islamic political militancy is thus integral to Islamic history. The modern Islamist movements, however, date from the period, since the eighteenth century, when a greater part of the Islamic world came under European colonial rule. Traditionalist revolts of the kind that had often succeeded in the past were no longer able to displace European conquerors or governments underpinned by European power. A new generation of reformers addressed itself to re-interpreting the law to accommodate modern reality without sacrificing Islam's ethical, spiritual and social values. The most influential of these reformers was Sheikh Muhammad Abduh (1849-1905) who was Grand Mufti (chief Islamic legal officer) of Egypt for much of the period of indirect British rule (1882-1919). In purging the *Shari'a* of accretions and innovations, Abduh drew partly in the methods of earlier reformers, notably Ibn Taymivya (d. 1327) and Muhammad ibn Abdul Wahhab (d. 1792) whose puritanical version of Islam became the official ideology of the ruling *Sa'udi* dynasty in northern Arabia. By returning directly to the *Qur'an* and the earlest traditions of the 'pious ancestors' (*al salaf al saleh*) Abduh was able to inject a new creativity in the interpretation of the law. He distinguished between its essentials (defined in terms of maintaining the social good of the Muslims) and the superficial details (such as attachment to particular social habits or details of dress), allowing for social growth and change within the overall framework of an immutable, divinely-ordained *Shari'a*. Abhuh's influence spread from the Maghreb to Indonesia. Throughout the Islamic world it helped inspire Muslim national resistance to colonialism by presenting a radical and progressive version of Islam which contrasted with the mystical or quietist versions encouraged by the colonial authorities. This type of fundamentalist or *salafi* thought thus entered the mainstream of the anti-colonialist struggle, becoming mixed with the emerging nationalist struggle against the British, French, Dutch and other colonial powers in the Muslim world.

The effect of this merging was to divide Muslim activists into two, eventually hostile, camps. On one side were the secularists, who adapted reformist ideas to largely nationalist purposes, effectively reducing Islam to a personal religion comparable to Christianity as practised in the West. On the other were the Islamic radicals who sought to reintegrate society into a comprehensive Islamic framework which would transcend the boundaries of the national state. The logic of the independence struggle and post-colonial history inevitably favoured the former, driving the latter into opposition. The fact that the struggle for independence was fought on a regional basis, and that independence, when won, was granted within the old colonial frontiers gave secularists the upper hand. In nearly every Muslim country it was nationalists of one kind or another who came to power after independence. Time and again, nationalists would collaborate with Islamic radicals when in opposition, only to ditch them on coming to power.

A classic example occurred in Egypt, one of the first Arab states to achieve formal independence. Throughout the period of British domination, nationalist leaders like Urabi Pasha, Mustafa Kamil and Sa'ad Zaghloul had enlisted Islamic feelings in their demand for an end to foreign or infidel rule. The limited independence won by Egypt in 1921, however, was entirely secular in character. The new constitution, adopted in 1923, embodied reformist principles that had been developing since the early nineteenth century. Egypt became a sovereign state under a constitutional monarch. This conflicted with the Islamic principle that sovereignty belongs only to God, and that the Muslim's only allegiance, after God, is to the *Umma*, the whole community of believers. Similarly, parliament was given full powers of legislation, untramelled by the *Shari'a*, which was effectively reduced to regulating questions of personal status, such as marriage and divorce. Moreover, by granting Egyptians equal rights before the law regardless of religious affiliations, the constitution abolished the time-honoured distinction between Muslims and *dhimmis* (non-Muslims from other religious communities, originally Jews and Christians but later extended to other scriptural religions, who were granted protected, but inferior, status in classical Islam).

Even before the Second World War a growing number of Egyptians began to perceive the new state as unIslamic and therefore lacking legitimacy. Their most influential spokesman was Hasan al Banna, founder of the Muslim brotherhood. Partly modelled on the traditional Sufi or mystic orders which had spearheaded resistance to European power in the eighteenth and nineteenth centuries, the Brotherhood combined the functions of evangelical society and pressure group. Its members, who came from all walks of life, from university professors to urban labourers, were pledged to uphold the *Shari'a* in their personal lives, by avoiding the evils of alcohol, gambling, fornication and so forth; their wider, more political aim was to rid Egyptian society of all foreign influences, particularly that of the British. At the same time Banna and his followers accepted some of the reforms of the *Shari'a* advocated by Abduh and his more conservative disciple, Rashid Rida. For example, they sometimes took the modernist view that the Quranic penalties, such as amputation for theft, should only be applied when the just Islamic society, in which no one might be tempted to steal for reasons of need, had been created. Although Banna had stated that he was prepared to work within Egypt's constitutional framework he was also responsible for establishing a 'secret apparatus' for the 'defence of Islam and society'. Its members were given military training which enabled them to enlist as volunteers in the 1948 Palestine War. Brotherhood members were prominent in the disturbances that followed the Arab defeat in that war, a defeat that was widely blamed on corruption, especially in Egypt. The Brotherhood's organisation was dissolved, and, following the murder of the Prime Minister, Nuqurashi Pasha in December 1948, Banna was himself assassinated by government agents. The rioting in Cairo which led to the fall of the monarchy in 1952 was largely inspired, and directed, by the Brotherhood; in recognition of their role the Free Officers led by Gamal Abdul Nasser who took power offered them a place in government. The collaboration, however, was short-lived. Within weeks the Brotherhood membership had left government; and following the general ban on the old political parties, their organisation was once again dissolved. An attempt on Nasser's life in 1954 provided the Egyptian leader with a pretext for turning on his former allies: six of the Brotherhood's leading figures were hanged; hundreds more were imprisoned or driven to seek asylum in Syria, Jordan, Sudan, Saudi Arabia and Pakistan, where they received some official encouragement and helped spread the movement's influence internationally.

It was Nasser's prisons, where its members were subjected to appalling conditions, including torture, that Sayyid Qutb, the Brotherhood's most infuential theorist, formulated the more radical politcal ideology of the modern Islamist or fundamentalist movement. Comparing the persecution experience by the modern Brotherhood to that suffered by Muhammad and his Companions at the hands of their Quraishite enemies in Mecca, Qutb argued that the entire

Muslim world was now in a state of *jahiliyya* corresponding to the 'period of ignorance' prior to the coming of Islam in seventh-century Arabia. Qutb was strongly influence by the ideas of Sayyid Abu'l ala Maududi, an ultra-conservative Indo-Pakistani thinker and founder of the *Jama'at-i-Islami*, a party which works in Pakistan and India for an Islamic state. Maududi had been a disciple of the modernist thinker and poet, Muhammad Iqbal, one of the founders of the Pakistan movement, who died in 1938. Although Maududi did not share Iqbal's liberal and intellectual outlook which combined a profound knowledge of Islamic religious tradition with wide reading in Western philosophy, he adapted Iqbal's vision of the *Shari'a* as a dynamic system of law which could be expanded to cover every aspect of modern life. For Maududi the struggle for Islam was not for the restoration of an idealised past, but for an Islamic order which could be brought about here and now. The *jihad* (holy war) was not just a defensive war for the protection of *Dar ul Islam* (the abode of Islam or Islamic territory). It might be waged offensively against those forces which threatened to undermine Islam at home or abroad, for the state of *jahiliyya* was everywhere present.

Drawing practical conclusions from Maududi's arguments, Sayyid Qutb advocated the creation of a new élite, or vanguard, among Muslim youth which would fight the new *jahiliyya*. Like the Prophet and his Companions, this élite must decide when to withdraw from society (as the Prophet did in AD 622, when he left Mecca to found the new Islamic state in Medina), and when to maintain contact with it (as the Prophet did during his early years in Mecca). Qutb's ideas established an agenda for Islamic radicals, not just in Egypt, but throughout the *Sunni* Muslim world. His ideas were also influential in Iran, where part of the *Shi'ite* religious establishment under the leadership of Ayatollah Ruhalla Khomeini took power following the fall of the Shah in 1979.

One group influenced by Qutb advocated a strategy of withdrawal. Led by Shukri Mustafa, a former Muslim Brother who had spent time in prison, they designated the whole of Egyptian society as infidel, defining themselves as the only true Muslims. They refused to pray in 'infidel' mosques (by which they meant those with government-appointed *imams* or preachers); they refused to serve in the armed forces, and married exclusively among themselves, creating a semi-autonomous counter-culture in Egypt, living off remissions sent by sympathisers working abroad. The Egyptian press dubbed the group *Takfir wa Hijra* (literally: 'Excommunication of Holy Emigration'). Mustafa was executed, and the group driven underground, after they kidnapped and murdered a former Minister of Religious Endowments, Sheikh Muhammad el-Dhahabi, who had denounced them as Kharijite heretics. (The Kharijite dissenters, now represented only in Oman and parts of North and East Africa, are the oldest sect in Islam, which split from the main body of the community in 660 following the claims of 'Ali, the Prophet's son-in-law, to leadership. Originally supporters of 'Ali, they became disillusioned with his decision to compromise with the Umayyad forces of Mu'awiya. Withdrawing from the ranks of 'Ali's supporters, they established separatist communities in remote parts of the Islamic world. Seeing themselves as the only true Muslims in a world of infidels, they regarded as legitimate to wage war on society, and kill other Muslims at will. Shukri Mustafa and his followers denied this charge, arguing that they were merely following the Prophet's example; in due course, they expected the mass of Egyptians to follow their strategy so that eventually the whole of society would be purified.

Another more celebrated group, though influenced by Sayyid Qutb, adopted the opposite strategy of attempting to seize state power in order to impose an Islamic order by force. This was the *Jihad* group responsible for the killing of President Anwar Sadat at a military parade in October 1981. In addition to Qutb's writings, their principal ideologue, Abdul Salaam Farraj, drew on legal rulings and theories advocated by the jurist Ibn Taymiyya to justify the Egyptian leader's execution on the ground that he had failed in his duty of 'enjoining the good and forbidding the evil' by applying the *Shari'a*. The group's intention appears to have been somewhat naïve; the assassins, led by Lieutenant Khaled Islambouli, had infiltrated the military parade with a view to killing the whole Eyptian government in the expectation that the population as a whole would support their subsequent bid for power. In the event, only Sadat and a few others were killed, and power passed peacefully to Sadat's constitutionally-appointed successor, Husni Mubarak.

Other Sunni activists who invoked the same medieval jurist to justify attempts to overthrow 'infidel' rulers include members of the Syrian Muslim Brotherhood, who seized control of the city of Hama in February 1982 in the most serious insurrection by *Sunni* militants yet faced by an Arab regime. The rebellion was suppressed by President Hafez al Asad and his brother Rifaat at the cost of at least ten thousand lives. A previous attempt by *Sunni* activists to seize power by *coup d' état* occurred in Egypt in 1974, when members of the Islamic Liberation Party tried to initiate a mutiny among cadets at the Egyptian Military Academy in Heliopolis. The same group, which aims at a restoration of the Caliphate, was accused of plotting against the Tunisian government in two major trials in 1983 and 1985.

In contrast to these revolutionary groups the main body of the Muslim Brotherhood has become increasingly cautious and politically conservative. During the period of persecution during the 1950s and early 1960s, many of the Egyptian leaders, such as Omar al-Talmassani and Said Ramadan, found refuge in Saudi Arabia; some of them made considerable fortunes in business through their connections with members of the Saudi Royal family which, during the reign of King Faisal (1964–75) actively supported their cause. When, soon after acceding to power in 1970, President Anwar Sadat found it expedient to turn against the former Nasserist left and their Soviet supporters, he needed the support of Islamist elements as an alternative power-base. He allowed prominent exiles to return and establish themselves in business where they became beneficiaries of his 'open door' economic policies. They thus found themselves in the anomalous position of tacitly supporting these policies whilst deploring their consequences, which was to open the floodgates of Westernisation, kept at bay by President Nasser's socialist policies. Although Sadat turned against the Brotherhood and other critics of his regime during the last two months of his life (a factor which certainly contributed to his assassination) the mainstream Brotherhood leadership still occupied the same anomalous position under his successor Mubarak. While pressing for the enforcement of the Shari'a, they remain in favour of political stability – which means, in effect, retaining the status quo. Though still technically banned, they are pressing for legal reinstatement, and have been permitted to air their views in their journal Al Da'wa ('The Call'). To overcome the ban in parliament, they formed an alliance with the pre-revolutionary secular nationalist party, the Wafd. By 1986 they disposed of a dozen parliamentary seats. However, the People's Assembly has repeatedly blocked or thrown out proposals for a wholesale re-enactment or restoration of the Shari'a in Egypt; and, frustrated in parliament, fundamentalists have turned to agitation in the streets. The leaders outside parliament, including the popular preachers Sheikh Hafez Salama in Cairo and Sheikh Omar Abdul Rahman of Assiut, remained thorns in the government's flesh throughout the mid-1980s, as did the university students' unions, which continued to be dominated by the militant Islamic Associations. There were few indications, however, that Islamic opposition forces would be able to topple the regime by mounting an Iranian-style Islamic revolution. In Egypt, as in other Sunni countries, the greater part of the religious establishment is under government control. Outside the universities the Islamic opposition lacks the leadership or organisation which could turn a wave of popular discontent inspired by deteriorating economic conditions into a successful bid for power.

A similar pattern, with many local variations, prevails in most of the states with Sunni Muslim majorities between Morocco and Indonesia. In general, the appeal of Islamic militancy had been strongest in counties like Egypt and Tunisia with the longest exposure to Western political, cultural and economic influences. It has been weakest in countries like Saudi Arabia and Yemen where the Shari'a continues to be applied in its traditional forms. (Thus while some Saudis may have sympathised with the motives of the young extremists who seized the Grand Mosque in Mecca in 1979 to protest against the prevailing corruption and proclaim the new millennium, many more were scandalised by the sacrilege done to Islam's holiest shrine.) An exception to this general pattern is Turkey, where the process of secularisation begun by the Ottoman Sultans and continued by Ataturk after the First World War has gone so far that an Islamic state has ceased to be on the political agenda. Islamist sympathisers among the urban youth have had to content themselves with purely symbolic gestures such as the wearing of beards and headscarves.

The parties and movements which continue to fight for the full implementation of Islamic law by the use of state power have usually been highly ambivalent in their attitudes towards democracy. When in opposition they have joined with other more secular oppositionists in protesting against the absence of democratic freedoms and himan rights. Yet in several important instances they have been prepared to collaborate with autocratic military regimes in furthering their aims. In Pakistan the *Jama'at-i-Islami* collaborated with the dictatorship of General Zia ul Hagg during the early years of his Islamisation programme, although later, as is regime became increasingly unpopular and isolated, they moved into opposition. In the case of Sudan, where President Numiri's September 1983 Decree replaced existing laws with a code based on the *Shari'a*, this strategy of collaboration seriously backfired for the Muslim Brotherhood, whose support the decrees were explicitly designed to win. The economic and political confusion brought about by the decrees contributed directly the Numeiri's downfall in April 1985, leading to a flight of foreign capital, the loss of essential revenues and an escalation of the civil war in the south. Following the restoration of democracy in April 1986 the Brotherhood, which won only fifty-two seats in the general elections, moved into opposition; but its prospects of achieving power by democratic means were permanently blocked by the predominance of two other Muslim parties, the *Umma* led by Sadeq el Mahdi and Muhammad el Mirgani's Democratic Unionist Party. In Tunisia the influential Islamic Tendency Movement's commitment to democracy was similarly doubtful; so long as it remained proscribed and sought legalisation, its leaders looked for allies among the secular opposition, stressing the common demand for a restoration of democracy and full human rights. However, a secret document published abroad revealed that the Movement merely regarded democracy as a stage on the road to power. The concept of the 'Sovereignty of God' (as distinct from that of the 'People'), if not explicitly anti-democratic, sets severe limitations on the exercise of democracy, since it inhibits any elected assembly from enacting legislation deemed contrary to the 'laws' decreed by God.

The ambivalence in the relationship between Islamism and democracy is most evident in the one country where the movement has been in power, the Islamic Republic of Iran. In one sense, Iran's government is one of the most democratic in the Middle East, having been elected in relatively free ballots, with the *Majlis* or parliament having the right to veto cabinet appointments. On the other hand the Constitution, by providing that all legislation should be approved by a Guardianship Council under the Supreme Jurist (Khomeini or his successor Ayatollah Montazeri), ensures that such legislation is confined within strict fundamentalist limits. Individuals or parties which stand outside the narrow consensus of the Islamist movement have been effectively excluded from political life. At the same time, however, the government has remained divided on the major issue of economic management; apart from the strictures on *riba* or usury, which are extremely difficult to apply under modern conditions, and a generally-expressed concern for the welfare of the poor, Islam offers no specific answers to the bread-and-butter questions which concern all modern governments.

Although the Iranian revolution has proved an inspiration for Islamist move-

131

ments further afield, especially in distant countries like Malaysia and Indonesia, there are several factors limiting its exportability. It is doubtful if any other country, whether *Sunni* or *Shi'ite*, can imitate the Khomeinist model, which was built on a clerical estate both well-organised and independent of the government. A possible exception is Iraq, where a major military collapse could lead to the defeat of the Baathist regime which is dominated by the *Sunni* Arab minority and the establishment of a pro-Khomeinist government drawn from the *Shi'ite* majority.

Unlike their *Sunni* counterparts, who have long been subject to state control and are generally despised by Islamic radicals, the Iranian *Shi'ite 'ulema* (religious scholars) have long enjoyed considerable spiritual authority and independent social power. The *Shi'a* (or 'Partisans') believe that the leadership of the whole Islamic community inheres in the descendants of the Prophet Muhammad through his son-in-law 'Ali and his grandson Husain who was killed while making an unsuccessful bid for the caliphate at Kerbala, Iraq, in 682 AD. In Iran, where *Shi'ism* has been the state religion since the sixteenth century, nationalist *'ulema,* known as *'usulis,* acquired the ascendancy over their more traditionalist rivals in the nineteenth century. This bolstered the intellectual authority of the religious establishment which already enjoyed a high degree of autonomy *vis-à-vis* the state by having the right to dispose of and collect religious taxes, to administer religious endowments *(awqaf)* and to give sanctuary *(bast)* to criminals or political fugitives. The fact that two of the holiest *Shi'a* shrines at Kerbala and Najaf lay in Iraq, in Ottoman territory, further increased the power of the *'ulema vis-à-vis* the Persian Shahs, as many of their leaders were beyond the reach of royal pressure.

As guardians of religious tradition the Iranian *'ulema* – who, unlike the *Sunnis,* are organised into a hierarchy comprising Grand Ayatollahs, Ayatollahs, Hojjat-ul-Islams and ordinary mullahs – played a prominent part in resistance to Western economic penetration, notably during the successful agitation against the tobacco monopoly granted to an English company in 1890 and the events leading up to the Constitutional Revolution of 1905-6 when a section of them joined with the liberal bourgeoisie in forcing the Shah to grant a constituent assembly.

This relative independence *vis-à-vis* the state enabled the Iranian clergy to take power in the chaos surrounding the collapse of the Pahlavi regime in 1979. The ground had been prepared by two very different thinkers – 'Ali Shariati, a modernist, and Khomeini himself, a radical neo-traditionalist. Shariati, who died in 1977, was a lay intellectual, partly educated in the West. He combined elements of Marxism and Islam in his thinking in a manner which attracted both the Westernised bourgeoisie and radicals from the 'traditional' classes. Khomeini, a theologian from the holy city of Qom, was in many respects a traditionalist who held to conservative interpretations of Islamic law. He first rose to prominence during the agitation against Shah Muhammad Reza Pahlavi's reforms and pro-Western policies in the 1960s, which threatened the interests of the mullahs, among others. Exiled to Najaf in Iraq, he became the Pahlavi regime's most outspoken critic, until his expulsion to Paris in 1978, which made him an international figure. Khomeini's radicalism lay in his view that the *ulema* should rule directly on the basis of religious law. In a now famous series of lectures to his students at Najaf, he outlined the doctrine of the *wilayat-e-faqih* (the trusteeship of the jurisconsult) according to which government should be under the direct supervision of the *ulema*. At the time of the revolution, Khomeini's ideas were known to relatively few people. What made him a powerful symbol of opposition was the uncomproming moral tone of his message and his jeremiads against the Shah, whom he often compared to Yazid, the Umayyad caliph responsible for the death of Husain, a traditional hate-figure in *Shi'ite* folklore. Even more significantly, perhaps, his prophet-like appearance fitted popular ideas about the Hidden Imam: and while he never claimed to be the Hidden Imam, there is no doubt that he and his supporters allowed eschatological ideas about the Imam to operate in his favour, enabling him to acquire a much larger following than other leaders. These factors, along with his own political astuteness, allowed him and his hard-line supporters to get the upper hand in the struggle for power with more liberal and left-wing elements that followed the triumph of the revolution in 1979.

Politically the Islamic revolution shares the same ambiguities as the Islamist movement generally. It is both radical and conservative, progressive and reactionary, democratic and authoritarian. As an ideology it is thus fraught with apparent contradictions. The movement, or rather movements, should not, however, be considered separately from the context in which they operate. Throughout the Islamic world wealth and power has been concentrated in the hands of relatively small, unrepresentative élites who have resorted to religious or nationalist arguments to justify their privileges. The vocabulary of Islam can be used to challenge these privileges, by drawing on the same repertoire of religious symbolism, and by invoking nationalist feelings that go deeper than patriotic allegiances to recently-formed national states. In most of the Muslim world the folk-memory of a golden age of Islamic civilisation before the West became dominant has a strong attraction, especially when the élites who took power after independence have been discredited by compromise with the West, or with the global system associated with Western domination.

The vocabulary of Islam has a powerful mobilising appeal for recently-urbanised people. It provides a familiar language or conceptual framework in which the unfamiliar can be addressed and coped with. It makes it possible for people with traditional village backgrounds to arrive in the cosmopolitan world of the city, with its largely 'Western' appearance in terms of buildings and motor traffic, without necessarily feeling lost or socially confused. Religious obligations such as prayer and fasting, which are taken lightly in the villages, acquire an added significance in the city where there exist people who neither pray nor fast. For the urban migrant religion becomes for the first time a matter of choice, a badge of identity.

The appeal is especially strong in the case of women and the whole area of male-female relations. Modern urban life has seriously disrupted the elaborate social codes governing relations between the sexes in traditional Muslim society. In cities like Cairo men and women are promiscuously herded together in appallingly overcrowded public transport systems, creating embarrassment, confusion, and unexpected sexual opportunities. Wearing 'Islamic dress' – which may come as a restriction of liberty for a westernised minority of women accustomed to greater freedom – enables the majority of women from traditional backgrounds to cope with those conditions more comfortably. The veil or *chador* becomes a barrier against unwelcomed advances, enabling these women to enjoy more mobility than previously.

Stated most broadly, the underlying desire of the Islamic movement is to modernise without becoming westernised, to achieve urbanisation and economic growth without loss of cultural identity. These very general aims do not fit easily any one clearly-defined social or political programme, which is why the various Islamist movements – outside the special case of Iran – seem more likely to succeed as pressure groups on Muslim societies than as parties of government.

Further Reading

Albert Hourani, *Arabic Thought in the Liberal Age*
Hamid Enayat, *Modern Islamic Political Thought*
Edward Mortimer, *Faith and Power: The Politics of Islam*
Roy Mottahadeh, *The Mantle of the Prophet: Religion and Politics in Iran*
Gilles Kepel, *The Prophet and Pharaoh: Muslim Extremism in Egypt,* trans. J. Rothschild
James P. Piscatori (ed.), *Islam in the Political Process*
E. I. J. Rosenthal, *Islam in the Modern National State*
Malise Ruthven, *Islam in the World*
Emmanuel Sivan, *Radical Islam: Medieval Theology and Modern Politics*
W. Cantwell Smith, *Islam in Modern History*

Isolationism

The term 'isolationism' is normally used to describe the doctrine which demands of a state that its government restrict relations with other states, especially political relations, to the barest minimum. The most extensive form of isolationism was that practised by Japan between the expulsion of western influence and the 'reopening' of Japan at the time of the Meiji restoration. More commonly, the terms has been used to describe the avoidance of political commitments to, and especially alliances with, other states. At the end of the nineteenth century Lord Salisbury described the policy he felt Britain should follow as one of 'splendid isolation'. The most common application of the term, however, is in discussions of American foreign policy, the doctrine of Isolation claiming as its origin the warning against 'entangling alliances' contained in President Washington's farewell address and confirmed in President Monroe's 1823 pronouncement against European intervention in the Americas.

In these discussions, distinction has been drawn between various types of isolationism; that which coupled non-involvement in European power politics with vigorous expansion westwards towards and across the Pacific, in search of America's 'manifest destiny'; hemispheric isolationism, which confined the operation of American power to North and South America; strict 'continentalism' which seeks to restrict American concern to the North American continent; and advocacy of 'Fortress America' which sees American power as potentially so great that, provided that power is properly maintained against external threats, Americans need not concern themselves at all with external affairs.

'Isolationism' as a label is used to cover a collection of often mutually incompatible attitudes to the external world including: a belief in the innate primacy of domestic political attitudes; xenophobia in general and Anglophobia in particular; an absolutism and simplism in relation to external relations as governable by simple moral standards, war being so evil that, if it is unavoidable, any means of winning war quickly is acceptable; a conviction of the irrelevance to America of all issues not directly touching American interests; a resentment of limitations on American freedom of action; and a willingness to impose restrictions on American action in the search for means of avoiding American involvement in war.

The policy of Isolationism could be advocated either on idealist or on realist grounds, either as a revulsion against the war and *Machtpolitik* of the old world, or on geopolitical grounds – the remoteness of America from the threat of invasion by the European great powers. Its opposite, 'Internationalism' (see INTERNATIONALISM) or 'interventionism' could equally be the product of idealist or realist arguments. The opponents in the Senate to American involvement with the League of Nations were in the main realists who felt the commitment, contained in Articles X and XVI of the League's Covenant, to the maintenance of the territorial *status quo* the world over, by force, if necessary, was contrary to American interests. They were by no means dedicated idealists, however, and favoured in fact American involvement in some other looser association of nations. By contrast, the advocates of American membership of the League in the 1920s turned in many cases a decade later to support American neutrality legislation which would have made American aid against aggression impossible.

Political isolation from Europe did not necessarily imply absence of economic entanglement. Economic isolationism expressed itself during the 1890s in the advocacy of silver coinage, and of effective separation from the gold-based European financial system. In the 'isolationist' 1920s, American intervention settled the reparations issue with the *Dawes plan* in 1924, and financed European recovery thereafter. President Hoover's personal diplomacy in the international financial crisis of 1931, the year which saw the collapse of Austrian and German banking systems and the near collapse of the Bank of England, marked its apogee. President Roosevelt, elected in 1932, took America into economic isolationism when he devalued the dollar in 1933 and broke up the London Economic Conference of June 1933. This was followed by the *Johnson Act* in 1934 which banned access to the American capital market to all states in default on existing war payments. Roosevelt's attempt from 1935 onwards to reopen America to world trade had only marginal effects in reducing the isolation of the American economy from a world breaking up into separate currency and trading blocks.

Isolationist sentiment expressed itself most strongly in the 1930s in the revision of American neutrality legislation in the years 1935-38, which abandoned most of the 'neutral's rights' enjoyed by non-belligerents in the nineteenth century. German violation of this, in the years 1914-1917, had done much to involve America in the First World War. The legislation sought to restrict both Presidential and Congressional powers to protect American interests where such protection might risk American involvement in war. Support for this gradually waned as American opinion came more and more to regard the expansion of Nazi Germany as a threat to American ideals and interests. Parts were repealed in the winter of 1939-40. The Nazi conquest of France was followed by the destroyer-bases deal with Britain and by *Lend-lease,* though Roosevelt was careful to stay within the letter of Isolationism by extending the no-war zone deep into the Atlantic. Isolationist opposition to his policy, now led by ex-President Hoover and the *America First* organisation, based itself essentially on grounds of *realpolitik,* arguing that America could best defend her interests by building up her defences and keeping out of the conflict ('Fortress America').

The Japanese attack on Pearl Habour and the American entry into the Second World War is generally taken, in retrospect, to have marked the final abandonment of Isolationism by the United States, though much of Roosevelt's thinking in the war years about post-war security was dominated by the fear that the end of the war would see its return.

However, America became host country to the United Nations in 1945. From 1947 onwards the needs of the Cold War brought the United States to enter one 'entangling alliance' after another, including, in the military field, the North Atlantic Treaty (1949), the Australia-New Zealand-United States Pact (1950), and the South East Asian Treaty (1954). These were justified by the public enunciation of 'doctrines' binding the United States, for example, to come to the aid of any 'freedom-loving' nation facing external threats to their sovereignty or independence, which were even more far-reaching in scope (e.g. the 'Truman doctrine' of 1947 and the 'Eisenhower doctrine' of 1957 in relation to the Middle East). This is not to say that Isolationist impulses did not continue to manifest themselves from time to time. The 'New Look' defence policy adopted by the Eisenhower administration in 1953, with its run-down of conventional forces in favour of nuclear weapons delivered by intercontinental missiles, represented at least in part a return to the concept of 'Fortress America'.

The amendments to successive defence budgets advanced annually in the late 1900s and early 1970s by Senator Mike Mansfield calling for the withdrawal of American troops from Europe can be seen in a similar light.

Underlying much of the classic formulation of isolationism was a sense of American moral superiority over the wicked corrupt European states from which American forebears had emigrated. With President Wilson, and again with American sentiment from 1941 onwards, that sense of moral superiority was coupled with the determination not to withold from the world that moral leadership for which their moral superiority most qualified them, if it did not indeed destine them to provide against a tide of corruption which threatened America itself. American opinion after 1941 was the more concerned to provide such leadership for its conviction that only American refusal to participate in the collective security system of the League of Nations had made its breakdown and the onset of the Second World War possible. The decline of that sense of moral obligation since the 1960s is one of the most disturbing of phenomena in current developments in the United States.

Keynesianism
(including the New Deal and Monetarism)

Keynesianism, as the term suggests, derives from the work of John Maynard Keynes, the famous British economist, whose book, *The General Theory of Employment, Interest and Money* (1935), is one of the most important contributions in the whole history of economics. It must however be emphasised that the term 'Keynesianism' goes well beyond Keynes's own work in both its economic and political implications, and it is doubtful whether he would have subscribed to many of the apparent implications of his work that his acolytes allege to have found. This is especially true of the political interpretation of his work.

As an economic doctrine Keynesianism consists of the following propositions:

(1) There is no natural tendency in capitalist market economies for the system to move towards equilibrium at full employment. This is in contrast to most of orthodox (classical) thinking before Keynes which tended to assume, implicitly or explicitly, that full employment of labour and capital was the norm. Moreover it was further assumed that should an economy be out of equilibrium it would quickly return to it.

(2) As a consequence of (1) it followed the capitalist economies would commonly experience general unemployment and there would be no tendency for natural forces to eliminate it. There would commonly be workers willing to

137

work at going wage rates but who were unable to find work. This is what Keynesians call *involuntary* unemployment. Prior to Keynes unemployment had been thought of in orthodox circles as a voluntary act undertaken by workers who had quit jobs to search for better pay and conditions.

(3) The failure to maintain the workforce in full employment is mainly due to lack of total spending. Once again, this view is in severe contrast to the classical position which emphasised lack of saving and excessively high wages as major causes of disturbance.

(4) These periodic total spending failures were mainly due to a shortfall of private domestic capital formation. The entrepreneurial group responsible for investment outlays were prone to bouts of deep pessimism about future profitability upon which its decisions were based. Often these pessimistic expectations were completely irrational, but, as a consequence of holding them, investment outlays would be cut, tending to a reduction in employment, income and spending, followed by secondary reductions as lower consumption spending added to the decline.

(5) It follows from points (1) to (4) that there is now a strong *prima facie* case for government economic intervention, not simply for traditional reasons of monopoly control, the provision of public goods that the market might not provide in adequate amounts, or to alter the pattern of income and wealth distribution, but a major, more dramatic reason of becoming *the* regulator of the whole economy. A shortfall of aggregate demand required an increase in government spending to fill the gap and, conversely, excessive private spending required a reduction in the public contribution. A key feature of this new economic philosophy was that government budgetary policy, far from being a fairly straight-forward exercise of balancing the budget, now became the centre of national economic policy. Aptly the new aspect of government economic policy became known via Abba Lerner (1) as the 'theory of functional finance'. It also seemed to end the traditional (Conservative) fixation with balanced budgets: correct economic policy now required sometimes a deficit and sometimes a surplus.

It should be noted here that in Keynes' own work there was room for the operation of both fiscal and monetary policy. This implied that to expand an economy a government had the options of increasing government spending and/or reducing tax rates (fiscal policy), or increasing the quantity of money and lowering interest rates (monetary policy). There is some evidence that Keynes himself preferred monetary policy. As interpreted by his followers – both in the United States and in the United Kingdom – however, Keynesianism became associated essentially with fiscal, budgetary policy.

The New Deal was the name given by Franklin D. Roosevelt to the economic policy carried out by his administration from 1933 onwards. Although he came to power with a mandate to reduce the budget deficit, his administration soon became associated with a massive programme of intervention in the market place, Government spending and large budget deficits. The first of these aspects

– interference with the working of competitive forces – was epitomised in the N.R.A. (National Recovery Administration) and the A.A.A. (Agricultural Adjustment Administration). As an example of a public spending programme, the T.V.A. (Tennessee Valley Authority) is perhaps the most famous example. Keynes had no direct influence on the form that the new deal policies took but towards the end of the 1930s some of the key advisors surrounding Roosevelt – for example, Alvin Hansen of Harvard – were converted to Keynesianism and preached it almost as divine revelation in the 1940s and 1950s. The real influence of Keynes on American economic policy came *after* the Second World War and reached its peak in Washington in the so-called 'Kennedy' years with the economics and politics of the New Frontier. As one of Kennedy's advisers put the matter: 'When the private economy is foundering because the goods being produced are not being taken off the market at profitable prices and hence, output falls below the potential – at such times the government should intervene through increased public spending (and) or reduced taxes. The objective of economic policy is a balanced economy, not a balanced budget.'(S. E. Harris, *Economics of the Kennedy Years,* Harper & Row, 1964 p. 22)

We refer earlier to the set of ideas – often called classical – that Keynes sought to destroy. In a very broad sense Monetarism is a return to these classical ideas. Thus its roots go back at least to the eighteenth century in the person of David Hume. Its recent revival very much associated with Professor Friedman and the Chicago School, only came to major prominence in the mid-1960s.

Monetarism may be thought of as both a political philosophy and an economic philosophy. As a political philosophy, exemplified in the British Conservative administration of Mrs Thatcher and to a lesser degree in President Reagan's Republican administration, it evokes a return to what may be termed a belief in the *minimal state* (see LIBERALISM). By this we mean that monetarists view most governmental activity – whether in industry or social welfare – as a substitute for what private agencies would otherwise provide. Moreover it is assumed that public provision will typically be inefficient and bureaucratic. There are very few areas of social and economic life, according to this view, where public provision is demonstrably superior to private provision.

The economics of monetarism consists of two key parts; firstly, as its designation suggests, the supply of money is regarded as the prime determinant of the general level of prices – hence inflation is due to the money supply increasing more rapidly that the supply of output. This is why Professor Milton Friedman – the main academic spokesman for the monetarists – refers to 'Inflation as always and everywhere a monetary phenomenon'. Politically this means that the governments are then *the* responsible agent since they control the money supply. Other alleged culprits – employers who seek to push up prices, or trade unionists pushing up wages – are found 'not guilty' by the monetarists!

Monetarists also emphasise the degree to which total output and the average standard of living is held in check *not* by the demand factors that Keynes had highlighted, but by supply factors. High rates of income and corporation tax

139

may discourage effort and initiative; social security payments may discourage the unemployed to search actively for employment. Government expenditure via deficit spending and monetary supply increases cannot ameliorate this sort of situation. It is the forces of supply that have to be liberated, not demand artificially stimulated. It is for this reason that monetarism is often termed 'supply-side economics'.

In general then, monetarism is a return to earlier, pre-Keynesian modes of economic and political thinking.

Should we now simply regard Keynesianism as at an end – as an historical episode in the development of social ideas? This is a difficult question to answer. The success of monetarism as a workable policy alternative has yet to be demonstrated. As the economic down turn moves from recession to long term depression, demands for government intervention are being resurrected on an increasing scale.

Kuomintang

The foundations of *Kuomintang* ideology, the ideology of the party that ruled over much of China from 1927 to 1937, are to be found in the writings of the professional revolutionary and patriot, Sun Yat-Sen (1866-1925). Sun, who spent much of his life outside of China, developed a complex set of political ideas in the course of a thirty-year career more noteworthy for its failures than its successes. At the heart of his teachings lay the *Three People's Principles* (nationalism, democracy and people's livelihood). Sun envisioned their realisation through the agency of an all powerful party that would represent the interests of *all* the Chinese people. This party would lead the nation through a period of military dictatorship and then a period of 'political tutelage' during which the prerequisites of democratic government would be established. Sun placed great stress on the period of 'political tutelage' because, in his view, millennia of despotism had deadened the political sense of the Chinese people.

He outlined a *Five-Power Constitution* that drew upon Western institutions for three of its powers (executive, legislative and judicial) and traditional Chinese institutions for the other two (examinational and censorial). The people would exercise control over this constitution through the *Four Powers Of Democracy* (suffrage, recall, initiative and referendum). Behind these complex arrangements lay Sun's concern that the administrative powers of government should not encroach upon what he perceived to be the sovereign rights of the people.

Sun proposed to insure the livelihood of the Chinese people through the gradual equalisation of land ownership by means of punitive taxes on excessive landholdings, an idea borrowed from the American Henry George (*Progess and Poverty*, 1879). He stood firmly against the application of 'either Communism (see COMMUNISM) or the Soviet system in China', for he believed that class struggle, upon which Communists had fixed their attention, was an abberration in social development. Interdependence and co-operation formed the basis of his naïve social and economic theories.

After Sun Yet-Sen's death, Chiang Kai-Shek (1888-1975) quickly and ruthlessly assumed the leadership of the Kuomintang, whose membership had come to be dominated by bureaucrats, businessmen and militarists. While some of Sun's followers had sought to place a progressive, leftward-leaning gloss on his writings, Chiang adhered to a traditionalist interpretation of his teachings and spoke approvingly of contemporary fascist movements in Europe (see FASCISM). Chiang believed that China's ills resulted from the degeneracy of the individual within Chinese society and that national salvation therefore depended upon the moral regeneration of the people. He sought to realise this conviction through the inauguration in 1934 of the *New Life Movement*. Even within the framework of this movement, Chiang dared not encourage the politicisation of the masses. As a result, the movement never became anything more than a campaign for good manners and personal hygiene.

Chiang and those about him were not opposed to change; they were committed to the reconstruction of China but did not understand the requirements of a modern state. All they could do was to fall back upon traditional methods and a conservative vocabulary. Much was proposed but very little realised. When, in the aftermath of the massive dislocation caused to Chinese society by the Japanese invasion, the Communists, who had been able to tap the energies of the peasant masses, rose to challenge the Kuomintang, the latter lacked the resources with which to resist and soon collapsed.

Further reading

Chester C. Tan, *Chinese Political Thought in the Twentieth Century*
Lloyd E. Eastman, 'The Kuomintang in the 1930's', in Charlotte Furth, ed., *The Limits of Change: Essays on Conservative Alternatives in Republican China*
Lloyd E. Eastman, *The Abortive Revolution: China under Nationalist Rule, 1927-1937*
Arif Dirlik, 'The Ideological Foundations of the New Life Movement: A Study of Counterrevolution', *Journal of Asian Studies*, Vol. 34, no. 4, August 1975.

Liberalism

Liberalism is historically a collection of ideas and attitudes, not a coherent body of theory. It cannot profitably be studied in any other way than through its meaning in practice. Its important theorists tend, revealingly, to be also classifiable as conservatives (see CONSERVATISM) (Burke, for example) or radicals (see FEMINISM; RADICALISM; UTILITARIANISM) (J. S. Mill). Or else they were, like

Guizot in France, politicians first. In the last century the United States of America stood for democracy; while Great Britain represented Liberalism, which essentially belonged to that age. The twentieth century has, however, lived with a Liberal legacy compounded of constitutionalism; doubtfully of pluralism; certainly of a belief in the virtues of economic freedom, and less certainly of a desire to restrict government intervention in most other aspects of life.

First, the nineteenth century: there was then a distinction in people's minds between democracy and Liberalism, as the European revolutions of 1848 and their outcome confirmed. Liberalism involved the explicit rejection of democracy. The first and second Reform Acts (1832 and 1867) in Britain were based on a conception of political responsibility which excluded a large majority of adult males from the franchise, and further limited popular power through extensive plural voting by the well-to-do. After 1832 one Englishman in five enjoyed the right to vote; although in Ireland, supposedly an integral part of the United Kingdom, the proportion was deliberately kept down to five per cent of the adult male population. Not until 1918 did Britain legislate for manhood suffrage at the age of twenty-one, giving the vote at the sane time to women of thirty. The character of British parliamentary government as late as 1887, after recent legislation had enfranchised male householders throughout the United Kingdom, was publicly described by the greatest of British Liberal politicians, W. E. Gladstone (d. 1898), in these candid words: 'The natural condition of a healthy society is that governing functions should be discharged in the main by the leisured class. . . whatever control a good system may impose by popular suffrage.' By 'the leisured class' he meant primarily the landed aristocracy and gentry who still formed an absolute majority of British MPs as late as the Parliament of 1880-85. This upper class had by that date acquired considerable wealth from non-agricultural sources and taken far the process of assimilating their natural rivals, the businessmen raised up by a continuing industrial revolution. But Gladstone distinguished between what another great British liberal, the thinker J. S. Mill (d. 1873) called 'the open aristocracy' of Britain and the plutocrats who came to the forefront of American democracy in the nineteenth century, to remain there ever since. The naked power of money without the restraining influence of aristocratic tradition was repugnant to Gladstone and Mill. The corruptibility, prejudice and ignorance of democracy in the contemporary United States led Mill, whose Liberalism was much more advanced than Gladstone's, to argue that the inevitable democratic franchise in Britain must incorporate a strong bias in favour of the educated by perpetuating and rationalising the practice of plural voting. An important legacy of Gladstone and Mill to modern British politics, notwithstanding its acceptance of democracy, has been the distrust of the merely rich on the one hand, and of populism on the other.

Liberalism in Britain cannot be narrowly identified with the historic Whig party (see WHIGGISM) that preferred the description of Liberal by the 1860s. The first British statesman to advertise the legitimate supremacy of public opinion, ten years before the Great Reform Act of 1832, was the Tory George Canning (d. 1827). In his view, the strength of public opinion in an increasingly numerous and prosperous nation was quite effectively expressed through the medium of a fast-growing and, as regards middle-class papers, free press. He considered it unwise to modify the existing medieval system of Parliamentary representation, and thus to reduce the independence of government and legislature by making them more directly answerable to the public. The two outstanding British Liberal prime ministers of the last century, Gladstone and Lord Palmerston (d. 1865), were both former Tory cabinet ministers and admirers of Canning's 'Liberal Toryism', who adapted his thinking to allow for moderate reform. The fourteenth Earl of Derby (d. 1869) and Benjamin Disraeli (d. 1881), who between them led the Tory party for over forty years, started on the other side in politics. As a Whig cabinet minister, Derby helped to frame the 1832 settlement. In 1867 he and Disraeli expanded it to take in the minority of the urban working-class who were deemed to have proved their social and political responsibility in such ways as their voting in municipal elections from 1835 on a ratepayer suffrage. The efficacy of the two Reform Acts in preserving the old order while broadening its social base inspired successive generations of European Liberalism. Already the French constitutions of 1814 and 1830 had attempted to reproduce much of the structure and spirit of British institutions; on the first occasion under the intellectual guidance of Benjamin Constant de Rebecque (d. 1830) and, on the second, under that of the connected group of French Liberals called *doctrinaires,* to which Guizot belonged. European Liberalism, however, differed significantly from the British model.

Firstly, in the Catholic countries of Europe and also in some Protestant states, notably the Netherlands, Liberalism was, above all, anti-clerical (see ULTRAMONTANISM). Except in relation to the special case of Irish Catholic nationalism (see NATIONALISM), this preoccupation was absent from British Liberalism. Nearly everywhere in Catholic Europe the advent of manhood suffrage, beginning with France (1848), and reaching Italy in 1912, undermined the Liberals and strengthened political Catholicism.

Another often overlooked feature of Continental Liberalism that set it apart from the theory and practice of British politics was its reliance upon likeminded dynasties. Louis Philippe on the French throne, the kings of the House of Savoy, especially Victor Emanuel II (1849-78) in Italy, the Coburgs Leopold I (1831-65) and II (1865-1909) in Belgium, were not constitutional monarchs of the British type, as described in Walter Bagehot's *The English Constitution* (1867), left with practically none but consultative and representational functions. They ruled as well as reigned, in conjunction with, not in subordination to, ministers whose selection remained partly, even largely, in their hands. The most eminent of nineteenth-century French Liberals, Adolphe Thiers (d. 1887), remarked that he would like to place a member of the Coburg family on every European throne. Manhood suffrage in France helped to prevent the restoration of Louis

Philippe's line, and considerably diminished the position of monarchy in Italy and Belgium. A third and better known characteristic of European Liberalism was its opposition to aristocracy. The hereditary second chamber in the French constitution of 1814 was replaced in 1830 by one composed of life peers. The crown nominated the senators of the Italian kingdom. The British Liberal states-man, Lord John Russell (d. 1878), who was twice prime minister, once asserted that Thiers and François Guizot (d. 1874) in France, Cavour and Gino Capponi (d. 1876) in Italy, and in Germany the political associates of Duke Ernst II of Saxe-Coburg-Gotha (1844-93) nephew of the Belgian King Leopold I, were Whigs like himself. But Whiggery was inseparable from aristocracy and the maintenance not only of the House of Lords but of the Established Church. 'I suppose the Church may be disestablished, but I should expect to see a republic in ten years after', wrote Russell in a moment of gloom. There were Liberal aristocrats on the Continent but no real counterpart to the aristocratic and Christian Liberalism of men like Russell and Gladstone.

A fourth and very important difference between British and European Liberalism of the nineteenth century lay in the attitudes to centralisation, bureaucracy and individual freedom. In the France of Louis Philippe and the Italy of Victor Emanuel II, government leant heavily in the provinces on the prefectoral system inherited from Napoleon I's European new order and on a para-military police with similar origins, the *gendarmerie* and the *carabinieri*. At Paris and Rome authoritarian bureaucracies under king and ministers controlled these local instruments. Freedom of the press, virtually complete in Britain after 1850, was circumscribed in Liberal France and, less so, in united Italy. Nothing like this governmental surveillance existed in Britain; although it did in Ireland where stipendiary magistrates and the armed, countrywide Irish Con-stabulary reported to the Dublin Castle administration, and a succession of exceptional measures curtailed the liberty of the subject and of the press. The tiny higher civil service in Britain reflected the principled aversion of its political masters to interfering with business or the landed interest; with the extensive freedom of town councils chosen by ratepayer electorates; and with the indepen-dence of the unpaid landowning magistracy that administered the countryside until the inception of elective rural local government in 1888. The extraordinary success of aristocratic Liberalism in Britain may be ascribed in large part to two things: the libertarianism typical of the country as a whole, and the cheapness of government. Conscription, which oppressed the Continental poor, and a national police on the lines of the *gendarmerie,* were alien institutions; outside the capital, municipal councillors and country magistrates controlled the unarmed local constabulary. Official regulation of the individual's actions was minimal. While the British working class had to wait until 1918 for full political democracy, their distinctive class activity of trade unionism received the sanc-tion of law nearly a hundred years earlier, in 1824-25 under a 'Liberal Tory' government. The labour legislation of 1871-76 confirmed and developed this statutory protection. The French working class, sweepingly enfranchised in

1848, was not given the right to strike before 1864, and their trade unions not legalised until 1884. Moreover, down to 1890, French workers, other than peasants and self-employed artisans, had to carry the *livret,* an industrial passport ordained by Napoleon I, which needed endorsing by the employer and the mayor of the commune on a change of job. Gladstone justified the rights secured to British trade unions on grounds of simple equity between capitalists and those whose sole marketable commodity consisted of their labour.

Fifthly, British Liberalism was bound up with free trade, which required far-reaching alterations to the country's fiscal system European Liberalism was divided as to the feasibility and desirability of the British achievement in these related fields. Gladstone's exemplar in matters of economic and social policy was Sir Robert Peel (d. 1850), the Tory prime minister whose party broke with him over the repeal of agricultural protection in 1846. It has been well said of Peel that 'he pursued social harmony through fiscal reform'. The repeal of the Corn Laws was the culmination of five years of tax reform, designed to shift the burden from indirect to direct taxation and to stimulate a depressed economy by increasing competition and purchasing power. Gladstone, who served in Peel's last cabinet and followed him out of the Tory party, carried on his work in budgets of 1853-54 and 1859-65, assisted in its completion by the Victorian prosperity to which it contributed as much by its political as by its economic effects. As a serious menace, radical social protest disappeared for a long time to come after the end of Chartism (1858) (see RADICALISM). The fiscal changes were accompanied by the insistence on governmental thrift for which Gladstone became famous. Cheap government and very modest levels of direct and indirect taxation underpinned the continuance of an aristocratic primacy that was paradoxical in the most highly industrialised and urbanised country in the world. The bourgeois democracy of the Third Republic in France did not introduce income tax before 1913, over seventy years after Britain, fearing that once established its incidence would rise. It was a reasonable fear in the absence of the parsimonious mentality of the British government and Parliament, and of their bias against state intervention. In nineteenth-century America the Supreme Court of the United States pronounced income tax unconstitutional by its decision of 1894. The general failure of Liberal and democratic states to emulate the British commitment to free trade owed something to reluctance to adopt the fiscal reforms of Peel and Gladstone, but more to the widespread feeling that the policy was unduly favourable to Britain's national and imperial interests in the heyday of her industrial leadership.

Britain was quite exceptional among the Great Powers in her steady Liberalism. The other Liberal states were minor powers, uneasily conscious of being overshadowed by their potent neighbours. As Emperor of the French (1852-70), Napoleon III combined an authoritarian régime with a democratic franchise for a tame legislature, although in the latter part of his reign he embarked upon a process of liberalisation cut short by the collapse of his empire in war. Prussia, which overthrew Napoleon III, had already paid him the compliment of borrowing the idea of his constitutional arrangements for the North German Confederation of 1867, the predecessor of the German Empire formed after Napoleon's defeat. The architect of the Confederation and Empire, Bismarck, wanted to 'kill parliamentarianism through Parliament'. Manhood suffrage for both confederation and empire was effectively neutralised by denying the Reichstag the initiative in legislation and taxation and control over the German emperor's ministers. Germany could claim to have a democratic foundation, legitimising the undemocratic structure built upon it. German Liberals co-operated in maintaining Bismarck's machinery of state. They were more opposed to the Catholic (see CHRISTIAN DEMOCRACY) and social democratic (see SOCIALISM) mass parties, whose expansion manhood suffrage made possible, than to Bismarck's authoritarianism. Austria did not follow Germany's electoral example before 1907; until then, although the franchise had been widely extended in the 1870s, voters were divided into classes with a vote in the highest class outweighing one in the lowest class many times over. After 1907, as previously, the Austrian Emperor retained and exercised the power to rule by decree; he was still an autocrat. In the last of the four Continental Great Powers, Russia, the Tsars upheld a cult of autocracy and no national representative assembly came into being before the turn of the century. The great conscript armies of France, Germany, Austria and Russia completely overshadowed the small regular force of Great Britain, seeming to proclaim the irrelevance of Liberalism to European realities. The British mixture of oligarchy and libertarianism, a hardy anachronism in peace, did not survive the 1914–18 war without profound changes.

Yet the influence of nineteenth-century Liberalism cannot be measured by the number and size of the states that tried it and adhered to it. Constitutionalism was not exclusive to them. To German, Austrian and Russian Liberals the idea of a *Rechtsstaat,* a polity based on the rule of law, did not necessarily imply the subordination of monarchs to parliaments. French, and of course American, democrats professed a deep respect for legality, natural in republics dominated by lawyer-politicians. Even the more traditionalist of Russian gentry Liberals, however, associated personal freedom with the existence of representative assemblies at local and provincial, but not national, level created by the Tsar Liberator Alexander II (1855–1881). D. N. Shipov (d. 1920), chairman of the Moscow provincial *zemstvo* (assembly) and long the leading spokesman of gentry Liberalism, saw little room for improvement in this compromise between Tsarism and the West. The West to which he looked in the context was Britain, where his kind, the landed class, possessed such enviable independence of bureaucracy in their own neighbourhood. British example had more fruitful consequences through the lasting impression it made on Napoleon III, who knew Britain from his period of apparently hopeless exile before 1848. He appreciated the way in which her political and social framework maintained an essential conservatism while allowing the free play of opinion and of different economic interests. In liberalising his régime after 1860, Napoleon endeavoured to take the best features of British government and society and graft them on to a true crowned democracy. Hence his reform of labour and press laws, and the final experiment of 1869-70 with relatively free elections and ministers commanding a majority of the resulting chamber. Napoleon III and his dynasty did not survive the war of 1870-71, but the authentic parliamentary democracy which received its start from him did so, thanks to the veteran Liberal, Thiers. For want of a suitable king, Thiers, a lifelong monarchist, established the Third Republic with a socially conservative bourgeois oligarchy depending on a conservative peasant vote to keep radicalised urban workers in their place. Had it not been for the bitter conflict of Catholicism and secularism which absorbed so much of its energies down to 1914, the Third Republic would more readily have appeared to demonstrate the general truth of the French anarchist thinker Pierre Proudhon's (d. 1865) (see ANARCHISM) pessimistic observation: 'Universal [i.e. manhood] suffrage is counter-revolution'. Nevertheless, republican France bore a greater resemblance to monarchical Britain than did the other Great Powers of Europe. The likeness certainly helped to draw the two countries together against Wilhelmine Germany. But almost universally in Europe by the second half of the century, whether assemblies were the basis of government or merely representative, Palmerston's dictum to Napoleon III's ambassador in 1863 held good: 'I said. . . the word "Constitution" all over Europe means a Parliament'.

It will be clear that the concept of pluralism – meaning the co-existence inside the state of bodies with contrasting principles – was not integral to nineteenth-century Liberalism. Liberals regarded Ultramontane Catholicism (see ULTRAMONTANISM) and Socialism (see SOCIALISM) as incompatible with their beliefs. In that age, Liberalism was strongly nationalist; sufficient reason in itself for the incompatibility with Rome. If Catholics, Liberals were anti-Papal and latitudinarian in their views. If Protestants, like Lord John Russell, Palmerston and Gladstone in Britain, they were even more hostile to Ultramontanism. These three all refused to grant state recognition and aid to a Catholic university for Ireland with its large, devout Catholic majority; they feared the political results of accelerating the growth of a Catholic middle-class in that peasant country. Successive British governments also upheld the symbolic legal prohibition on the appointment of a Catholic viceroy to head the Irish administration. The disestablishment of the Protestant State Church in Ireland made no difference to the fundamental anti-Catholicism of British Liberals. Hence Irish Catholicism and Irish nationalism (see NATIONALISM) became more than ever inseparable. Where Continental Liberalism came to terms with the resurgent Catholicism of the time, as in Spain with the Concordat of 1851, it imposed severe conditions on the Church. Uttering the commonplaces of Liberalism and democracy, military dictators came and went in Spain and Spanish America; usually they served the interests of small landowning minorities. Mexico experienced forty-three changes of régime between 1821 and 1853. Spain herself kept this 'military Liberalism' in the background after the shortlived republic of

1873-74. The stage management of Don Antonio Canovas del Castillo (d. 1897) produced an artificial parliamentarianism copied from Britain. Canovas may have known by heart many of Gladstone's speeches and Disraeli's, but he dealt in Spanish realities. Elections were systematically and monotonously rigged; the advent of manhood suffrage in 1890 altered nothing. By a friendly arrangement, the *turno pacifico,* Canovas's Liberal-Conservatives and the other Liberal party alternated in office. The price of civilian rule was the falsification of parliamentary government preventing the rise of great socialist and popular Catholic parties like those well established in Germany within a few years of manhood suffrage.

Pluralism arguably came with democracy secured by free elections, and was not a product of Liberalism. German elections were not conducted on Spanish lines, although the Reichstag's authority was so limited. The Catholic Centre party and the Social Democrats both weathered Bismarckian persecution and in turn reached an accommodation with the state. Each party was an entire sub-culture with its associated organisations, which the state had eventually to accept as such. For their part, German Catholics and Social Democrats moderated their Ultramontane and Socialist ardour, respectively. In Belgium, the creation of Liberalism and a country very advanced in its economic and social development, democracy displaced the Liberals in favour of continuous Catholic government from 1884 to the Great War. The Belgian Socialists obtained more seats than the fallen Liberals in 1894, in the first elections after manhood suffrage. The experience of these two countries prefigured that of most European states in which political Catholicism has since been a power. Except in republican France, Liberalism lacked a broad electoral base; there its vigour, chiefly under the name of Radicalism, depended largely on the strength of anti-clericalism in the land where it originated in its modern form, and on the wide diffusion of small property. Generally, Liberalism in Europe and beyond derived from more or less enlightened oligarchies. Count Cavour foresaw the alliance of Ultramontanism and Socialism. The prophecy was fulfilled to the extent that the popular Catholic parties, particularly after the 1914-18 war, increasingly adopted policies of social welfare which encroached upon private property (see CHRISTIAN DEMOCRACY). Where a Liberal party exceptionally possessed mass appeal to urban workers, that is, in Edwardian Britain, it was due to a combination of religious activism, quite alien to Continental Liberalism, with embarkation upon the politics of welfare.

Twentieth-century Liberalism, as an organised political movement, has been eclipsed by its rivals. In the aftermath of the Great War, the huge social disruption arising from the internal demands of the conflict on the participants made Liberalism seem outdated. The propertied classes, feeling themselves threatened, turned in Germany and Italy to different brands of Fascism (see FASCISM), setting the fashion for some smaller states, notably General Franco's Spain. In Britain the archetypal Liberal party collapsed with astonishing suddenness between 1918 and 1924, although the French Liberals/Radicals retained their prominence until 1940. Russia passed from Tsarism to Communism with an interval of only a few months of confusion when the bid to establish a parliamentary republic failed. The Communist (see COMMUNISM) parties that proliferated quickly outside Russia varied greatly in size and influence, but their impact was out of all proportion to their numbers. Following the 1939–45 war, Continental Europe west of the Soviet bloc was largely divided between Christian Democracy and the parties of the Left. The electorates of West Germany, Austria, Italy, Belgium and the Netherlands made Catholic parties the principal and, more often than not, the successful rivals of Socialists, and always, to date, of the Communists. In France, also, a quarter of the votes in the first elections (1944) under the Fourth Republic were cast for the new Catholic party – over a quarter went to the Communists. On a superficial view, Liberalism had retreated to the periphery of this clash between ideologies equally opposed to it. In fact, both political Catholics and the non-Communist Left revealed the pervasive influence of Liberal ideas, like the Gaullist and Giscardien Right in France more recently. Similarly, British Toryism and Labour bore out the famous aphorism of Sir Harold Wilson, prime minister in two Labour administrations, that whether his party or the Tories held office, the Liberals were forever in power. Wilson had in mind the economic policies he was implementing at the time as a minister in the first majority government (1945–51).

It has been seen that *laisser-faire,* or the wish to minimise governmental interference, especially in economic life, went with external free trade in nineteenth and early twentieth-century Britain, but not usually in other major states of the period. Wilson's removal in 1949 of numerous controls on industry and commerce, maintained after the end of the Second World War, was not accompanied by departure from the protectionist system that replaced peacetime free trade and comprised Britain and her trading partners in the Empire-Commonwealth from 1932 to 1973. Continental Liberals had been keen advocates of internal freedom for businessmen, if not for workers seeking to unionise. Their nationalism (see NATIONALISM) and dislike of direct taxation stood in the way of free trade such as Britain had for nearly a hundred years. It took Napoleon III to force through an appreciable relaxation of French tariffs in 1860 with the object of applying British methods to the economy. The Third Republic, like Bismarckian Germany, found higher tariff barriers consistent with industrial advance and indispensable to saving peasant agriculture from North American competition. If the formation of the European Economic Community after 1945 was in the tradition of Continental Liberalism rather than of British free trade in the Victorian and Edwardian eras, it plainly testified to the hold of Liberal economic thinking over the Catholics and Democratic Socialists who concluded the agreement. They identified liberty and prosperity with a vigorous capitalism, subject indeed to social control, but accepted as the best security for individual rights. This attitude came easily enough to Catholic politicians, whose socio-economic doctrine, broadly laid down in a series of Papal encyclicals from the late nineteenth century, emphasised the crucial importance of private property to the individual, the family and the Church when faced with the modern state, as firmly as the same teaching stressed the imperative necessity of counteracting the abuse of property-rights under the conditions of industrialisation. Western European social democrats arrived by the middle of the next century at a practically indistinguishable position. The totalitarian nature of thoroughgoing State Socialism in Eastern Europe under Communism propelled them towards acceptance of a predominantly capitalist economy and its Liberal assumptions about man and society.

One requirement of Liberal economics now quite commonly overlooked, or played down, was unequivocally set forth in the most celebrated of its foundation texts, Adam Smith's *Wealth of Nations* (1776): 'Upon the power which the leading men, the natural aristocracy of every country, have of preserving their. . . importance depends the stability and duration of every system of free government'. The unfettered operation of market forces, as Smith and a great many others understood it, assumed a ruling class, a 'natural' aristocracy, possibly but not necessarily one institutionalised to some extent, as in Britain with her House of Lords. That the existence and persistence of this class could be reconciled with democracy, given the proper working of a free economy, was shown decisively in the United States when the country was massively industrialised after the Civil War. In twentieth-century Europe the opponents of unbending Socialism and Communism were ideologically sustained by the ability and willingness of private wealth in America to fill its commanding role in business and politics. Political Catholicism (see CHRISTIAN DEMOCRACY) had little difficulty in learning the lesson; although its critics have constantly remarked on the incongruity between Catholic morality and that of the market. The Church has always dwelt on the social obligations of wealth. British Toryism, divested today of its close Anglican links, welcomed unreservedly the reinforcement of its secularised philosophy by American example. It is the Social Democrats and British Labour (see SOCIALISM) who have been embarrassed. On the one hand, there was, and remains, their theoretical commitment to socialist egalitarianism. On the other hand, they have their experience in government of the benefits to the working class from economic freedom and their perception that a collectivist economy inhibits, if it does not stifle, personal liberty. They have continued to pay lip service to the egalitarian ideal while co-operating fruitfully with capitalism.

In its hostility towards anything resembling Socialism, nineteenth-century Liberalism shrank from the idea of a comprehensive welfare state which the Marquis de Condorcet (d. 1794) envisaged as the corollary of democracy based on private property and a free market. Condorcet's conclusions in the final chapter of his brilliant summary of the Enlightenment's social and political thought, *A Sketch for a Historical Picture of the Progress of the Human Mind,* are no doubt to be viewed as those of a Radical rather than of a Liberal. Radical, too, rather than Liberal was the *Constitutional Code* of Jeremy Bentham (d. 1832) (see UTILITARIANISM); but Bentham's Radicalism, less in advance of its time, affected the social policy of contemporary Liberalism in a constructive fashion. The *Constitutional Code* proposed an extension of governmental functions to provide, or oversee the provision of, the infra-structure, from roads and canals to elementary schools and poor relief, without which democracy and a free economy would not work. The impulse behind Benthamite Radicalism, as behind Liberalism, was enlightened self-interest. The pressures of industrialisation, urban growth and a wider franchise broadened the understanding of what constitutes enlightened self-interest in Britain and other Liberal states. In this way, Liberalism made a slow approach to the welfare state before 1900. The trend must not be exaggerated. A British colonial democracy, New Zealand, was well ahead of Britain herself in the field of social legislation. The definitive emergence of the welfare state, as such, did not come in Britain and some European countries before the inter-war period in this century.

The profoundest of democratic thinkers, J. J. Rousseau, made the point in his *Social Contract* (1762) (see THE ENLIGHTENMENT; RADICALISM) that democracy, taken literally, was an impossibility. The government of the people, by the people, for the people proclaimed in Abraham Lincoln's Gettysburg Address (1863) cannot be realised: there must be delegation of power, with the unavoidable separation of rulers from the ruled. But democracy embodies a compelling truth, expressed by Rousseau when he said that natural inequality should be rendered tolerable by building the recognition of moral equality into the state, instead of leaving its assertion to the Church, as hitherto. It is the achievement of Liberalism to have formulated the still, and perhaps eternally, incomplete attainment of this noble aim. For all its oligarchical nature and its tendency to preoccupation with getting and enjoying wealth and power, Liberalism rejected the social pessimism running through Edmund Burke's (see CONSERVATISM) immensely influential writing which Gladstone otherwise revered, in common with most English Liberals of his sort. A belief in progress, however qualified by apprehension and scepticism, comprehended men who differed as widely from one another in their outlook and methods as did the leading Liberals of nineteenth-century Europe mentioned in the course of this essay. The ablest of their conservative antagonists, Bismarck, the third Marquess of Salisbury (d. 1902), for thirteen years prime minister of Britain, and Count Taaffe (d. 1895) in the Austrian Empire, opposed Liberalism because it led inexorably to democracy. They were statesmen playing for time; and in that respect, among others, there was little to choose between them and the great names of Liberalism. The democratic idea was bound to triumph in the long, or not so long, term; de Tocqueville's prediction in the 1830s was not an isolated one, only the most intellectually distinguished of many such prophecies. The concern of Liberals, in a sentence, was to tame democracy. They wanted to rid it of the frightening and oppressive tendencies amply displayed in the United States, and to prevent it from becoming the means of domination by Socialism and political Catholicism.

151

Further reading

Gerald Brenan, *The Spanish Labyrinth*.
Raymond Carr, *Spain, 1808-1939*.
R. A. Dahl (ed.), *Political Oppositions in Western Democracies*.
G. Fischer, *Russian Liberalism, from Gentry to Intelligentsia*.
E. Kossmann, *The Low Countries, 1780-1940*.
W. E. H. Lecky, *Democracy and Liberty* (2 vols).
J. McManners, *Lectures on European History, 1789-1914*.
J. S. Mill, *Considerations on Representative Government*.
L. Robbins, *The Theory of Economic Policy in English Classical Political Economy*.
J. J. Sheehan, *German Liberalism in the Nineteenth Century*.
D. Mack Smith, *Victor Emanuel, Cavour, and the Risorgimento*.
J. R. Vincent, *The Formation of the British Liberal Party, 1857-1868*.
T. Zeldin, *France 1848-1945*, vol. I.

McCarthyism

On February 9 1950, Joseph R. McCarthy, an obscure Republican senator from Wisconsin worried about his prospects of re-election, announced in a speech to the Ohio County Republican Women's Club that he held in his hand a list containing the names of two hundred and five Communists employed by the State Department. McCarthy had no list and none existed; the number of supposed Communists in the State Department later changed to eighty-one, fifty-seven, or 'a lot'. Nonetheless, he had catapuled himself to national and international prominence. He played the press, radio, and television for all they were worth and soon the word *McCarthyism* was coined to describe the mudslinging which charged, for example, that the Democrats were responsible for 'twenty years of treason', or that Secretary of Defence, George Marshall, was part of a 'great conspiracy' to aid the Soviet Union and was 'always and invariably serving the world policy of the Kremlin'. McCarthy never exposed a single Communist in the government. (The campaign to clean Communists out of the government had been running so long that it was extremely unlikely that there were any to be found.) When McCarthy was finally forced to be specific on one case, that of Owen Lattimore, it turned out that Lattimore, whom McCarthy charged as 'Alger Hiss's boss in the espionage ring in the State Department', was not even a government employee, but an academic at Johns Hopkins University. He was also no Communist. However, Lattimore was indicted for perjury in denying he was a 'Communist sympathiser' and found his academic career in the United States ruined.

It seemed that, as McCarthy's charges grew wilder, his influence grew. For the next four years scarcely any important decision could be made by the government without worrying about his reaction. After Eisenhower became president in 1953, an agreement was reached with McCarthy that gave the senator the power of approval over all State Department appointments.

McCarthyism has become a general term of opprobrium, a term used in particular by liberals to attack certain manifestations of the extreme right. But, in spite of the importance of McCarthy, the tactics he used and the movement that bore his name were no aberration. McCarthyism was in the mainstream of political discourse in the United States of the late forties and early fifties. Among conservatives, Richard Nixon used similar tactics to gain national attention in the Alger Hiss case, while a liberal like Hubert Humphrey could introduce a bill to make Communist Party membership a crime and support the rounding up of Communists into concentration camps in times of national emergency. The Cold War, and the image of a 'Red menace' that accompanied it, provided conservatives with a convenient weapon against radicals in all walks of life – in the arts, in the professions and, perhaps most important of all, in the labour movement, where Communists and other radicals had gained ascendancy in several of the CIO unions organised in the 1930s. Not only could any radical potential for the future be eliminated, but here was an opportunity to roll back some of the gains of the New Deal, gains which had led to a certain limitation on free enterprise and on the power of business. The New Deal had expanded government intervention on the economy and provided new groups with access to power, sometimes within the government, as in the case of the liberal intellectuals, and sometimes from outside, as in the case of the new industrial unions of the CIO.

By 1950 the counterattack on the New Deal had already won massive victories. The new industrial unions had either been beaten into conformist submission or persecuted into impotent opposition. Education and the media, government and the professions had been purged and repurged. But, to some, any vestige of liberalism remained a threat. A ragtag collection of veterans' organisations, Texas millionaires, Catholic ethnics and others constituted McCarthy's main support. McCarthy himself never had any coherent ideology beyond his own self-aggrandisement. Unlike the Fascists of the twenties and thirties, he made no attempt to build an organisation. He remained in the Republican party throughout. Rather than being a 'new American Right', McCarthyism was in large part a weapon for Republicans in the battle against their traditional enemies, the Democrats. Thus an old-line Republican like Senator Robert Taft could advise him: 'If one case doesn't work, try another.' When, in 1953, he began to attack his own party's administration, his usefulness was at an end and his career was stopped.

Further reading

David Caute, *The Great Fear: The Anti-Communist Purge Under Truman and Eisenhower*
Earl Lathan (ed.), *The Meaning of McCarthyism*
Richard H. Rovere, *Senator Joe McCarthy*
David M. Oshinsky, *A Conspiracy So Immense: The World of Joe McCarthy*
Thomas C. Reeves, *The Life and Times of Joe McCarthy*

Nationalism

Nationalism means asserting the primacy of a group affinity based on a common language, culture, and descent – and sometimes on a common religion and territory as well – over all other claims on a person's loyalty. As a political doctrine, it claims to provide the ideological basis and justification for the right of all the world's people to organise themselves into independent or autonomous entities. These have, for the most part, taken the form of the independent national state, although there have been instances where some form of cultural or territorial autonomy has been instituted instead. This has been especially the case in countries, such as Yugoslavia, Switzerland or Belgium, comprising two or more smaller national groups which would find complete independence difficult or impossible

The terms *nationalist* and *national,* which are derived from the Latin word meaning 'born in', sometimes overlap with their Greek counterpart *ethnic.* The latter term, however, is generally used to mean a shared descent, language and culture outside of any political context.

The origins of the doctrine of Nationalism lie in the culturally united but politically fragmented milieu of eighteenth-century Germany and in the European-wide upheaval occasioned by the French Revolution.

What comprised Germany in the late eighteenth century was a patch-work of states, principalities and kingdoms which appeared to have little in common other than a shared language and cultural heritage. Although earlier in the Century several German writers, such as Leibnitz, had emphasised the importance of a common literature in overcoming disintegration, and the great French philosopher and critic of society, Jean-Jacques Rousseau (see THE ENLIGHTENMENT), had stressed both the significance of customs and traditions in fostering group identity and the role of patriotism in achieving a society based on harmony of self and communal interests, it was the German philosopher Johann Gottfried Herder (1744–1803) who gave the notion of cultural patriotism its first positive and coherent expression. In isolating the singularity of human endeavour and diversity of its expression as positive values, he not only challenged the rationalist belief that absolute criteria could be found to measure human happiness, but accorded supreme importance to the activity of each individual and each nation in the flow of history. This was the basis for his argument, first put forward in *Fragments of a New German Literature* (1767), that every people is intrinsically and peculiarly different, none being superior to any other and each having something unique to contribute to human experience. This singularity, or *Volksgeist* (folk-spirit), was realised by each nation through its culture, of which language was the most important attribute, as well as its customs and

154

institutions.

Herder's writing took on a wider significance by maintaining additionally that a people did not have to comprise a political entity in order to be recognised as a nationality. It furnished the intellectual impetus for a period of self-discovery on the part of peoples and ethnic groups which had previously often been only barely conscious of a collective identity. Encouraged by Herder's own pioneering work in the field, the submerged nationalities of Northern and Eastern Europe – the Finns, Norwegians, Czechs, Slovaks, Serbs and Croats – discovered the attributes of nationality in their own folk traditions – their songs, dances, legends, art, craft, customs and architecture. National revivals ensued, which, despite their ostensibly esoteric purpose, rarely lacked a political dimension. This could hardly have been otherwise, as a nationality almost always became 'submerged' through the domination of another.

Thus, for example, the Bohemian nobility supported the renaissance of Czech language and culture of the 1820s and 1830s not just as an end in itself, but also as a means for justifying and bolstering their own claims for political autonomy within the Habsburg Empire. In a similar vein, German writers and publicists in the period before 1848 took up the cause of national independence for the Poles, Greeks, Irish and South Slavs not just on its own merits, but as a means of fostering the national consciousness of their own people, because at the time a direct appeal to German national feeling would have hardly escaped the censor's blue pencil.

Still, it was the great transfiguration brought about by the French Revolution which bridged the gap between the cultural patriotism of Herder and nineteenth-century Nationalism. Although patriotism, love of one's country or group, loyalty to its institutions and dedication to its defence, never lacked a political dimension, only after the Abbé Sieyes and his fellow revolutionaries in Paris proclaimed the concept of popular sovereignty did a people's collective identity take on a higher meaning. The State was no longer simply the totality of persons in a given country under a single government, but a manifestation of its democratic will. The State was sovereign with the people. Rather than a territorial or patrimonial accident, the State was, according to this line of thinking, an expression of the popular will.

The idea of national self-determination, the belief that each poeple had the right to will its own collective destiny, had in effect come into being. Like most of the other ideas produced in the French Revolution, it spread quickly throughout Europe and the Americas as if on a propagandistic magic carpet. Mainly for reasons of expediency, moreover, successive French governments, and especially that of Napoleon, encouraged movements of national liberation. On the other hand, the Napoleonic system of political domination and economic system provided a new cause – liberation from French oppression – around which nationalist movements could grow. This was the case in Germany as well as in Spain and to some extent in Italy also. National feeling combined too with almost paranoic fears of Jacobinism (see RADICALISM) to convert once staunch supporters of the French Revolution to its sworn enemies. This was particularly so in Germany where a kind of Francophobia took hold amongst the dominant section of the nation's intellectual elite following Prussia's defeat by the armies of Napoleon at Jena in 1807. While the philosopher Johann Gottlieb Fichte (1762-1814) reminded his fellow Germans of their historic mission, as the only major European nation whose culture had not been completely dominated by French influence, to launch a crusade against France, nationalist agitators such as Friedrich Jahn (1778-1852) who went on to father the German gymnastics movement, and Ernst Moritz Arndt (1769-1860) called on their fellow-countrymen to expunge French influence at home. Jahn went so far as to suggest that allowing one's daughter to learn French was tantamount to delivering her up to a life of prostitution.

Fichte, of course, was no mere nationalist propogandist. He was just as concerned as Rousseau and Herder with the dilemma of how to overcome the atomisation of society while at the same time maintaining, if not enhancing, individual freedom. As early as 1800, in *The Closed Commercial State,* he argued that this could only happen in a state which regulated every aspect of human endeavour. For, as for his fellow German Adam Müller (1779-1829), the individual could only experience fulfilment by achieving oneness with the state. Having conceived of the state in organic terms, they thus regarded it as an absolute prerequisite for the attainment of human freedom and happiness. As with Rousseau, for them the force which wedded the individual to the state was nationality. Moreover they, like Herder, viewed language as its most important attribute. It was that which created the 'multitude of indivisible bonds' making a people that they belonged together, of forming 'by nature one and inseparable whole'.

For Fichte, what is more, geographic boundaries between peoples were only meaningful in so far as they defined the area inhabited by a given linguistic group. In other words, a people, according to his analysis, constituted a nationality because they spoke the same language and shared the same culture, and not because they lived in the same area. The ramifications of this doctrine need only be imagined, as will be seen later. Of perhaps equal importance was his notion regarding the primacy of the state in human endeavour, which was elaborated on by the great philosopher Friedrich Hegel (1770-1831).

In challenging the old order – the Europe of supra-national dynastic states and traditional society – Nationalism inevitably became linked with other emancipatory movements, being, at the same time, a manifestation of the ascendancy of the bourgeoisie. Clearly, this was so when in the French Revolution the principle of national self-determination developed out of the concept of popular sovereignty.

It was evident too in the movements of national liberation which arose primarily as a response to the rigours of Napoleonic rule in Italy, Spain, Germany and Belgium. Having experienced at least some measure of reform under the French, they were reluctant, if not unwilling, to exchange foreign domination for a return to domestic tyranny of the old order. Although the general period of reaction and restoration dampened their hopes of national independence and individual liberty, by no means did it extinguish them.

Despite the system of political repression introduced in the wake of the Congress of Vienna in 1815, especially in Germany and Austria, under the guiding hand of the Austrian Foreign Minister Prince Metternich, groups, some secret, soon emerged throughout Western and Central Europe which challeged the *status quo*. In both the early German student societies (the *Burschenschaften*) and the Italian secret organisations (the *Carabonari*) liberal and national goals seemed virtually inseparable. This trend became even more pronounced after the Revolution of 1830 brought a measure of constitutional reform to France.

In Italy and Germany national unity became increasingly conceived of as a vehicle for reform as well as an end in itself. The nascent middle classes, especially of those two societies, began to regard it as a means of achieving larger home markets or overcoming the intransigent obscurantism and outmoded policies of the local princes and breaking the stronghold of the aristocracy.

Amongst the middle classes of the supressed nationalities – for example, the Finns, Norwegians, and Czechs – support for the national cause was virtually unanimous, since they usually endured economic as well as political disadvantages. As industrialisation took place, they were joined by elements of the working class, and in one way or another the social and national questions became inexorably intertwined.

Nobody perhaps embodied the nationalism of the post-Napoleonic period better than the Italian Giusseppe Mazzini (1805-1872). Fleeing to Marseilles in 1831, he founded the 'Young Italy' movement which he hoped would endow the revolutionary movement of his country, as exemplified by Carabonari, and of which he had been a member, with both a spiritual mission and an overall plan.

His aim was the unity not just of Italy but the whole of mankind. Only by each nation realising its unique potential did he believe that his ultimate goal of universal harmony could be achieved. Otherwise, frustration and dissension would prevail. The influence of Rousseau, if not Herder and Fichte, should be apparent (see ROMANTICISM).

Despite his avowed internationalist convictions, Mazzini did claim for Italy, as the Heir of Rome, the role of leading humanity towards universal regeneration: 'Italy is the chosen people, the typical people, the creative people, the Israel of the modern age.' The messianic element in nationalist thought which was already apparent in the writing of Fichte, Arndt and others was now fully developed. What he perhaps failed to see was that by holding up Rome as a symbol, if not an example, he was undermining his own goal of equality amongst national and unwittingly nurturing a myth, that of Italy's mission as the new Rome, which helped bring under the Fascist rule of Mussolini, untold misery for a future generation of Italians, Europeans and Africans (see: FASCISM).

Mazzini, none the less, distinguished himself from Fichte and the other theorists of German nationalism in maintaining that the goals of national independence and individual liberty were unthinkable on their own; you could not have one without the other. While he also rejected French political cultural domination, he never relinquished his belief in the ideals of the French Revolution (see RADICALISM). National unity and independence at the expense of individual freedom were, for him, not worth having.

He continued to believe, moreover, that the political and individual rights achieved during the French and English Revolutions were the best means available to safeguard liberty, even though his faith in democracy was more religious than rational and his stress on the need for unity and a sense of community perhaps left too little leeway for dissent and opposition.

Not surprisingly, Mazzini's influence went far beyond his native Italy. Although he was the archtype of a political revolutionary, his ideology proved attractive to moderates and radicals alike (see LIBERALISM and RADICALISM). A good deal of his appeal had to do with the style of his writing, being highly emotional and readable at the same time. His cosmopolitanism notwithstanding, what made Mazzini's programme so attractive outside Italy, or for that matter Europe, was his insistence on the inseparability of national and democratic aims. The dilemma confronting most emerging societies, whether in Europe, Africa, South America, Asia or the Middle East, of how to maintain democratic values in the face of overwhelming demands for national independence and unity seemed to solved (see ANTI-COLONIALISM).

In concrete terms, Mazzini was himself responsible for the founding in 1834 of 'Young Europe', 'an association of men believing in the future of liberty, equality and fraternity for all mankind. . .'. Although it soon languished in dissent, the idea lived on and gave birth to similar groups, if on a national basis, throughout Western and Central Europe, for example, 'Young Spain', 'Young Switzerland', 'Young Germany' and 'Young Bohemia'. It was, perhaps more significantly, many years later the inspiration for the 'Young Turkey' and 'Young China'.

While Nationalism inevitably became interconnected with Liberalism throughout Western, Central and Southern Europe, the liberal component in the admixture was not everywhere as strong as it was in Italy, where the influence of Mazzini endured at least until the First World War. In Germany, to take the most obvious case, between the Revolutions of 1848 and National Unification in 1871 it virtually disappeared. German Liberals, quite simply, were too weak and found it economically as well as politically expedient to sacrifice the goals of representative and responsible government in favour of political unity.

Even if German Liberals for the most part wholeheartedly supported the creation of a unified German state under Prussian direction and leadership, there were still those who looked to a different solution. For a good many Germans, especially those from the middle-sized states of the South and West (for example, Baden and Hessen), local and regional bonds remained much stronger than national ones. Politicians as well as many ordinary people feared not just a loss of their local identities in a unified Germany, but a dimunition of their hard-won political rights in a state dominated by Prussia. Even though their hopes were dashed by Austria's defeat by Prussia in 1866, they still clung to the possibility of achieving some sort of loose confederation of German states in which a large measure of local autonomy would be maintained. It is in this direction in German politics after 1848 that we find the origins of particularism, the doctrine proclaiming the necessity of maintaining local traditions and institutions, especially in newly constituted or unified states. The political expression of this doctrine is usually a demand for some form of federalism or regional autonomy (devolution) (see FEDERALISM).

Although the case for the creation of such institutions has often been argued on its own merits, it has also been used to defend local vested interests against incursions by a central power. This was so, for example, when Southern politicians in the United States, anxious to defend the continued separation of the races in public life, rallied behind the banner of 'states' rights'.

Closely related to the concept of particularism is that of separatism, originally meaning the advocacy in seventeenth-century England of the separation of Church and State, but referring in the nineteenth-century to the policy of Home Rule, or provincial autonomy, for Ireland. As it was coined by its opponents, the term took on a negative connotation which it has never lost. Witness the labelling of, for instance, the movement of French Canadians to achieve greater autonomy for the province of Quebec in the English-speaking press on both sides of the Atlantic as 'separatists'.

Put forward from the 1870s onwards (and supported later by the Liberal Prime Minister of Great Britain, Gladstone) by Charles Stewart Parnell's Irish Parliamentary Party, which purported to speak for Ireland's impoverished and politically under-represented Roman Catholic majority, it led to a fundamental realignment in British politics, with many former Liberal stalwarts joining the Tory (or Conservative) Party, thereby paving the way for Liberal defeat in the election of 1887. The opponents of the Home Rule Bill of 1886 from both the Liberal and Conservative Parties came to be known as 'Unionists' because they sought to uphold the legislative union between Great Britain and Ireland operating since 1816. Ever since the establishment of the Irish Free State in 1921 'Unionism' has meant advocating the continued membership of the predominantly Protestant (Presbyterian) six counties of Northern Ireland, or Ulster, in the United Kingdom. Those on the other side of the divide in Northern Ireland, claiming to represent the Catholic minority in the province and advocating an independent and united Ireland, have become known as 'Republicans'.

While particularism became a lost cause with the consolidation of the German Empire in the 1870s, German Nationalism as such remained in a state of fermentation. In the first place, unification had been achieved on the basis of a *Kleindeutsch* (lesser German) as opposed to a *Grossdeutsch* solution, which meant that many millions of ethnic Germans, mainly in the Habsburg Monarchy, were

159

not part of the new German state. What is more, by the later 1870s the enthusiasm which greeted the foundation of the new *Reich* gave way to disappointment, anxiety and disenchantment. Following the financial crash of 1873, economic difficulties beset the new state and in the eyes of a good many people, especially younger intellectuals, the political system of Chancellor Bismarck, instead of fostering the integration of German society, had done just the opposite by encouraging the wheeling and dealing of petty politicians and financiers.

While Austria faced some of the same economic problems as Germany (stagnating development, falling commodity prices, etc.), she too found herself in a permanent state of national strife. The situation was most poignant in the Bohemian Crownlands, where the rise of the Czechs meant that the German element was constantly on the defensive. It was in this nexus of problems associated with the inability of both the German and Austrian Governments to satisfy the national aims and aspirations of many of its citizens that origins of Pan-Germanism as well as anti-Semitism (see ANTI-SEMITISM) can be traced. As a political doctrine, it aimed to gather together in one state all persons of German nationality and all those areas in Europe where the German element predominated, if not numerically then politically, economically and/or culturally. It cannot be denied that supporters of the Pan-German doctrine, who by 1914 accounted for a sizeable proportion of middle class voters in Germany and Austria, realised that what was proposed was in fact the domination by the German Nation of large numbers of non-Germans.

In a sense, therefore, Pan-Germanism in Wilhelmine Germany can be seen to have gone hand in hand with the nation's imperial aspirations, or perhaps their lack of fulfilment. The aim of domination over a vast area of Central and Eastern Europe, in this light, became an alternative to the quest for colonies overseas. In Austria the situation was somewhat different in that many Germans saw in the Pan-German a way out of national strife at home and a means of becoming part of a Greater German State.

Quite clearly, in proposing the domination of one people by another, the doctrine of Pan-Germanism was closely connected with the rise of the notions of racial superiority in Europe. They helped give the movement its original impetus and furnished it with a form of higher justification.

Yet racialism, the set of beliefs maintaining the existence of a casual relationship between physical characteristics and personality, and, usually, the assertion of one group connected by common origin or descent over one or more other such groups for the most part on the basis of supposedly scientific criteria, was by no means a purely German phenomenon. Although racial distinctions have been made by all peoples since time immemorial, and various writers began to construct notions of race in the late eighteenth century, it was not until about 1850 that the first systematic attempts to argue that racial distinction was a key factor in the unfolding of human experience appeared in print. The most notable, if perhaps idiosyncratic, of these was by the French diplomat and Renaissance scholar Count Arthur de Gobineau (1816-1882) and was entitled *Essay on the Inequality of the Races* (1853-55). In drawing together the various strands of anthropological, linguistic and historical research on the subject, he asserted one basic premise which has guided writers on race ever since: 'The basic organisation and character of all civilisations are equal to the traits and spirit of the dominant race.'

Like his predecessors, he believed that there existed in the world three main races – the white, the yellow and the black. While distinguishing between them primarily on the basis of his own observations and considerable knowledge of linguistics, he attempted to transpose the eternal struggle in which he regarded them to be locked to the France of his own time. He took the nobility, who in his eyes stood for the true ideals of France (love of freedom, honour and spirituality), to represent the White Race, while the bourgeoisie represented the Yellow Race, whom he saw as for ever crass, materialistic and solely interested in trade and commerce. On account of its supposed fecklessness, inherent stupidity and sensuality he identified the mob, or lower classes, without whose support the bourgeoisie would not have been able to perpetrate its supposedly evil deeds, with the Black Race.

In attempting to prove his thesis, de Gobineau argued, mainly on the basis of linguistic evidence, that the French nobility, to which he naturally claimed he belonged, was of Teutonic/Aryan (Germanic/Central Asian) origin. What had happened, however, not just in France but throughout Europe, was that the White, or Aryan, Race by superimposing itself on the original 'yellow' inhabitants of Europe through inter-marriage, had lost its true vigour and character. It had, in fact, become degenerate, tainting itself with the materialism and sensuality of the Yellow and Black Races. The only hope for the White Race, forlorn though it was, was to reassert itself.

Had it not been for his friendship later in life with the renowned German composer Richard Wagner (1813-83), who had himself done so much to propagate racist and anti-Semitic (see ANTI-SEMITISM) notions in Germany if not the whole of Europe, the ideas of de Gobineau might not have received the currency they did. That Wagner should take such an interest in the French Scholar's writings and hardly surprising. In his *Jewry in Music* (1869) he had already ascribed to the Jews many of the same characteristics Gobineau observed amongst the so-called 'yellow' peoples of the world. Being devoted by their very nature to the materialistic pursuits of trade and commerce, the Jews, according to Wagner, were completely lacking in passion and the depth of feeling of the Aryan soul. Jews, Wagner went on to argue, were, therefore, incapable of composing music, the ultimate expression of human feeling. (In this polemic, he was no doubt venting a grudge against the Jewish composers Mendelssohn and Meyerbeer, of whose success he was inordinately jealous).

Wagner gave a more positive expression to his racist notions in his operatic work. In *Lohengrin* and *Parsifal,* especially, he tried to endow the Germanic race with a unique mission in the redemption of Christ, a messianic purpose, if you

161

will. What he, in fact did, was to interpret the Medieval legend of the Holy Grail in such a way that the vessel containing the blood of Christ as he died on the Cross was entrusted to Germanic knights, who were pledged to defend it with their swords and moral purity. This enabled the composer to combine the notion of Aryan racial destiny with the concept of Christian salvation, thereby also divorcing Christianity from its Jewish origins.

His influence grew in Germany as well as throughout Europe not only by way of the performance of his operas and the publications of his prose, but through the phenomenon of Bayreuth, the medieval Franconian city where the Wagner family made its home and where the well-known annual festivals of his operas were held from 1876. The aura of the place and the conscious efforts of the Wagner family soon made it into the seat and veritable Mecca for racist and anti-Semitic ideology in Germany.

One of those who was to play a key role in the Bayreuth Circle's activities was Wagner's young English son-in-law Houston Stuart Chamberlain. In its midst he became an apostle of racial and anti-Semitism and 'Aryanised' Christianity. In his notorious *Foundations of the Nineteenth Century*, first published in 1899, he put forward the view that the world was witnessing the climax of the apocalyptic struggle for its control between Germans and Jews. He depicted the conflict, like de Gobineau, as one between a race whose soul was full of love, honour, creativity and compassion, and a race whose spirit was materialistic, legalistic, uncreative and lacking even an ounce of tolerance or mortality. Instead of the Yellow Race, he singled out the Jews as the racial enemy of the Aryan Germans.

While he was quite clearly accepted the physical stereotypes of other ideologues of race, his notion of race had an almost mystical character to it. For him the struggle between Aryan and Jew was not merely a clash between two physically distinct races, but one between two distinct diametrically opposed cultures, two different race-souls as he put it.

Despite his British origin, Chamberlain was an emphatically German thinker on Race. Not only his almost mystical attitude towards the subject, but his anti-Semitism distinguished him from the vast majority of his colleagues in his country of origin. In so far as British writers on race were preoccupied with questions of struggle and racial inferiority, their attentions for the most part turned towards the Black Race. After all, not only did Britain have a relatively small Jewish population, by which it hardly felt threatened, but the experience of exploration, slavery and colonisation meant that any British interest on the subject of racial distinction usually turned in quite a different direction. The only major exception was the well-known Scottish anatomist Robert Knox (1798-1862) who in his well-known treatise of 1850, *Races of Man*, besides proclaiming quite independently of Gobineau that "Race is everything, civilisation depends on it" drew the all-too-familiar stereotype of the Jews as a person lacking spontenaity, ingenuity or in any attachment to the land or a craft, who existed solely on the basis of cunning, stealth and deceit.

162

A much more representative British thinker on race was James Hunt (1833-1869). The founding president of the Anthropological Society, he believed, as did many others, including Knox, that the Negro was incapable of attaining the intellect of more than a fourteen-year-old. However disturbing his conclusions, the tone of his argument was always scientific and reasonable. An opponent of slavery as well as the mixing of the races, Hunt first put forward the notion of 'separate development', which foresaw the peoples of Black Race in Africa and the Caribbean being left alone in their native environments to live their lives according to their own capabilities.

Although some of his ideas, especially those regarding the breeding of a hereditary aristocracy, already denote the influence of Darwin's theories of 'natural selection', it was only with the research of Sir Francis Galton (1822-1911) regarding the continuity from one generation to the next to be found in the germ plasm of reproductive cells that Darwinism lost its original emphasis on the importance of environment on the evolutionary process. Often regarded as the founder of Eugenics, the science of controlling heredity, Galton, for all his emphasis on scientific investigation and the importance of health in the hereditary process, also put forward ideas which led to the formation of stereotypes and a hierarchical classification of the races.

In a sense, this rather disturbing turn in Galton's thinking points to the dilemma faced by all serious scholars on subjects even remotely relating to race: when making distinctions between one racial group or another, or even studying the characteristics of different groups side by side, how can one avoid thinking in hierarchical terms? This is evident from the work of medical practitioners concerned with the role of housing and sanitary conditions on heredity amongst the more disadvantaged sections of the population in Britain, Germany or France in the inter-war period and, more recently, from the studies on the different degrees of academic attainment by minority groups in Britain.

At any rate, by the end of the nineteenth century racist ideas were commonplace throughout Europe, North America and, to a large degree, amongst the European settlers in Africa. Although they took on a particular virulence within the context of German anti-Semitism and the continued separation of the races in the United States or Southern Africa, they were taken for granted elsewhere as well. It was indicative, for example, that the liberal British crtitic of Imperialism John Hobson (1858-1940) could not deny the need for at least some form of European domination of colonial peoples of Africa and Asia.

Where Nationalism and Racism found their most negative expression, however, was in the various forms of Fascism which developed in Europe after the First World War. Altogether, in fact, notions of nationality and race, primarily because of their supposed transcendence of social strife and the justification they furnish for expansionist policies, have tended to become incorporated in the ideology and propaganda of right-wing movements throughout the world. This explains why such movements, whether in China or Spain, have either called themselves 'nationalist' or have been referred to as such by friends and adversaries alike.

Just as in the case of racism, Pan-Germanism cannot be viewed in a purely German context. In point of fact, it was neither the first nor the only movement or doctrine to seek a form of national expression transcending existing geographical, political or even linguistic limitations. Pan-Slavism, the movement and doctrine proclaiming the unity of all peoples of Slavonic speech, actually came into being before its German equivalent, during the Czech, Slovak and other Slav National Revivals of the 1830s and 1840s.

Under the impact of Herder's praise of the Slavs for their supposedly democratic, peaceful, musical and poetical virtues, and as a consequence of increasing contact with Russians and other Slav groups, Czech and Slovak scholars, initially concerned with their own languages and cultures, soon turned their interests further afield. The Slovak Lutheran Pastor Jan Kollar (1793-1852), for instance, claimed that the Slavs comprised one single nation with a common heritage of literary and cultural interaction. He believed, moreover, that in order to achieve their full potential the Slavonic peoples would have to strive for both physical and spiritual unity.

Although at the time many Slav intellectuals agreed with the broad outlines of Kollar's remarks, differences of approach and attitude along national lines soon developed. Polish Nationalism, with its strongly messianic element, gave birth to a form of Pan-Slavism in which Poland was the guardian of the lesser Slav nations. This was, in turn, in marked contrast to that of the Czechs, Slovaks and South Slavs who continued to emphasise the need for co-operation on the basis of equality. For their part, the Russians, whom the Poles did not even consider a Slav nation but an agglomeration of Finns, Tartars, Mongols and other nationalities of Slavonic speech, also had their own form of doctrine which reflected their country's sheer size and power. By asserting their role as the natural leaders of the movement in highly emotive and religious terms, the Russian Pan-Slavists, despite being regarded for that very reason with suspicion by successive Tsarist governments, nevertheless furnished the ideological justification for Russia's intervention in the Balkans during the 1870s and 1880s. It also provided the basis for a good deal of Soviet propoganda in the Second World War.

Despite the various attempts at forging Slav unity, of which the most notable examples were the Slav Congress held at Prague in 1848 and the bid by some Czechs and Poles to reconcile Russia and Austria, Slav solidarity in the political sphere remained an elusive, if not impossible, goal. Linguistic similarities and some common folk traditions notwithstanding, the individual Slavonic peoples possessed identities and interests which were very much their own. Old rivalries and new *ressentiments,* whether of religious, social, economic or political origin, finally emerged stronger that the bonds which united them.

Although a good deal of the impetus for the idea of Pan-Slavism, as in the case of the Pan-Arab and Pan-African (see BLACK CONSCIOUSNESS) movements of more recent times, came from the sincere belief that peoples of similar culture and descent should achieve some form of political unification, the same could not be said of the efforts within the Italian national movements after unification (1870) to redeem the territory which it claimed belonged within the new Italian State. This is the origin of the term Irridentism, the notion asserting the necessity of a nation redeeming territories and/or populations under foreign dominion to which it supposedly has historic claims based on common descent, culture, religion and/or former possession. Thus, the provinces of Trento (Aldo Adige or the Südtirol) in the North, with its large German-speaking population, and the city of Trieste, both of which remained under Austrian rule after 1870, as well as Istria and Dalmatia, which in spite of their overwhelmingly Croation and Serbian majorities were likewise under Habsburg rule, became known as *Italia Irridenta*.

As can be imagined, the slogan became almost a war-cry amongst a large section of the Italian public. Only the Radical Democrats, Socialists and, later, the Communists remained faithful to the Liberal tradition of Mazzini which preached brotherhood with Italy's neighbours, especially the South Slavs, and resisted the temptation to incorporate irridentist planks into the party programmes. The Fascists (see FASCISM) were particularly adept at exploiting the emotions which were thus aroused, especially after Allied promises of territorial gains to be given to Italy in return for her entry into the war failed to materialise. Still, even Mussolini at the height of his power and influence was unable to redeem all of *Italia Irridenta,* and the gains that he actually made proved short-lived on account of the outcome of the war. Ironically, the only territory claimed by the Italian Irridentists and now part of Italy is Aldo Adige, which was denied to Mussolini by Hitler, and the city of Trieste, which she was given following the result of a United Nations plebiscite shortly after the end of the Second World War.

Having originally developed in Europe when society was in a state of transition from a system characterised by the domination of aristocratic/dynastic elites and the maintenance of semi-feudal or feudal economic organisation to one increasingly influenced by commercial and entrepeneurial élites and industrial economic development, nationalism and its associated doctrines have in our time enveloped the whole world. They continue to underpin the efforts of various peoples around the world to achieve national independence as well as to provide the ideological focus for a good deal of the conflict between states and the internal strife in states which are composed of more than one national group. Our newspapers and television screens bear witness to this fact only too well.

Further reading
Hans Kohn, *Nationalism: Its Meaning and History*
George L. Mosse, *Toward the Final Solution: History of European Racism*
L. L. Synder, *German Nationalism: The Tragedy of a People*

Non-violence

In the past hundred and fifty years or so the idea of abstention from violence has attracted significant numbers of followers. So also, to an even greater extent, has the actual use of non-violent action in political affairs. In view of the very violent character of twentieth-century history this may seem paradoxical, but in many cases non-violence has been a response to violent events or to potentially violent situations.

'Non-violence' can mean two distinct things:

1) A general principle of abstention from violence, for example on ethical or religious grounds; and

2) The behaviour of people using non-violent action who neither initiate, nor retaliate with, violence. Such behaviour may derive from adherence to the general principle of abstention from violence, or indeed from the closely-related principle of pacifism (see PACIFISM), but it does not always do so.

Cases of non-violent action can be found in the history of most countries at most times. But it was in the nineteenth century that non-violent action began to assume its contemporary forms and names. The term 'the strike', referring to an organised withdrawal of labour, appears to have originated in the USA at the beginning of the nineteenth century. The term 'passive resistance' (which is roughly synonymous with the newer term 'non-violent resistance') was used in its modern sense at least as early as the 1840s. The term 'boycott' originated in Ireland in the autumm of 1880. Some nineteenth-century movements consciously used non-violent methods – for example, the Hungarian movement led by Francis Deak which campaigned effectively against Austrian domination between 1849 and 1867. And in the nineteenth century too a number of writers, most notably Leo Tolstoy in Russia, articulated a belief in non-violence.

In the twentieth century, non-violent action has been used in a wide variety of struggles, including some of those against colonial rule. (see ANTI-COLONIALISM). Between 1898 and 1905 such methods were used extensively and effectively in Finland against Russian domination. Then between 1906 and 1914 similar methods were used in South Africa, when members of the Indian community resisted various forms of exploitation and discrimination. In the course of these events a young lawyer, Mohandas Gandhi, emerged to prominence and (dissatisfied with the English term 'passive resistance') organised a newspaper competition as a result of which he hit on the term *satyagraha* meaning 'firmness in truth'.

In the struggle for the independence of India, between roughly 1907 and 1947, non-violent methods, including boycotts, strikes, mass defiance of laws, etc., assumed some novel forms and attracted unprecedented publicity.

Gandhi's astute generalship of many of the campaigns, with the able assistance of colleagues such as Jawaharlal Nehru, contributed to the pressures on Britain to withdraw from the sub-continent. The event had a far-reaching significance: India's independence in 1947 was the beginning of the end of other European colonial empires as well. However, non-violent methods played the main role in liberating only a few other colonies at the time, one such case being the 'positive action' campaign in the Gold Coast (now Ghana) in 1950.

Non-violent action has also been used in several twentieth-century struggles against military occupation, including the 1923 struggle in the Ruhr area of Germany against Franco-Belgian occupation; and in several of the resistance movements in the Second World War (see COLLABORATION AND RESISTANCE), most notably and successfully against particular policies of the occupation authorities in German-held Norway and Denmark. Such methods have also been used, with considerable effect, in struggles against initially-successful military *coups d'état,* for example in Germany in March 1920 and in Algiers in April 1961. In several countries of Eastern Europe since 1945 the use of non-violent action has been particularly prominent, the initial popular Czechoslovak resistance to the Soviet-led occupation of August 1968, and the *Solidarity* movement in Poland in 1980-81 led by Lech Walesa, being the clearest examples. Within Western states, too, non-violent methods of struggle have been used extensively, most notably in the US civil rights movement which was led by Martin Luther King between 1955 and his assassination in Memphis, Tennessee, in April 1968.

Despite the very wide use of non-violent action, it has run into many difficulties. For example, the widespread and peaceful struggles against *apartheid* in South Africa between 1945 and 1965 failed to secure a change in the system, and there was pressure thereafter to turn to sabotage or guerrilla warfare as other possible means of achieving results. To make withdrawal of labour and similar methods work, non-violent action tends to require a high level of support, commitment and discipline.

There have been many attempts in the twentieth century to devise a general philosophy of non-violence. 'Gandhism', for example, refers to a nexus of beliefs, not just in the avoidance of the use of political violence, but also in simple living, vegetarianism, and various other ethical precepts. However, in many countries supporters of a philosophy or life style based on non-violence did so in rather general terms, without supporting any particular 'ism' other than pacifism.

The sheer complexity of many of the actual cases of non-violent action goes some way to explaining the difficulty of enunciating a general philosophy of non-violence. In some cases non-violent action achieved results, not on its own, but in conjunction with other factors: for example, Russia's defeat in the war with Japan in 1905 probably helped the Finns achieve a measure of independence; and perhaps in India the possibility that violence might break out if the British did not make concessions in face of the non-violent struggle led by Gandhi contributed to the ultimate outcome – namely Indian independence. Moreover, many non-violent campaigns have been accompanied or followed by outbreaks of violence – as in the communal violence in India in 1946-47.

But if there are some difficulties in the way of a general philosophy of non-violence, it remains true that non-violent action in its various forms often offers a practicable means of achieving change. The reasons for the avoidance of violence can be various, deriving not only from ethical or religious beliefs but also from habit, from legal considerations, from the political culture of a state, or from a practical assessment of the political and military realities of a situation.

Further reading

Richard Gregg, *The Power of Nonviolence*
William Robert Miller, *Nonviolence: A Christian Interpretation*
Adam Roberts (ed.), *The Strategy of Civilian Defence: Non-violent Resistance to Aggression*
Gene Sharp, *The Politics of Nonviolent Action*
Mulford Q. Sibley (ed.), *The Quiet Battle: Writings on the Theory and Practice of Non-violent Resistance*

Pacifism

Pacifism has, since about the time of the First World War, been a word with a specific and widely-accepted meaning: it is a belief that the waging of war by a state, and the participation in war by an individual, are wrong; that states should abandon military preparations; and that participation in civil wars or violent revolutions is also to be rejected.

Pacifists (i.e. people who support the idea of pacifism) hold differing opinions on certain issues connected with the use of violence. Some may reject its use in all circumstances. Others may accept its use in certain defined situations, for example against an insane and violent individual; in defence on one's own home or family; or when used in a controlled and legally prescribed manner by police forces within states or even, conceivably, by a world government. Despite such differences, the central idea of Pacifism – the rejection of organised mass violence, especially between states – is reasonably clear.

The word 'pacifism' has not always had this meaning. In its early uses, mainly at the beginning of the twentieth century, the word was used in connection with the movements which sought peace between states, the use of arbitration as a means of settling disputes, the setting up of international courts, and the reduction of armaments. Such advocacy by no means necessarily involved a belief that all participation in war was wrong; and although it was at one time labelled pacifist, it would be unlikely to be so labelled now.

Although the term 'pacifism' is relatively modern, the system of belief it describes is not. The rejection of participation in organised mass violence has been a feature of many religious systems and sects through the centuries. It can be found, for example, in ancient Buddhism, in the Essenes in Palestine before the time of Christ, and in the early Christian church. Since the time of the Reformation, many of the smaller Christian sects have been pacifist, including Anabaptists, Mennonites and Quakers.

Twentieth-century pacifism has differed from its religious forebears in three main ways. First, since the First World War it has included an element of rationalism, basing itself on pragmatic arguments about the alleged futility of war rather than on absolute religious prescriptions. Second, it has become the basis of several political movements seeking not just to witness to the pacifist faith, but also to bring about a radical change in the policies of states. And third, as a reaction to the wide use of conscription (i.e. compulsory military service) by states in the twentieth century, Pacifism has often led to conscientious objection (i.e. a principled refusal to be inducted for military service).

Pacifist movements which sprang up in many countries in the 1930s were a reaction not only to the obvious international instability of that decade, but also to the terrible experience of the First World War, in which the numbers of lives lost had seemed out of all proportion to the issues at stake. Fear of the possible consequences of full-scale war from the air further strengthened pacifist arguments that it was time to make a break from the vicious spiral of arms races and war. Pacifist movements were strongest in Great Britain and in the USA, but were far from negligible in many of the smaller states of northern Europe and elsewhere.

In the 1930s, as also in more recent times, pacifists were often asked how they intended to defend their country or political system if it was attacked. The emerging menace of Fascism (see FASCISM) in Italy, Spain and Germany added weight to such questions. In response, pacifists sometimes urged the possibility of negotiation as an alternative to war, an answer which came to be discredited because of the failure to contain Nazism of appeasement policies in the 1930s. Sometimes they stressed the potential of non-violent resistance as a means of countering violence. But the pacifist answers on these points, often put in a vague and general way, were not widely regarded as adequate. After the outbreak of the Second World War in 1939, there was some tendency (rightly or wrongly) to blame pacifists for having contributed to the lack of military preparedness of several states, and/or for having led Hitler to believe that he could attack certain countries with relative impunity.

Pacifist movements, and the cause of conscientious objection against military service which they had espoused, emerged considerably weakened from the Second World War. True, there had been thousands of men, in Britain and the USA as well as in some other countries, who had refused to be conscripted for the war. But the conduct of the war had shown that military methods were not entirely outmoded and ineffective; and the aggression and inhumanity of German policy had forced many to the conclusion that against powers as evil as those of the Axis, the use of force was legitimate.

The position of Mohandas Gandhi, leader of the Indian independence struggle, illustrated some of the difficulties which pacifists had in facing up to the Second World War. In a letter 'To Every Briton', published in the journal *Harijan* in July 1940, he said: 'I want you to fight Nazism without arms, or, if I am to retain the military terminology, with non-violent arms. I would like you to lay down the arms you have as being useless for saving you or humanity. You will invite Herr Hitler and Signor Mussolini to take what they want of the countries you call your possessions. Let them take possession of your beautiful island, with your many beautiful buildings. You will give all these but neither your souls, nor your minds. . .'. However, during the next two years Gandhi modified his position, and in 1942 he went so far as to say: 'I do not want the united powers [i.e. the Allies] to go beyond their obvious limitations. I do not want them to accept non-violence and disarm today.'

After 1945, pacifist movements continued to exist; and indeed many saw in atomic weapons a symbol of the utter destructiveness and futility of warfare. In the late 1950s and early 1960s, after both the United States and the Soviet Union had developed thermonuclear (H-bomb) weapons and the means to deliver them, there was a new wave of revulsion against war in many countries, taking particularly the form of nuclear pacifism – i.e. the rejection of all preparation and threatened use of nuclear weapons. In Britain, the change from pacifism to nuclear pacifism was perhaps best symbolised by Bertrand Russell, who had been a conscientious objector to military service in the First World War, and who, while not supporting complete pacifism in later years, became a leading figure in the British campaigns against nuclear weapons between 1958 and his death in 1970. There was a revival of nuclear pacifism in many countries, especially in Western Europe, following the December 1979 decision by NATO to deploy land-based, nuclear-armed, intermediate-range missiles in several member states.

The balance sheet of the various pacifist and nuclear pacifist movements of the twentieth century is not encouraging. Such movements have played some part in bringing about an awareness of the futility of war and the dangers of nuclear weapons; they constituted one of the many pressures which contributed to the conclusion of an important measure of nuclear arms control, the *Partial Test Ban Treaty* of 1963; and they participated in effective campaigns against particular involvements in war – for example, against the French role in Algeria (1954–61), and the US intervention in Indochina (for over a decade up to 1973). On the other hand, on their central issue of concern, the renunciation of military preparations by states, they have not been successful. Indeed, in no major state has anything approaching a majority of popular opinion been persuaded of the case for complete unilateral disarmament. While many states (including Sweden, Switzerland and Japan) have not developed nuclear weapons, despite a technical capacity to do so, such states have generally followed a non-nuclear approach for limited pragmatic reasons; and have maintained large conventional military forces, or allied themselves with a nuclear power, or both.

Further reading

Peter Brock, *Twentieth-Century Pacifism*
Christopher Driver, *The Disarmers: A Study in Protest*
Martin Ceadel, *Pacifism in Britain 1914-45: Defining of a Faith*
Aldous Huxley, *Ends and Means*
Sybil Morrison, *I Renounce War: The Story of the Peace Pledge Union*
Lawrence S. Wittner, *Rebels Against War: The American Peace Movement 1941-1960*

Popular sovereignty

Popular sovereignty exists when the people rule – when individuals possess equal rights of participation in political processes and when the sole object of government is to safeguard the interests of the *people* as a whole, rather than those of particular sections or interest groups.

This is a theoretical position. Its practical importance is that it represents an objective that political regimes which claim to respect popular sovereignty should aim for. In practical terms sovereignty has to be expressed through institutions which are far from perfect, but which at least allow the people (normally all adults, but with the frequent exclusion of criminals or the insane) to elect representatives, and, directly or indirectly, to select a government. Election is the source of political legitimacy.

Constitutional arrangements vary, but the function of elected representatives is both to initiate policy and exercise continuous control over government. Both representatives and members of government should be subject to regular and frequent re-election so as to provide the people, as voters, with opportunities to express their opinion on the effectiveness of both legislators and members of the executive, and to secure their replacement if this is felt to be necessary.

On the eve of the American and French revolutions Britain was the only major country in which political institutions were based upon election rather than hereditary rights. The development of the English common law, and the gradual strengthening of Parliament's authority had substantially limited the power of the monarchy: 'The king reigns but does not govern' was already close to becoming reality. Liberal ideas had emerged elsewhere, however, particularly in France, as an aspect of resistance of the nobility to royal power. Montesquieu's ideas provide a clear illustration of this situation. They were given more coherent form in the eighteenth century by a group of intellectuals including Rousseau, Diderot, d'Alembert and Condorcet. Equality (see ENLIGHTENMENT) and freedom of thought, expression and association, together with the freedom to engage in economic activity, were basic concepts employed to criticise and to condemn the existing social and political orders. Through them and more directly under the influence of Tom Paine the American Declar-

171

ation of Independence proclaimed the establishment of an egalitarian republic in which all citizens should participate in public affairs. In 1789 this new ideology was proclaimed in France in the Declaration of the Rights of Man, heralding the beginning of a period of Revolution and war which was to have a tremendous impact on the whole of Europe.

The first article of the Declaration summarised this new ideology: 'All men are born and remain free and equal in their rights'. During the following century men were to continue to argue over this thesis and were repeatedly to struggle to transform ideals into real institutions (see LIBERALISM). There was considerable disagreement over what this reality should be but gradually it was extended from freedom of speech to freedom of association and into free elections and universal suffrage, and the right of the most deprived to form trade unions and to engage in strike activity in order to protect their interests. Subsequently, in this century, the rights of women were finally recognised. Resistance was strong at all stages as defenders of the old order sought to protect what they took to be vital interests against 'the vile multitude' (see CONSERVATISM). Where parliaments were established, this was initially on the basis of a limited franchise. Voting rights were granted only to those with property which was taken to be the necessary guarantee of a proper sense of responsibility. In Britain the franchise was extended by a series of laws, most notably in 1832 and 1867; in France, following the revolutions in 1830 and again in 1848 when universal male suffrage was introduced for the first time in Europe. This was an important precedent.

1848 had another important consequence. Demands were made by socialists (see SOCIALISM) and the more radical republicans in France and elsewhere for a Social and Democratic Republic, that is for social reforms to complement political democracy. To conservatives this appeared to herald social revolution. The brutality with which the left was repressed was indicative of fears shared by conservatives and many political democrats. This conflict emphasised vital differences of opinion concerning the nature of popular sovereignty. Did it involve simply equality before the law and rights of political participation which were conditional upon tacit acceptance of the social order or, as socialists insisted, was greater economic equality essential to make democratic political rights meaningful?

Although developing liberal democracies extended popular rights through elections, democratic freedoms and education, it has been argued that one objective, and the main consequence of this extension of liberty together with the improvement in living standards, was to integrate the masses into political systems which continued to be dominated by narrow élites.

Universal suffrage has in fact, in certain conditions, proved to be an effective means of social stabilisation. Democratic institutions have had the double-edged effect of extending popular rights and imposing effective institutional restraints upon the exercise of popular sovereignty. This can often be seen in key characteristics of the institutions.

Conservative suspicions of democracy were expressed by the establishment

of bicameralism, with upper houses composed of hereditary peers, or deliberately constructed to facilitate the dominance of essentially rural and small town
social groups which were felt to be politically conservative (see CONSERVATISM).
Efforts were frequently made to limit the effects of election by universal suffrage
through electoral manipulation, e.g. the system of official candidature in Second
Empire France, or through the careful designation of electoral districts (gerry-
mandering), or unequal distribution of votes between town and country, as in
numerous state legislatures and the Federal Congress in the USA.

Political parties are an obvious feature of modern parliaments. Competition
between them has helped to extend popular rights, but again has also imposed
institutional restraints on the exercise of popular sovereignty. The emergence
of parties was gradual. Interest groups of like-minded individuals were always
likely to form, but these had weak structures and left considerable freedom to
individuals. Elections stimulated the establishment of electoral committees
whose importance increased with the emergence of a mass electorate. In most
of Continental Europe, the evolution of socialist groups with more permanent
organisation stimulated counter-organisation by liberal and conservative
groups. These socialist parties sought to develop a more genuine democracy
by encouraging mass participation in political processes, and the election of
political leaders at all levels (see SOCIALISM). This was an important step forward
in the political education of the masses, and in the emergence of democracy,
but, as early as 1912, Michels criticised the emergence of oligarchical control
even within these parties. In all parties it seemed that candidates for election
tended to be selected by small inner groups. The electorate as a whole was
permitted to choose only from amongst the small number of candidates previously selected by oligarchies within political organisations. This was true even
of the American system of primaries designed to increase popular choice.

Another serious restriction on popular sovereignty has been identified by
numerous witnesses on the left, of whom Marx is only the most notable. They
have argued that electoral and parliamentary procedures remain essentially formal in their effects, for as long as those with wealth are able to control the
means of propaganda, information and instruction, and thus to influence the
process by which individuals are socialised in the family, school, church, and
wider society – to accept certain basic values based upon private property and
social inequality. The more discreet and subtle techniques of persuasion are
vital to the establishment and preservation of a conservative political consensus
and make the use of more overt and brutal means of repression unnecessary.
Even where, as in Europe in the last third of the nineteenth century, socialist
parties developed with systems of values opposed to and challenging the *status
quo,* they either adopted an overtly reformist stance, as in Great Britain, or
were revolutionary in word rather than action. Class conflict was thus muted
by the development of a general consensus based upon the acceptance of political
pluralism and moderation, which had the effect of facilitating continued social
dominance by élites based upon wealth.

173

The virtues of a pluralistic society in which organisations in all spheres of life compete with one another, inculcated in one form or another are often proclaimed as an important safeguard for democratic freedoms. It is important that centres for the mobilisation of public opinion exist which are independent of government agencies, such as trade unions, employers' associations, pressure groups.

It is also important, however, to be aware of the limits placed upon both pluralism and freedom of expression. In part these are financial. The ability to organise and distribute propaganda depends upon financial backing. In part the limits are informal based on commonly accepted modes of social behaviour. In part they are political and institutional. Tolerance is extended only to groups which do not threaten the social *status quo*. In a period of crisis the limits of tolerance are likely to be circumscribed and narrowed.

Popular sovereignty has frequently been under threat – most notably perhaps during those years of crisis between 1918 and 1939 when the period of progressive extension of political freedom came to an end. In these inter-war years economic depression caused massive discontent and social tension, and stimulated the search for political alternatives. The Russian Revolution of 1917 had led to the creation of an alternative social system which its propagandists claimed established for the first time a genuine popular sovereignty on the basis of an increasingly classless and egalitarian society (see COMMUNISM). The establishment of this model posed a threat to those who subscribed to the values of individual effort and rewards in the form of private property. The restriction of political freedom was a price many were prepared to pay in order to defend established privilege. The violence of the ensuing political crises varied between countries according to the depth of the economic crisis they experienced and the character of their political cultures, but everywhere democratic rights were restricted. Dominant élites revealed again their determination to resort to whatever means were necessary to maintain the *status quo*.

In any society, groups whose nonconformity has become intolerable are liable to repression, which varies in severity according to the intensity of the threat they are felt to pose. Repression can thus take the form of social ostracism or involve the use of legal sanctions, usually with the willing support of judges selected from amongst the dominant élite. If necessary, although normally only as a last resort, the military can be employed in a politically repressive role. These stages might well reflect the progressive decline of consensus.

Since the Second World War prosperity and the establishment of welfare societies in the western world have provided stable social conditions in which the restoration of political consensus has been possible. However, the problems of preserving the realities of popular sovereignty have been as great as ever. Domination of the mass media by oligarchy continues to reduce the number of channels by which information is diffused. The increase in the role of the state in the economy and in the provision of social services – and in the scale and complexity of its operations – has made control of its activities increasingly difficult. Access to accurate information is to say the least difficult. Legislatures can in general only act on the basis of information which governments choose to provide for them. Although the rigidity of party systems should not be exaggerated, it remains true that a government supported by a stable parliamentary majority can remain in power for long periods, often in spite of public opinion – and this is the situation in relatively favoured areas of the world, in which, with all its faults, democratic pluralism has deep enough roots in political culture to survive, at least in the absence of another severe socio-economic or political crisis. The virtues of popular sovereignty stand out in comparison with those political systems which place even more restrictions on individual political freedom. Democracy is no doubt less complete than is practically possible, but it nevertheless offers to citizens greater opportunities to influence government than those offered by the existing alternatives. It is far more than merely 'formal'. Governments remain subject to parliamentary criticism, elections continue to allow an infrequent, limited, but nonetheless real, expression of public opinion. Popular sovereignty is limited by the entrenched position of social and political élites in the western democracies, but is unfortunately even more restricted, where political pluralism exists only within the bounds of a single ruling party.

Further reading
T. B. Bottomore, *Élites and Society*
G. Duncan, *Marx and Mill*
B. Holden, *The Nature of Democracy*
J. Lively, *Democracy*
D. Thompson, *The Democratic Citizen*

Populism

Few labels in American political history have been used more vaguely than 'Populist'. When virtually any recent politician who is not a member of the eastern establishment (from George Wallace, the white supremacist former governor of Alabama, to Jimmy Carter, the conservative peanut farmer turned president, to Fred Harris, the hope of the left wing of the Democratic Party in 1976) can be called Populist, the term would appear to have lost much of its analytical value. Populism has not only been used as a convenient label for the journalist to pin on many a politician; it has also been the centre of an academic debate which had political overtones. Richard Hofstadter, writing just as *McCarthyism* (see McCARTHYISM) had begun to recede as a political force, saw in Populism a movement that was tinged with paranoid theories of conspiracy (by the international gold ring of Jewish and English capital, the money trust, and Wall Street). Hofstadter saw a tradition of conspiratorial theories in American politics and traced that tradition to his own day, thus implying that Populism helped lay the groundwork for McCarthyism

But historical Populism is hard to recognise through Hofstadter's distorted lens. And it is as a historical movement that we must analyse Populism, for Populism was a specific movement with a specific ideology that arose out of a particular set of historical circumstances. Its period of existence was less than twenty years, from around 1879 to 1896, but it was able to create a mass movement that challenged the predominant industrial capitalist ethos and threatened, albeit briefly, to supplant one or other of the major political parties just as the Republicans had earlier supplanted the Whigs.

Populism was an agrarian movement and arose in reaction to the grinding poverty suffered by farmers throughout the South and in many of the newly-settled areas of the West. The movement first began in the cotton states, and it was in those states that the farmer found himself in perhaps the deepest poverty, trapped in a system of monoculture and debt from which there was no escape. 'The basest fraud on earth is agriculture', wrote one Mississippi farmer. 'No wonder Cain killed his brother. He was a tiller of the ground.'

What kept the farmer in a state of peonage was the lien system whereby the farmer, whether tenant or landowner, pledged his next crop to a merchant in return for credit on supplies in the current year. The interest rate was unspecified, and even the prices of the goods supplied were frequently unfixed. The credit price was at least 80 per cent and often 70 per cent above the cash price. The merchant thus made a double profit: from a price substantially higher than the cash price and from frequently usurious rates of interest – rates of over 200 per cent were not unknown. Once his crop was pledged to a merchant, no other sources of credit were available to the farmer, for his crop was the only security he had to offer. At harvest time, he took all his crop to the merchant, who bagged it and weighed it. The farmer would then commonly be told what he had failed to pay off his accumulated debt. Thus the cycle would begin all over again. Because his crop was worth least at harvest time, the farmer sold in the lowest market. Because he had no choice of supplier, he bought in the highest market. The merchant would only accept one crop for credit; in most of the South that crop was cotton. Monoculture produced all the attendant problems of exhausted soil and fickle markets.

With the variation one would expect, a similar situation existed in various areas of Europe, most notably in western and south-western Germany, where peasants found themselves constantly in debt to cattle dealers.

To compound the farmer's misery, the price of cash crops fell steadily. The price of cotton dropped by 48 per cent between 1874–77 and 1894–97, while that of corn declined by 33 per cent. The return from the 23.7 million acres of cotton planted in 1894 was less than that from the 9.4 million acres planted in 1873. The cause of this steady decline lay in the hard-money, deflationary policy of the federal government.

During the Civil War the federal government had issued $450 million of treasury notes, known from the colour of their ink as 'greenbacks'. These notes were not backed by any gold or silver reserve. At the end of the war, orthodox banking circles, believing such a paper currency was unsound, advocated a return to a gold currency. Similarly, those who had purchased union bonds with greenbacks pressed for a return to a gold currency so that they could redeem their bonds for gold at a tidy profit. Under these twin pressures (frequently from the same source) the government resolved on a gradual return to the gold standard. This was achieved by 1879 but only at the cost of a massive contraction in the amount of currency in circulation and consequently a severe deflation. This deflation produced the general price decline.

Two early movements arose in reaction to the plight of the farmer – the one predominatly social and economic, the other political. The first was the *Patrons of Husbandry*, better known as the *Grange*, which was founded in 1867 as a social organisation for farmers. Since most rural communities had few social amenities, the Grange proved popular, spreading to fourteen states and reaching a membership of some 800,000 in 1874. The Grange established co-operatives stores to supply goods to farmers at reasonable prices, but since these were cash stores on the English model and one thing many farmers lacked was cash, the stores were of limited appeal. The Grangers did move into politics to some extent, particularly in the Midwest and in certain states in the South. They concentrated on railroad regulation in an attempt to reduce the high rates charged by the railroads for shipping farm products to market. But the Grangers were too timid to challenge the established political parties and after 1875 the movement declined.

More radical and more overtly political was the *Greenback* movement. Greenbackers, as their name implies, believed in a 'people's currency' of paper notes issued by the government. The currency would have no previous metal backing, and the amount in circulation could be expanded as the population and productivity of the nation grew. Such ideas are relatively commonplace in the twentieth century, but at the time they appeared to many to border on the lunatic. The Greenbackers held that labour, whether rural farmers or urban workers, would benefit from a paper currency. A series of parties such as the Greenback National Party of 1876 and the Greenback Labour Party of 1878 espoused this platform. But on the defensive ideologically, with the labour movement weak and farmers still tied to the Republican and Democratic parties, the various Greenback parties made little headway. They did, however, leave in their wake a number of agrarian radicals who were to carry Greenback ideas into the Populist movement.

These agrarian radicals did not have long to wait: the Populist movement was already under way. The *Farmers' Alliance* began in 1877 in the frontier district of Texas as a secret social and political organisation which aimed at the betterment of the farmer. The Alliance soon divided over the issue of whether to support the Greenback Labour Party, but in 1879 it was reformed, shorn of

177

party political features. Once again it faltered, but in 1883 a system of organisers was set up, headed by a 'travelling lecturer' who oversaw sublecturers. The principal organising tool was the encouragement of concerted efforts by Alliance members to force merchants to give them special terms, and thus to escape some of the impact of the lien system. Soon the Alliance began to organise its own cotton sales in which the product, conveniently gathered into an Alliance warehouse, could sometimes be sold at a premium. In another attempt to combat the lien system, a statewide purchasing agent was appointed to deal directly with the manufacturers of farm implements and machinery.

Hoping to escape the shackles of the lien system, farmers flocked to the Alliance. By the summer of 1886, membership was over 100,000, organised in 2,700 suballiances. In August of that year a statewide convention met in Cleburne and adopted a series of 'demands' calling in part for federal regulation of railroads, the recognition of trade unions, and limitations on foreign and domestic land syndicates. Finally, the convention adopted a currency demand calling for a federal paper currency 'that shall increase as the population and business interests of the country expand'. This was the Greenback ideology in a nutshell.

What distinguished this movement from subsequent American reform movements, and what caused it in some ways to resemble past and present-day European opposition movements, such as the Social Democratic Party of Imperial Germany (see SOCIALISM) and the French Communist Party (see COMMUNISM), was its ability to establish a daily round in which the individual Populist lived and breathed the movement. The Populist family could maintain an existence almost wholly encapsulated within a Populist alternative society or counterculture. They could attend classes given by the travelling lecturers who numbered some 35,000 by 1891. Here they could assimilate Populist economics, history and political theory. They could read the Populist press which consisted of over a thousand weekly papers in the 1890s. They could meet twice a month in the local Alliance lodge, there to have their determination reinforced by the secret ceremonies of the ritual. And once, twice, or three times a year, they could attend a county, district, or state convention. These conventions, frequently held in the open air, resembled camp meetings. Hundreds or thousands of wagons would be driven along dusty roads to a meeting that was part revival meeting, part festival, part huge barbecue, and part educational experience. But most important of all was the series of Alliance-run co-operatives – the Alliance warehouse, the Alliance store, and on top of the pyramid, the Alliance Exchange. Through these co-operatives the member could learn an ethos that was diametrically opposed to the prevailing ethos of competition and individualism.

But the co-operatives were soon in trouble, foundering on the same problem that caused the individual farmer so much misery – access to credit. Aware that the farmer could not participate in a co-operative based on cash, Macune endeavoured to set up a scheme for his Exchange that would allow the farmer to purchase on credit. Capital would be raised through joint notes from sub-alliances in which the Alliance members that owned land would pledge their land as security for the supplies received from the Exchange. The Exchange in its turn would use the notes as collateral to secure capital from banks. But, in Macune's words, 'the moneyed institutions. . . did not choose to do business with us'. The Texas Exchange was forced to retreat into operating on a cash-only basis. The exchanges that had sprung up in other states suffered similar difficul-ties. In 1889 the Texas Exchange collapsed.

Undaunted, Macune unveiled a new plan, one that was even more radical than the Greenback plan. This proposal, the sub-treasury plan, was to become the centrepiece of the People's Party platform. The logic of the plan was simple: if the banks refused to lend to the co-operatives, the power of the banks woud have to be short-circuited. Macune believed that his plan would 'secure such changes in the regulations that govern the relations between different classes of citizens'.

The plan called for the federal government to establish local warehouses or 'sub-treasuries' to which the farmer could bring his products for storage. The farmer would receive fully negotiable sub-treasury notes or greenbacks for up to 80 per cent of the market price of his product and could order his goods sold when market conditions were suitable. Interest would be charged at 2 per cent. This scheme would have injected several billion dollars of federal notes into the economy.

The need for Macune's radical plan – in effect, social control of credit – could easily be explained to a farmer mired in debt. He himself had no access to credit, and he had seen the co-operative schemes of the Alliance fail because of lack of credit. But a major problem remained: such a programme could only be enacted if adopted by a major political party. In the 1890 elections, the Alliance had considerable success sending Democrats who had run on the Alliance platform to Washington. But the chances of either major party adopting the programme were virtually nil. The logic of the situation propelled the Alliance into the formation of a third party. The People's Party achieved somewhat disappointing results in the election of 1892 – the Populist candidate for president, General Weaver, received 8.5 per cent of the total vote – but party adherents were realistic enough to be aware that victory required organising.

In that organising, the People's Party attempted to cement an alliance between black and white: blacks were elected as delegates to national conventions, lynch laws were attacked, and black organisers like John Rayner of Texas were employed to win blacks from Republicanism. The white Populist leader, Tom Watson of Georgia, declared: 'The accident of colour can make no difference in the interests of farmers, croppers and laborers'.

The People's Party also attempted to build an alliance with urban workers. But here, in spite of their strong support for the rights of unions to organise, they were far less successful. The labour movement was weak: the mass organis-ing of the Knights of Labour had been beaten back and the conservative Ameri-

179

can Federation of Labour was restricted to a few crafts. The Populist programme of credit for farmers had little appeal to urban workers who felt their grievances to be distinct from those of the agrarian poor.

The Populists faced other difficulties too, in particular the wholesale stealing of elections by the major parties. But when depression struck in 1893-94, it seemed as though victory were possible. The hard-money Democratic administration of Grover Cleveland was totally discredited. But it was not the Populists that benefited, but instead a group of quasi-Populists within the Democratic Party whose slogan was 'free silver' or *Bimetallism*. To most Populists the coinage of silver as well as gold was a false panacea: the amount of currency in circulation might increase somewhat, but the value of money would still be subject to vagaries in the supply of precious metals, and the problem of credit would not be solved. But in the West, where silver was mined and where farmers were not subject to the lien system, Bimentallism had considerable appeal.

In 1896 the Democratic Party rejected Cleveland and nominated the free silver advocate William Jennings Bryan. The pressures in the People's Party from Western farmers who believed in free silver and from political officeholders who were worried about being swamped in a Democratic tide proved irresistible. The Party joined in nominating Bryan for President. Although the Party rejected the Democratic candidate for vice-president and nominated Tom Watson instead, the People's Party had lost its separate identity (and the Democrats lost the election). Watson himself spoke the Party's epitaph: 'Our party as a party does not exist any more. Fusion has well nigh killed it.'

Further reading

Lawrence Goodwin, *Democratic Promise: The Populist Moment in America*
   The Populist Moment: A Short History of the Agrarian Revolt in America
   (abridged ver. of the above)
Richard Hofstadter, *The Age of Reform From Bryan to F.D.R.*
C. Van Woodward, *Origins of the New South: 1877-1913*
   Tom Watson: Agrarian Rebel
Donna A. Barnes, *Farmers in Rebellion: The Rise and Fall of the Southern Farmers Alliance and People's Party in Texas.*
Bruce Palmer, *'Man Over Money': the Southern Populist Critique of American Capitalism.*

Radicalism
(including Jacobinism, Terrorism and Chartism)

The term 'Radical' used as a substantive noun to define a person's political attitudes, dates from the last years of the eighteenth century. In the context of British politics, Radicalism orginally denoted the political attitude deriving from the conviction that, since the Constitutional Settlement of 1689, successive ministries had undermined the independence of the elected House of Parliament by means of the abuse of patronage, systematic bribery and other unlawful or tyrannical practices, with the result that the entire British Constitution had become perverted. The aim of Radicals was therefore to reassert what they believed to be the genuine spirit of the 1689 Settlement, or even to return to the democratic principles which they attributed to the Anglo-Saxon 'constitution' before the Norman Conquest. The first practical step in this direction was to be achieved by restoring the independence of the House of Commons. As the Radicals ascribed the growing opposition of the American colonies to the mother country to the disregard of constitutional rights and liberties on the part of George III 'and his ministers, they also supported the American cause and, ultimately, American independence.

The main concern of Radicalism, however, was to find a basis for the political independence of the people's elected representatives. The search for such a basis gave rise to the specific demands for which British Radicals agitated vigorously and consistently for the next century – manhood suffrage and annual parliaments. As these demands were far removed from the received opinion of the time, it was important to evolve a theoretical framework of justification for them. Among the first systematic attempts to do this were James Burgh's *Political Disquisitions* (1774/5) and Major John Cartwright's *Take Your Choice* (1st ed. 1776). Cartwright believed 'that personality is the sole foundation of the right of being represented and that property has, in reality, nothing to do in the case'. Property, he went on, 'is a very fit object of (a person's) representative in parliament, but it contributes nothing to his right of having that representation'. As for the duration of a parliament thus elected, Radicals believed, following Jonathan Swift, that only annual parliaments would render the cost of the 'commerce of corruption between the ministry and the deputies' sufficently high to put an end to it.

To secure the widest possible dissemination for their views, and to create a basis of popular support for the reform agitation, a group of Radicals founded the *Society for Constitutional Information* in 1780, which sponsored and distributed a considerable body of radical political literature during the next two decades. Radicalism had a particularly strong appeal for the Dissenters, who identified their own lack of political rights with the perversion of the constitution and expected complete equality from a successful assertion of Radical principles. Despite their commitment to manhood suffrage and their campaign to popularise radical political aims, the majority of this first generation of British Radicals did not believe that the equality of rights which they asserted necessarily implied social equality. The majority, gentlemen themselves, 'accepted the normality of a stratified society' (Bonwick). Cartwright believed, on the basis of his own experience of the lower orders, 'that they preferred confiding their interests to persons of more consideration than themselves'.

Radicalism, however, was not a homogeneous school of political thought. It contained a stream which did challenge the hitherto generally accepted stratification of society. This stream did not derive from any notions about the authentic British or Anglo-Saxon Constitution, but from that old tradition of egalitarian utopianism which periodically comes to the surface in the history of European political thought, and which was developed and deepened in the eighteenth century by Mably, Morelly and above all by Jean-Jacques Rousseau (see THE ENLIGHTENMENT). According to these thinkers, political rights are not only innate but also inalienable. Hence they cannot be legitimately surrendered to a 'sovereign' set above the people. Sovereignty must continue to reside where it originates – with the people as a whole. The theory of popular sovereignty and inalienable rights had to offer an explanation of how these rights had historically been lost. The attempt to do this helped to link the notion of social equality with that of political equality, in as much as the stratification of society and the desire for unlimited material wealth were identified as important factors facilitating 'clandestine and villainous attempts of princes to ruin liberty' and to clamp onto their peoples the 'chains of slavery'. The true merchant, 'concerned with making profits, a stranger to all other considerations, closes his heart to all the noblest affections', and thus becomes a willing instrument of the would-be tyrant (Marat). The egalitarian Radicals therefore opposed large-scale commerce and capitalist industry in general as corrupting forces in society which, by virtue of their divisive effects, facilitated the tyrannical designs of princes. Would-be tyrants, they argued, cunningly divided their subjects into different classes with conflicting interests. Conversely, a society concerned with the maintenance of freedom must 'prevent extreme inequality fortune' (Rousseau). To this end, Rousseau advocated a graduated income tax and luxury taxes, and such economic regulations as would ensure that plenty was within the reach of all in such a way that 'labour is always necessary and never useless for its acquisition'. This explicitly egalitarian and democratic Radicalism, with its systematic hostility to the aristocracy of wealth and its condemnation of all princes as would-be tyrants, was propounded in Britain by Jean-Paul Marat in his *Address to the Electors of Great Britain*, also entitled *The Chains of Slavery*, and published at the time of the 1774 General Election.

Though non-democratic Radicalism could on occasion rouse mass enthusiasm for its cause, as during the crisis resulting from the government's refusal to accept the election of Wilkes in the late 1760s and early 1770s, the political mass movements which arose in some European countries in the wake of the French Revolution were inspired by democratic Radicalism. The doctrines of inalienable popular sovereignty, of the corrupting role of wealth, and of social equality, appealed strongly to the growing number of literate artisans, and could be invoked in the struggle to defend the livelihood and independence of artisans and others threatened by the onset of capitalism and industrialisation. The strength of this appeal was dramatically demonstrated in the course of the French Revolution. The first revolutionary Constitution of 1791, which reflected the attempt to combine the principle of popular sovereignty with the maintenance of a socially stratified society, was soon challenged by a mass movement insisting on social equality as a precondition for the full exercise of popular sovereignty. The leaders of the movement, notably Marat, who returned to France after a ten-year stay in Britain, argued that in order to make equal political rights a reality, and to secure them effectively against the developing Counter-Revolution, the people must go on from the destruction of noble privilege, achieved in 1789, to the destruction of 'the prerogatives of wealth'. The journals of Marat, Hébert and Jacques Roux brilliantly articulated an inspired egalitarian and democratic radical aspirations in the French Revolution. But the political leadership of the mass movement was assumed by Maximilien Robespierre and the Parisian Jacobin Club, which derived its name from the former Jacobin monastery in which it held its regular meetings. In the context of French revolutionary politics, democratic Radicalism is therefore known as Jacobinism. The outbreak of the Revolutionary Wars, in 1792-3, swiftly followed by the advance of hostile armies towards Paris with the proclaimed objective of wreaking vengeance on active revolutionaries and restoring the Old Order, made it imperative to mobilise the entire nation for the defence of France and the revolutionary achievements, and brought the Jacobins temporarily to political power (1793-4). Their successful channelling of the revolutionary mass movement into the war effort added a strong patriotic element to the Jacobin tradition in France.

The popular movement during the French Revolution was not only inspired but was deeply pervaded by Rousseau's political thought. Its influence found clearest expression in the new Constitution of 1793 which was based on manhood suffrage and spelled out the 'sacred obligation' of society to provide for 'the subsisence of indigent citizens, either by the provision of work, or by the provision of the means of subsistence if they are incapable of work'. In its practical activity, the popular movement also reflected the Rousseauist principle that sovereignty cannot really be delegated. The primary electoral assemblies became the organs through which ordinary people like artisans, workshop masters and shopkeepers – the so-called *sans-culottes* – asserted and exercised

183

their right of participation in political affairs, including the right to acquaint their deputies in the National Convention with their opinions and claims.

Under constant pressure from the popular movement, the Jacobin government had to try to provide for the subsistence of indigent citizens within a context of war, inflation and Rousseauist political economy. Forced loans and *ad hoc* taxes on the rich, and legal maximum prices on basic foods and necessities of life helped to slow down the pace of inflation. But the difficulties experienced in enforcing these policies consistently were ascribed in accordance with egalitarian assumptions to the corruption and selfishness of the rich exploiters, whose lack of public spirit was thought to make them half-hearted in the cause of revolution, if not downright sympathetic to counter-revolution. In the tension and hysteria following the French military reverses of 1793, this attitude stimulated a desire for revenge, and encouraged the notion that popular government could maintain itself against the intrigues and resistance of the rich only by terrorism, by 'putting terror on the order of the day' (Hébert). A popular insurrection in Paris on 4 and 5 September 1793 compelled the Jacobin government to make terror official.

Jacobin terrorism, like all other varieties of terrorism, was a many-edged weapon. The *sans-culottes* were as unsuccessful in making the rich bear the brunt of its impact, as were Robespierre and Saint-Just in confining its employment to the elimination of the most active opponents of Jacobin government. The victims of the terror were a cross-section of the whole of French society, ranging from royalist nobles to highway robbers. Whether terror contributed significantly to the Jacobin government's victory over counter-revolution and foreign invasion (1794), is an open question. It certainly strengthened the opposition to democratic Radicalism everywhere by giving currency to the idea that democracy could not be prevented from degenerating into anarchic mob rule, an idea which Rousseau had explicitly rejected, but which became deeply embedded in the politics of nineteenth-century liberalism (see LIBERALISM). Within the camp of democratic Radicalism, the retrospective attitude to terrorism was varied. Many attributed it to the brutalisation of the majority resulting from centuries of injustice and oppression inflicted by the rich and powerful minority. The Austrian Jacobin Andreas Riedel thought that revolutions were great acts of justice in which the most oppressed section of humanity raises itself to its natural human dignity, but in which it also 'calls its oppressors to strict account, compels them with clenched fist to surrender their usurped privileges, and sits in judgment over those who have made themselves guilty of proven crimes of violating humanity which call out for vengeance'. The catastrophic worsening of the condition of the poor in France after the end of the Jacobin terror and after the suppression of the popular movement, amounting to actual famine in the winter of 1794/5 and 1795/6, led some radical critics of terror to revise their attitude and to conclude in retrospect that terrorism was an essential weapon in the armoury of egalitarian democracy. François Noël (Gracchus) Babeuf was one of these. In the *Tribun du Peuple*, which was eagerly read in this period in

Parisian cafés frequented by the poor, he wrote: 'In order to govern judiciously, it is necessary to terrorise the evilly-disposed, the royalists, the papists, and the starvers of the people. . . and one cannot govern democratically without this terrorism'. Babeuf's failure to resurrect the popular revolutionary movement with the slogan 'Bread and the Constitution of 1793' prompted him to join Filipo Buonarroti in a secret revolutionary conspiracy, the *Conspiration pour l'Egalité*, and to elaborate plans for a temporary revolutionary dictatorship of the minority of 'consistent and energetic republicans' with the task of destroying the influence of the rich and enlightening the poor, thus laying the foundation for lasting democratic rule. Babeuf thus became the first democratic leader to develop a strategy of revolutionary dictatorship. His strategy, however, was not, as is often assumed, identical with that of Louis Auguste Blanqui who envisaged a much longer period of dictatorial rule, still less with that of Karl Marx, who used the term 'dictatorship of the proletariat' precisely in order to clarify the distinction between his strategy of majority dictatorship and that of minority dictatorship exercised on behalf of an immature or unenlightened majority.

Babouvist conspiracy and perspectives of minority dictatorship were specific products of the desperation and demoralisation of the defeated democratic forces after Thermidor (July 1794) and the consolidation of ostentatious bourgeois rule in France. The conspiracy was betrayed by a government spy and Babeuf executed in 1797. Though Buonarroti's reprieve and longevity and the publication of his book *La Conspiration pour l'Egalité dite de Babeuf* (1828) ensured the survival of a Babouvist tradition into the nineteenth century, a tradition of which Blanqui and Mazzini were the most important representatives, the mainstream of nineteenth-century democratic Radicalism developed along the very different lines of popular agitation and mass organisation.

In Britain, the progress of industrialisation, coupled with the economic dislocation resulting from the long war against Revolutionary France, undermined the prosperity of an ever-increasing proportion of the labouring population, especially in the clothing industry. This economic distress provoked a predominantly political reaction, with the disaffected artisans taking up the well-established radical programme of manhood suffrage and annual parliaments as the best hope for an amelioration in their condition. Thus the *Corresponding Societies* of the 1790s with their mainly aritisan mass membership replaced the radical societies of the 1780s whose members were predominantly gentlemen of fashion. In the 1780s it had been possible for the King's ministers to claim that Parliamentary Reform was the cry of a factious opposition impatient for offices to which the King did not wish to appoint them. In the 1790s, Parliamentary Reform was the programme of a mass movement impelled by the conviction that the distress of the labouring majority was the inevitable result of the rule of a minority corruptly exploiting their governmental and legislative monopoly for their own enrichment, and that consequently a democratically elected Parliament would inaugurate an age of better and cheaper government and thus of general prosperity. In this process of the popularisation of the radical programme among the artisans in all parts of the country, Tom Paine's *Rights of Man* (Vol. I 1791, Vol. II 1792) was probably more important than any other radical publication. The new movement for Parliamentary Reform culminated in two mass meetings organised by the *London Corresponding Society* in 1795, a year of particularly acute economic distress. The size of crowds caused such alarm – 100,000 were reported to have assembled at Copenhagen House in Islington – that the Cabinet of the Younger Pitt decided to make this form of radical agitation illegal by means of the *Seditious Meetings Act* of 1795. A few years later, in 1799, the *Corresponding Societies* were themselves declared illegal. As in France, failure and suppression pushed Radicalism into underground conspiratorial channels.

In 1815, after the ending of the war with France, which event brought with it the shock and disappointment of the post-war depression, Radicalism revived the tradition of popular agitation and mass organisation under a new generation of leaders (William Cobbett, Henry Hunt, Thomas Attwood). The programme of manhood suffrage and annual parliaments re-emerged unchanged, and indeed Major Cartwright's activities for a time provided a direct link with the movement's origins. But the centre of gravity of the movement was noticeably changing with the growing contribution of the working population in new industrial centres like Birmingham, Manchester, Leeds, Newcastle and Barrow. The social basis of Radicalism was changing as it established links with the emerging modern labour movement. By 1829, mass reform organisations, now calling themselves *Political Unions*, were established in every major industrial centre. The model was Thomas Attwood's *Birmingham Political Union*. The leaders' proclaimed intention was to keep the agitation within legal and peaceful limits. But the growing numbers who joined the *Political Unions*, the widespread attacks on property resulting from the acute economic distress of the late 1820s, and the enthusiasm with which Radicals received the news of the successful July 1830 Revolution in France, were symptomatic of a potentially revolutionary situation. When the simultaneous agitation in Ireland resulted in the enactment of Catholic Emancipation and the disintegration of the Tory Pary (the principal bulwark against Radicalism since the days of the Younger Pitt), concessions could not be delayed much longer.

The new Whig ministry under Earl Grey, a survivor of the gentleman Radicalism of the late eighteenth century, adopted the strategy of forestalling a serious upheaval by enfranchising the wealthier industrial middle class (the '£10 householders') through the Reform Act of 1832. It was the first major concession to radical agitation in Britain. The Whigs argued that the Reform would strengthen the British Constitution against any further challenge from democratic Radicalism by uniting all property-owners in its defence. The Radicals immediately rallied those who were disappointed and still unenfranchised by the Reform Act of 1832 – the majority of the working population – in support of a programme designed to ensure effective political power for this majority. The *People's Charter*, drawn up by William Lovett and the *London Working Men's Association*, contained not two points, but six. To the familiar radical demands of manhood suffrage and annual parliaments were added vote by ballot, abolition of property qualifications for M.P.s, payment for M.P.s, and equal electoral districts. The additional points expressed a new emphasis: they reflected a new concern to dissociate Radicalism from middle-class elements and to spell out the full egalitairan implications of democracy After the Whig manoeuvre of 1832, working men were not going to confide their interests to persons of more consideration than themselves.

The characteristic features of Chartism in its agitation during the period 1838 to 1848 were indeed its specifically working-class basis and consciousness and its increasingly explicit hostility to middle-class reforms and movements. This was a direct result of the sense of betrayal at the limitation of the 1832 Reform Act, which was reinforced by the bitter resentment of the working class, especially in the North, against the harsh new Poor Law enacted by the first reformed parliament in 1834. This feature made Chartism an important milestone in the political development of the British working class. It gives Chartism a claim to be considered as the first nationwide working-class political organisation in Europe. As such, it naturally reflected the comparatively undeveloped state of the British working class at that time. The emergence of the unrealistic *Co-operative Land Plan* as a central concern, reflecting as it did the nostalgia for the land felt by a newly urbanised working class, was an example of this. Another example was its rejection of any kind of bargaining for a common opposition platform with the middle-class *Anti-Corn Law League*, which might have brought Chartism closer to wresting some concessions from Parliament.

The decade preceding the Revolutions of 1848 witnessed the development of popular democratic Radicalism in other countries as well. In France its leading spokesman was Ledru-Rollin and its most important organ *La Réforme*. Here, too, the movement became increasingly critical of liberal reform movements campaigning only for a limited extension of the franchise. The 1848 Revolutions revealed the strength of the democratic challenge and its effectiveness in a situation where the governing classes were divided among themselves. In Britain, the Chartist challenge in 1848 was ineffective only because the Repeal of the Corn Laws two years earlier had restored the unity of the possessing classes and taken the industrialists out of the camp of radical opposition for the time being. In France, where Guizot's government refused to reconcile the unenfranchised sections of the middle class and faced a liberal as well as a democratic opposition, the democrats could impose manhood suffrage and the proclamation of the republic. In Germany, Austria and Italy the democratic challenge was contained only with difficulty, and ultimately only at the price of a reconciliation between liberalism and the old order. Democratic hopes of a second chance vanished when the triumph of radical democracy proved to be short-lived even in France. The fears of the propertied classes, legitimist and conservative as well as liberal, gave Louis Bonaparte the opportunity of imposing a

187

personal dictatorship at the modest price of paying lip-service to democratic principles by seeking retrospective plebiscitary endorsement for his *coup d'état* of December 1851.

It took Radicalism a long time to recover from its failure in 1848 and 1849, and to re-emerge as an autonomous movement from the gilded cage of Bonapatist patronage. When it did, it had effectively attached itself to the developing labour movement, and its further history cannot really be separated from the history of socialism (see SOCIALISM). The bulk of the socialist movement, following the strategy outlined in the *Communist Manifesto*, continued the struggle for democracy as the essential first step towards the emancipation of labour.

Further Reading

C. Bonwick, *English Radicals and the American Revolution*
F. D. Cartwright, *Life and Correspondence of Major Cartwright*
J. Epstein and D. Thompson (eds.), *The Chartist Experience*
A. Goodwin, *The Friends of Liberty*
S. Maccoby, *English Radicalism* (5 vols)
R. B. Rose, *Gracchus Babeuf*
A. R. Schoyen, *The Chartist Challenge*
A. Soboul, *Short History of the French Revolution*
J. T. Ward (ed.), *Popular Movements c. 1830-1850*

Romanticism

As a movement, Romanticism in its many and often contradictory forms resulted from the attack upon and collapse of the two great Western traditions, classical and Christian, and from the decisive victory of the Moderns in the seventeenth-century debate between the Ancients and Moderns. A prodigious attempt to discover the world spirit through the unaided efforts of the solitary soul (Fichte's 'Transcendental Ego'), a response to emergency created by the break with the canonical conception of the historical past (Providence, Natural Law) and its inherited modes of experience, and a fundamental transformation of Western thought and society, many of the principles and practices of Romanticism remain with us today. Producing an unprecedented range of styles to encompass an unprecedented scale of human emotion, extending from unbounded utopian optimism to radical anxiety, Romanticism forged the connection between artistic and social forms, replacing the dissolution of faith as a guiding principle with this substitute form of belief. The Romantic crisis furnished the model and impetus for the successive artistic, literary, and political movements of Realism and Nationalism, Symbolism, Impressionism, Imagism, Naturalism, Transcendentalism and Vitalism, Post-Impressionism,

Futurism and Fascism, Orphism, Surrealism, American Abstract Expressionism, and so on.

Romanticism has been variously defined by its protagonists (whether or not they considered themselves as being among the Romantics) – Goethe, the Schlegel brothers, Novalis, Heine, Eichendorff, Hugo, Stendhal, Delacroix, Berlioz, Byron, Coleridge, Carlyle – and by Georg Brandes, Irving Babbitt, and many others. Equally authoritative, the definitions necessarily conflict. Arthur O. Lovejoy, despairing of finding a satisfactory definition of Romanticism, proposed using the plural 'Romanticisms' in order to express the multiple variations and inconsistencies, the widely differing aspects and modes of thought and behaviour embraced by the movement. The inherent difficulty in defining Romanticism – in pinning it down – partly derives from the frequently self-contradictory, divided, and elusive aims of the movement which favoured sentimental intolerance and conflicting loyalties rather than a stance grounded in a systematic belief. Some of the attitudes and dispositions which psychologically and philosophically characterise perennial (as opposed to historical) Romanticism can be found in other widely different periods and cultures (such as the Chinese primitivism of Lao Tsu or twelfth-century modernism): faith and reason in opposition to the authority of tradition.

Romanticism as a literary, artistic, and philosophical movement began to gather momentum in the late eighteenth-century from a number of converging trends such as Neoplatonism (Young, Shaftesbury, and Winklemann), Pietism (Hammann, Jacobi, and Möser), the Protestant revival (Schliermacher), Methodism and other forms of 'Enthusiasm', the moral teaching of Rousseau and Diderot, the Catholic reaction against the Enlightenment, the English tradition of satire and sentimentalism (Swift, Sterne, Richardson), and the German *Sturm und Drang* (Herder, Goethe, Schiller). These already marked the break with Neoclassical authority and the transition from the eighteenth-century mimetic to the expressive theory of art in an age of irony, estrangement, and alienation. Most of all, the French Revolution supplied, as Shelley expressed it, 'the master theme of the epoch in which we live'.

As a term, Romanticism acquired the extended sense of liberation from rules and traditions, conventional forms or genres in art, literature, music, feeling, and behaviour. At times a caricature of the believer (the expressionist), at other times a caricature of the scientist (the impressionist), it grew into a mode of life concerned with the primacy of the imagination and the integrity of feeling (often accompanied by violent 'conversions') rather than with rectitude of judgment. Every human activity was seen as a form of individual self-expression born of impulse and emotion. The Romantic dwelt upon the concrete 'minute particular' (Blake) in thought and experience, affording a deep insight which transcends the oppositions and polarities of the subjectivity of human consciousness and objective existence.

Both the outcome of and the reaction against the dramatically increased abundance of rules, Romanticism was a rebellion against the levelling demands of social convention and conformism inherent in fast-expanding mercantilism. Romanticism became the modern – and particularly the northern European – expression of humanism, and remained predominantly Christian as opposed to classical in its bias and cast of mind (Mme de Stael, Chateaubriand, Coleridge). 'The generation rising among us has nothing to continue; it has everything to create. The great merit of Napoleon is to have 'cleared out the house' (Stendhal).

Romanticism was not a new set of norms but an abolition of norms. It constituted a cluster of beliefs based upon disbelief: both deep epistemological and social uncertainty and a longing for a myth to replace revealed religion. Poetry became the autonomous subjective; the theatre and the novel offered the education traditionally supplied by the church.

The tendency of the Romantic movement to model itself upon archaic feudalism (Scott, Wagner, the Gothic Revival) was found in the cult of the hero (Napoleon, Berlioz), the idealised libido (Byron, Edgar Allen Poe, Baudelaire), the formal realism of the novels which began to appear after 1814 (Manzoni, Hugo, Balzac, Dumas), the hero of consciousness populating historical writings (Carlyle, Michelet), and social philosophy (Ballanche). Romantic art was predominantly 'aesthetic education': it strove to occupy a providential place in the making of men and the development of true social form. Even when the Romanticist, like Scott or Carlyle, preached a feudal and patriarchal order, Romanticism exhibited populist tendencies, resulting from an ill-adjusted effort to replace hierarchic aristocratic forms or genres with democratic ones. History, no longer seen as sublime in the former sense, became restricted to progress and myth.

Romanticism involved appreciating – and reappraising – other periods and places according to their own standards, seen as differentiated but equal in merit: 'Every age has its own style' (Herder). Past cultures, literature, and arts were re-evaluated in terms of their Romantic qaualities, stressing the irrational, unconscious, supernatural, legendary, mythical, surviving forms of popular art, and folk culture. This entailed not only a shift of emphasis, for example from classical to archaic Greece, but also an attempt to compare archaic phases with both contemporary tribal society and the child, guided by the assumption that all three constitute the crucial poetic and truly creative phase of human development.

With the French Revolution, the Napoleonic wars and the wars of liberation, the use of indigenous sources developed beyond a revival of themes and forms heralding the first important original literary epoch since the Renaissance. Nationalism found its expression and cause in the vernacular languages, espoused by Mickiewicz and Niemcewiscz in Poland, Pushkin, Gogol, and Lermontov in Russia, Manzoni in Italy. The humanitarianism which anthologised and encouraged the national literature of every folk became the fountainhead of aggressive pan-Germanism and pan-Slavism.

It was in Germany that the reaction against the philosophy of the Enlightenment and the threat of the French Revolution took its most systematic form, in an attempt to replace political rationalism. Cultural nationalism (see NATIONALISM), a form of resistance to Napoleon, took the form of political reaction. Romanticism formulated a body of doctrine which served as a basis for the German ruling élite to justify its struggle against French hegemony, both political and cultural, over the Continent. Fichte, for example, insisted that there would never be a cultural Germany until there was a political Germany. Departing from Kant's subjective idealism, the Idealist *Weltanschauung* (Fichte, Schelling, Hegel) produced a new concept of man as a developing being whose nature could only be grasped historically, taking its shape in successive patterns of life and culture. 'The Romantic mentality, considered in its everyday forms, was not the Romanticism of the philosophers and poets. It found its expression in a variety of manners, in a variety of events, in the collective reactions of social groups' (Brunschwig). When transferred from the middle classes to the masses, Romanticism in Germany became a revolt against Western civilization.

Free from the stifling imposition of an alien Neoclassical pattern, Romanticism in England at first followed pastoral and nostalgic forms. In the works of Blake, Coleridge, and Wordsworth it became a vehement reaction against the mechanistic interpretation of nature and society in a fast-expanding market-economy and industrialisation, a loss of the communal bonds of solidarity, a search for visionary innocence, and a renewed affirmation of faith. This produced not only the philosophy of Carlyle and the literature of the Brontes but also innovations in form which combined the poetry of common speech, a calculated poetic diction, and the supernatural.

French Romanticism arose later than Romanticism in Germany and England, due to the strength of a more militant classicism able to portray the ethos of Revolution, its patriotic ideals, and its republican view of freedom. It was shaped by the violence of the classical opposition to it, and became an aggressive exponent of the new as against the established order (Lamartine, Vigny, Musset, Hugo); but in its concern for the people French Romanticism remained social, with its protagonists seeking their own revolutions (Blanqui).

In the 1830s, following changes in political regimes, the Polish and Italian risings and the English Reform Bill, Romanticism became allied with political liberation (see RADICALISM) and socialism (see SOCIALISM), embracing visions of utopia and terror (Babeuf, Proudhon, Marx). Gradually, after 1848, Romanticism declined into a frantic protest, an attempt to salvage culture in decline (the German Nazarenes in Rome, the Pre-Raphaelites, the Oxford movement, and the Aesthetic movement).

In the belief that one might attain contact with ultimate reality through an act of immediate intuition, the Romantics saw themselves not as adherents of a school or movement but as practitioners of a creative discipline or mode of being. 'We live in a world we ourselves create' (Goethe). In line with the assertion in Goethe's *Faust* of the primacy of action ('in the beginning was the Deed'),

Romanticists adopted, both in literature and in life, the themes of suicide (Goethe's *Werther*, Kleist), early death (Keats, Büchner, Pushkin, Byron, Schubert, Chopin), imprisonment (Beethoven's *Fidelio*, Baudelaire, Dostoevsky), exile, either voluntary or forced (Heine, Hugo, Marx, Nietzsche), drugs as a form of escape (Coleridge, De Quincey, Baudelaire, Rimbaud), the double (Hoffmann, Gogol, Heine, Dostoevsky), and madness (Hölderlin, Schumann, Gogol). Novalis asserted that 'Life should be a *Roman*' – the German word combines both the sense in English of 'romance' and the 'novel' – 'not given to us but one made by us'.

'All the species of animals are perhaps not as distinct from one another as a man is from men' (Herder). These words took on metaphysical shapes in the hands of Fichte, Shelling, and the idealist philosophers, followed by the sociological insights of Dilthey's *Geisteswissenschaft*, Simmel's irrationalism, Georg Sorel's doctrine of violence, and Bergson's *élan vital*. Romanticists protested sometimes demagogically and sometimes sincerely against capitalist materialism and asserted the alleged supernatural and unconscious forces of *Urvolk*. The idea of living nature in Carlyle or Dostoevsky or the use of the term *Metapolitik* by Wagner's circle show a Romantic critical refusal to accept the humanist measure, resulting in a preoccupation with 'either/or' positions, countered by dialectical theology (Kierkegaard), the rebirth of the tragic vision (Nietzsche), and the dialectic of reason (Sartre).

Romanticists showed a belief not only in moral freedom as it had been established by Kant but also in absolute freedom of action. Therefore they did not espouse any single political programme. Among Romanticists there were those who supported Metternich and those who opposed him. Some Romantic visionaries dreamt of the revival of the Holy Roman Empire, while Romanticists such as Erndt, Jahn, and Müller dreamt of a united Germany. Shocked and inspired by the political ideal of the French Revolution, Romanticists were diverse and divided – often alternating between conservatism and liberalism (or *vice versa*) – in their political practice: for example, Wordsworth, Byron, Hugo, Carlyle, Wagner. Pervasive uncertainty, coupled with an insatiable desire to bridge the gap between the subjective self and objective world, the real and the ideal, produced an incomparable creative renewal in painting, music, and literature, but also frequently left Romanticists occupying positions at the extreme ends of the theoretical and political spectrum.

Further reading
Irving Babbitt, *Rousseau and Romanticism*
Jacques Barzun, *Classic, Romantic and Modern*
M. H. Abrams, *The Mirror and the Lamp*
D. Thorburn & G. Hartman, (eds.), *Romanticism: Vistas, Instances, Continuities*
Hugh Honour, *Romanticism*

Socialism

It would be possible to write a history of man's striving to create a more egalitarian society which went back to time immemorial. It was not only the Nazi lunatic fringe who believed in the existence of 'Bolshevism from Moses to Lenin'; a Marxist as distinguished as Karl Kautsky, the most important populariser (and vulgariser) of the master's work after Engels in the late nineteenth century, also wrote of 'Communism from Plato to the Anabaptists'. Even in the twentieth century some socialists still seek inspiration in what they see as the essentially egalitarian message of Christianity. To provide a great chain of being of socialist thinkers stretching back to Biblical times is obviously not possible here. More important, however, is that such an enterprise would be most misleading; for modern socialism is perhaps best understood as a product of and a reaction to a set of relatively recent historical phenomena: the Enlightenment, the French Revolution and the Industrial Revolution. Although some of the early socialists, especially the social Romantics in France in the 1830s, disputed some of the individualist thinking that lay at the root of the Enlightenment, most inherited the belief in progress, science and man's ability to transform the world according to the dictates of reason. They also learnt from the writings of Jean-Jacques Rousseau, who realised that democracy implied a certain degree of equality in possessions and whose *Discourse on the Origins of Inequality* of 1755 saw inequalities in the distribution of goods and property as one of the major sources of corruption in the society of his time. Rousseau's solution to the problem, however, was not social ownership of property but rather its redistribution, preserving rights of ownership for citizens essentially conceived as independent peasant producers. Two of Rousseau's contemporaries, the Abbé Bonnot de Mably (1709-85) and Morelly (see RADICALISM; THE ENLIGHTENMENT), whose *Code de la nature* was once attributed to Diderot, accepted his essentially moralistic critique of inequality and took the solution a stage further, advocating on occasion public expropriation followed by the egalitarian redistribution of property, a kind of primitive communism. However, certain characteristics of the thought of these three *philosophes* distinguised it from that of later socialists. All three conceived society along lines that were primarily agrarian. No critique of the operation of industrial capitalism is to be found here; which is hardly surprising given that France still awaited her industrial revolution. It is also difficult to detect in Rousseau, Mably or Morelly any idea of how a social revolution could be engineered, other than the archetypal enlightenment belief that education would remove superstition and prejudice and enable all right-thinking men to agree upon a rational and indisputable course of action. In a sense, the mechanics of revolution could only be understood after practical experience of revolutionary upheaval; and this is what happened almost immediately in the wake of the great French Revolution of 1789.

The revolutionary events that seized hold of French and European imagination between 1789 and 1794 were important for the subsequent development of socialist ideology in a number of different ways. For some later commentators, especially the Romantic historians Guizot, Thierry and above all Michelet, the French Revolution revealed class conflict, and Marx studied them and by his own admission, learnt from them. In the second place, the outcome of the Revolution left a trail of disappointment and disillusion: it became clear that equality before the law and formal equality of opportunity did not solve the immediate problems of the 'menu peuple'. It became clear that 'bourgeois liberalism' (see LIBERALISM) did not mean universal liberation and this sense of having been cheated explains much of the thinking of the early socialists in France. Finally, and most immediately, the great French Revolution offered a concrete example of how men could seize power and use it to change society. Contemporaries like François Noël Babeuf and Phillipe Michel Buonarotti now possessed not only a critique of existing society but an image of how it could be transformed, an image they attempted to realise in the ill-fated 'Conspiracy of the Equals' of 1795 – see RADICALISM). For Babeuf, history demonstrated that wealth was becoming increasingly concentrated in the hands of a few privileged individuals and was approaching a point at which such inequality and mass poverty was becoming intolerable for the populace at large, a populace now ready for revolution. What would ignite that revolutionary spark, however, was the seizure of power by a small tightly organised, conspiratorial group of committed revolutionaries. These would then institute a revolutionary dictatorship which would dispossess the wealthy and create an egalitarian society, although whether Babeuf then believed simply in the redistribution of property or in its communal exploitation is a matter of some confusion and debate. Here, then, was a theory which combined a critique of existing society with a model of action for its destruction. It was a model which was to have a profound impact upon what might be described as the communist, as distinct from the socialist, tradition, espousing a belief in the efficacy of violence and the necessity of at least a temporary dictatorship, as distinct from a commitment to change along peaceful and essentially democratic lines. It was also the tradition that subsequently inspired Blanqui and, some would say, Lenin (see COMMUNISM). A final point to note about Babeuf's ideas, however, is that they were firmly rooted in a society whose pursuits were still primarily agrarian. We are still in the land of agrarian communism.

Modern socialism, the theory concerned to free an industrial working class from the shackles of industrial capitalism, truly emerged in Britain and France in the 1820s and 1830s. Its emergence reflected those changes in social organisation induced by industrialisation, a process which had begun in Great Britain in the mid-eighteenth century and which took off in France under the July monarchy (1830-48). It also coincided with the emergence of an organised labour movement in Britain, especially after the liberalisation of the laws against combination and association in 1824, and with the appearance of revolutionary secret societies and working class insurrections in France in the 1830s and 1840s. Some of the horrors associated with the early days of the industrial revolution – slum housing, insanitary factories, long hours, child and female labour, disease, pauperisation – provoked a variety of hostile reactions. Many conservatives and some of the first-generation Romantics (see ROMANTICISM) looked back with longing to an imagined pre-industrial idyll of social hierarchy and harmony which was now beyond recall in real terms. Later Romantics, the Social Romantics like Sue, Sand and Hugo in France, concerned themselves with the miseries of the lower orders, as did many middle-class philanthropists. In this period the 'social enquiry' appeared, as in Dr Villermé's study of the differences in mortality rates between upper and lower class residential areas in Lille. Finally, some of those who disliked the naked exploitation of the new, bourgeois order conceived of change not in terms of a return to a former golden age but in terms of a future socialist society built upon certain gains of industrialism.

The Saint-Simonians, the followers of Henri de Saint-Simon (1760-1825), were perhaps the most important socialist sect to emerge in France at this time. Saint-Simon himself claimed descent from Charlemagne, was incarcerated in the lunatic asylum of Charenton along with the Marquis de Sade and has variously been claimed as the father of technocratic modernisation, Christian Socialism, female emancipation and free love. It is certainly true that his work was diffuse and certainly not clear that he was ever a socialist, as is witnessed by the large following he attracted from bankers and industrialists and by the fact that Comte, that staunch anti-socialist, claimed to be his true intellectual heir. His thought did have a huge importance for future socialist thought however. Firstly, Saint-Simon saw industry as a force that could regenerate a decadent world, rather than as an unmitigated curse. To achieve spiritual and economic revival however, it was essential that those in charge of this industrial world and the gigantic productive forces unleashed by it should be men of the new order, the 'industriels', by which he meant both workers and industrialists. What transformed this relatively innocuous message into a revolutionary doctrine, however, was that Saint-Simon placed the functioning of the economic system above any commitment to the maintenance of private property. From this, it was not difficult for his followers to turn to socialism when they saw in the midst of economic crises and social conflict that private property relations conflicted with the rational organisation of production. This crucial step was taken by many of Saint-Simon's followers, including an odd assortment of Romantic visionaries around Bazard and Enfantin, who followed their master's call for a Christian revival and created a kind of socialist monastery at Melimont. It was a step also taken by his most impressive disciple, Paul Leroux, whose works first brought the term socialism into circulation in France in the early

1830s. Leroux combined a belief in industry as the basis of a new society with a profound critique of existing property relations and social inequality.

Saint-Simonians were only one of the many 'utopian' sects that sprang up in France in the 1830s, utopian not only because of some of their more fanciful notions – Enfantin's search for the female Messiah, Fourier's strange cosmological beliefs – but because they lacked really concrete ideas of how social reorganisation could come about, apart from their own powers of persuasion and what they regarded as the eminent rationality of their ideas. Above all they are to be distinguished from Marx and from some of their British contemporaries in failing to identify the emergent industrial working class as a potential motor of social revolution. Perhaps the archetypal 'utopian socialist' was Charles Fourier (1772-1837), who claimed that one philanthropic millionaire could solve contemporary social problems by supporting his schemes and who waited vainly in his rooms at a specified hour every day until the end of his life for such a saviour to appear and offer his services. Not all of Fourier's thoughts encompassed such eccentricity: he provided a trenchant critique of the operations of the new capitalist economy and the *laisser-faire* economics which sought to explain and justify it. In particular he identified two phenomena which were later to emerge as central to Marxist theory: the concentration of capital into fewer hands and unemployment as a consequence of cyclical depression. His solution, however, once again revealed the transitional nature of French society and the incompleteness of its industrial revolution. Primarily, Fourier looked to the creation of small-scale, independent communities in which all would lead similar lives: the institution of the family would play no part here, much to the disgust of many of his contemporaries, children would be cared for by the community, and the social product would be divided amongst its members in the following proportions: five twelfths to labour, four twelfths to capital and the remainder to talent (i.e. these *phalansteries*, which were to consist ideally of no more than one thousand eight hundred citizens, did not abolish private property as such but rather treated all their members as share holders). Again one can detect nostalgia in this model solution: Fourier had no time for modern techniques of production and based his *phalansteries* on skilled agriculture.

Such small-scale solutions to the problems of early capitalism were shared by innumerable contemporaries of Fourier: by Lammenais, who advocated a Christian socialism based upon the gospels and looked to producer co-operatives to bypass the mechanisms of the market, and by the poet Buchez. None of this is very surprising in a nation of artisan manufacture which was only beginning to feel threatened by organised big business. For some the producers' co-operatives were to be funded by the state. Louis Blanc (1811-1882) advocated the creation of *ateliers nationaux* (national workshops), initially funded by a central bank charging no interest, but which would then become self-governing and autonomous units. Within these there was to be a gradual abolition of wage differentials. Blanc, who had an opportunity to put some of these ideas into practice in the revolutionary government of 1848, believed that these workshops would prove superior to private enterprise and come to be imitated more or less automatically. He refused to see the need for any form of violent intervention to dispossess the wealthy, remained wedded to democratic values and may thus be legitimately regarded as one of the founders of the reformist tradition of socialism in France. Blanc's view of the state as an instrument of social change was shared by another of his utopian contemporaries, Étienne Cabet (1788-1856), whose *Voyage en Icarie* was widely read and quite influential. Cabet's vision of the future, however, was made of much sterner stuff, envisaging a completely egalitarian system including manners of dress and diet. Indeed, it was he who coined the slogan later adopted by the makers of 'scientific socialism': 'from each according to his capacity, to each according to his needs'. Although Cabet's followers attempted to establish some small scale communities in the New World in a way reminiscent of the Fourièristes, it is fairly clear that his imaginary utopia would constitute a self-sufficient nation embracing as many as a million citizens in its rigid equality.

On this last point, as on the question of state aid, Cabet would have found himself at odds with one of the most significant of his thinking contemporaries: Joseph Proudhon (1809-1865) (see ANARCHISM). Proudhon began as a critic of the bourgeois economy and bourgeois economics. Capitalist society was unjust because the workman did not receive the full product of his labour. To rectify this injustice a series of small-scale independent communities of craftsmen and peasants – we have still not arrived at solutions approriate to advanced capitalism – were to be established producing directly to satisfy the needs of their own members or engaging in the free exchange of goods according to the labour-time embodied in them. This system of 'mutualism' would thus establish a parity of supply and demand which could not be realised under private capitalism. Proudhon's importance for the history of socialist, or rather anarchist, thought in France, however, rests upon two other central tenets of his theory. In the first place, he distrusted all activities of the state and all theories of socialism which conceived of some kind of centralised state aid or direction in the new society: hence his belief in independent, small-scale communities and his claim to be the father of French anarchism. He also embraced a strict *ouvrierisme* a belief that only the working class could liberate itself and that bourgeois politics were necessarily corrupt and self-interested. It is hardly surprising that such views found a powerful resonance amongst the Parisian working class who had been shot down by the bullets of a supposedly democratic, bourgeois national guard in the 'June Days' of 1848.

What Proudhon shared with the other French theorists of the 1830s and 1840s who have appeared in this short account, however, was an image of a society still far from liberated from its agrarian shackles, together with a moralism which eschewed any real study of the mechanics of social change. Such could hardly be said of Auguste Blanqui, who engaged in several abortive attempts to seize power in France under the July monarchy and whose attitude towards social revolution was marked by an extreme voluntarism. With Blanqui we return to the communist tradition of Babeuf and Buonarotti, to a belief that a small group of professional conspirators, a revolutionary élite, could seize power and institute a revolutionary dictatorship to expropriate the owners of private capital and constitute some kind of egalitarian state (see COMMUNISM); although it has to be admitted that Blanqui said little about the precise structures of an ideal future. It is true, of course, that his image of a revolutionary *coup d'état* was located in a particuar historical situation, namely the necessary instability of capitalism caused by a recurrent imbalance between production and consumption; but it is also true that his theory of exploitation said no more than that producers overcharged consumers, and did not identify a conflict of interest between capital and labour in the arena of production, despite his remark that France was a nation of thirty million 'proletarians'. At the end of the day, therefore, the Frenchmen of the July monarchy did construct a biting critique of existing social relations but their economics remained relatively primitive and their visions of the future still bore the imprint of a past of small scale agriculture and manufacture.

At the same time as these intellectual developments were taking place in France, British thinkers were grappling with similar problems, albeit in a way which perhaps reflected the greater degree of industrial advance and the earlier onset of modern industrial protest on this side of the English channel. At first sight, this might seem a rather odd description of the work of Robert Owen (1771-1838), factory owner and philanthropist. Owen believed that he had discovered an ideal scheme for the solution of society's problems, a scheme whose moral rectitude would be recognised by all enlightened men. At first he hoped that government could be persuaded to implement it. When it failed in this task, and only then, Owen turned to labour to emancipate itself. In fact, in the end, he came to advocate a union of the whole working class which would, upon some central directive, lay down its tools and peacefully take over the means of production. Again we confront 'utopian' schemes. As Owen's thought developed, however, it did provide the basis for other variants of socialism. In the first place, Owen did not regard machinery and the new industrial order as a curse; which is perhaps to be expected given his role as an entrepreneur. He did recognise, however, that the present organisation of production led to long hours, periodic unemployment and pauperism. All of these phenomena he saw as unnecessary, as a consequence of imbalance between production and consumption, itself a product of a system in which the worker was not paid the full value of his labour. To rectify these problems, therefore, the worker was to be paid in labour certificates commensurate to the amount of value he had created. What we have here, therefore, is a theory of exploitation based upon the labour theory of value, which in turn is used to explain crises of underconsumption.

It was this economic theory which was developed by Owen's followers in the 1820s and 1830s, by men who sometimes self-consciously saw themselves as the economic theorists of the burgeoning labour movement. Starting from the labour theory of value as expounded by the classical economists Adam Smith and, in particular , David Ricardo, they put it to very different uses. They argued that labour was not merely the measurement but the creator, and in some cases the sole creator, of value. This then gave rise to the belief that labour, as the creator of wealth, should also be its owner, i.e. to 'socialism', a term which first appeared in the Owenite *Co-operative Magazine* in November 1827. George Mudle advocated co-operative ownership of the means of production, as did Francis Bray, who thought that these commonly owned enterprises could produce goods outside the capitalist market. Some Owenites went so far as to say that the capitalist had become a parasite and was unproductive, a conclusion not shared by Thomas Hodgskin, who still believed that the capitalist should have some share of the final product and did not envisage the abolition of private property in the means of production. He seems to have developed an idea of a society of independent producers exchanging their products. But Hodgskin did develop a theory of class conflict which asserted that capital and labour were destined to confront one another as hostile groups until labour did receive the whole of its product.

Significantly, these British critiques of industrial capitalism were studied avidly by Marx and obviously formed the background to his own economic theory. On their own, however, they lacked another central element of the 'Marxian synthesis', to use George Lichtheim's phrase: the moment of political intervention, of revolutinary action. This, as we have seen already, could be derived from developments in France, from both the study of the French Revolution and the writings of Blanqui and his contemporaries. Residing in Paris in 1843/4, Marx encountered these at first hand. He also came into contract with the radical French working class movement, and there is some evidence that it was this contact that led Marx to identify the proletariat as the motor of revolutionary change, as he did in his essays on the *Jewish Question* and the *Introduction to the Critique of Hegel's Philosophy of Right* in 1843. The third component of Marx's theory, following Engels' famous schema, was German Idealist philosophy. From the writings of the Young Hegelians and, above all, those of Ludwig Feuerbach, Marx inherited the concept of alienation. In its original religious context – and Marx continued to believe that the 'criticism of religion is the premise of all criticism' – this stated that God had not created man in his image. Rather the reverse was true: in an uncertain world man had projected upon an imagined supernatural being his own faculties for love and his own capacity to change the world for the better. Man's own creation thus became alien to him and came increasingly to dominate him, robbing him of the opportunity of self-fulfillment in this world. Marx and his contemporary Moses Hess (1812-1875) both extended this critique of religion to the real world of the state and, above all, economics. They saw in the role of money and the cash nexus an analogue of God in the Feuerbachian schema: man created an economic order and money to provide for his needs but increasingly the market and money came to dominate man. The relationship between subject and predicate were reversed and mankind became the slave of an increasingly impersonal economic machine.

The aspects of this economic 'alienation' were most extensively developed by Marx in his so-called *Economic and Philosophical Manuscripts* of 1844. Analysing the operations of the capitalist economy and the limited understanding thereof in bourgeois economics – and it is important to realise that Marx's theory of alienation is not concerned with a general existential malaise but located in a particular arrangement of industrial capitalism – Marx identified several interlocking aspects of economic alienation. Logically the whole structure of alienation begins with the separation of the producer from his product, i.e. the capitalist system in which the worker's product is not his own but is appropriated by the capitalist. This *alienation from the product* engenders a number of consequences. Because the product belongs to the capitalist, whose interest is in its sale for a profit and not in the satisfaction of human needs, the activity of its production ceases to be truly satisfying, according to Marx. Men now work not to satisfy needs and thus to be fulfilled but simply in order to obtain wages. Work becomes a means rather than an end in itself. This renders it 'involuntary' and constitutes a second aspect of alienation: *alienation from the work process.* From this follows a further aspect: *alienation from the species being.* What Marx means by this is that men have ceased to be truly human under capitalist relations of production; for according to him what separates mankind from the animal world and constitutes the essence of humanity is satisfying human labour, labour to transform the natural world according to human needs, one's own and those of others. Finally there is man's *alienation from other men*: in a world in which men work simply in order to live, market relations determine human relations. Men relate to one another not as one human being to another but as workers competing for employment or as wage-payer to wage-earner. The end product of these relations is that mankind has become nothing more than a cog in a giant economic machine. Economic imperatives dominate human imperatives; and this is reflected in bourgeois economics, which treat human relations as relationships between things, between comodities.

There are a number of things to be noticed about this model of alienation. Firstly, its validity does not depend upon an empirical study of psychological malaise. In this schema a man can be happy and yet still alienated. Indeed, this is precisely what Marx means when he talks about 'false consciousness' and claims that the capitalist is alienated as well as the worker. This alienation, therefore, is not analogous to Durkheim's concept of 'anomie': for Durkheim propounded his concept to explain an observed psychologicl problem, namely suicide, whereas Marx's theory rests upon certain assumptions about what it is to be truly human. This is not to say that Marx's concept of alienation is utterly lacking in any empirical substance. He himself prepared a questionnaire for workers to express their attitudes towards their jobs on one occasion. He also recognised that the performance of exclusively mechanical tasks, the way in which modern techniques of production reduced the worker to a mere 'appendage of the machine', was profoundly unsatisfying. Modern sociology, especially in the United States, has adopted some of these insights in a campaign to make the performance of various tasks more appealing to the industrial work force. Yet it must be stressed that a contented workforce does not necessarily mean an unalienated one in Marxian terms. As long as production is for profit not use, then the whole structure of alienation as described by Marx remains; for work remains a means not an end, not the fully human realisation envisaged in the *Economic and Philosophical Manuscripts*.

In so far as Marx's theory of alienation locates its origin in the primacy of economic laws under capitalism, it also renders nonsensical those interpretations of Marxism which have reduced it to a vulgar economic determination. What Marx is saying is that economic laws dominate human activity under capitalism. But he is also saying that this is precisely what is wrong with capitalism, that man has ceased to be the active subject of history and has become its tool. This is why he describes history before the socialist revolution as 'pre-history'; for real history only begins when mankind reappropriates its own fate. This is the sense of Marx's repeated assertion that 'the proletariat must liberate itself'. This is so not only because no other class will do it or has an objective interest in doing it, although Marx certainly believed both these propositions, but because self-liberation, the worker's seizure of control over his own fate, is precisely what the revolution is about. As Marx wrote in the *German Ideology* in 1845/46: 'this revolution is necessary, therefore, not only because the ruling class can only be overthrown in such a way but also because only in a revolution can the class overthrowing it rid itself of the muck of ages and become fitted to found society anew'.

Now this concept of revolution is clearly at odds with the kind of Marxism subsequently popularised by Karl Kautsky and other German Social Democrats who expected the mere operation of the economic laws of capitalism to usher in the new order: for to wait upon economic laws clearly is a function of alienation. The revolution is not simply about the transition from one economic order to another, although it is certainly that as well. It is about the conquest of economic by human imperatives. If proletarian action is central to the Marxian image of socialist revolution, however, this also raises problems for certain Leninist conceptions which to a certain extent ascribe the prime revolutionary role to a vanguard of professional revolutionaries (see COMMUNISM). If revolution is about the *self*-liberation of workers, then it must be they who act and not their surrogates. Indeed, this was precisely the argument which Rosa Luxemburg deployed against Lenin's arguments in 1902 and which was repeated by the advocates of 'council communism', Anton Pannekoek and Gorter, in the wake of the Russian Revolution.

That the concept of alienation has such immediate import for revolutionary strategy perhaps explains why there has been a heated debate about the precise role of the concept in the later work (i.e. post 1844) of Marx. Some would argue that Marx's early humanism had little to do with his later economic and political theories which constitute the real core of 'scientific socialism'. This is especially true of the structuralist followers of the French Communist Party intellectual, Louis Althusser, who argued in the 1960s that there was an 'epistemological break' in the work of Marx which insinuated itself between the ahistorical humanism of the 1844 manuscrips and the repudiation of that past in the *Theses on Feuerbach* and *The German Ideology* of the following year. It is certainly true that Marx's later work embodies theories which are analytically distinct from the concept of alienation, in particular the materialist conception of history, which finds its clearest enunciation in the first hundred pages of the *German Ideology*, and an economic theory of exploitation, which culminates in *Das Kapital*. But this does not mean that Marx simply abandoned the concept of alienation: in fact the word and its substance recur throughout the *Ideology* and above all in the *Grundrisse* of 1859, in which notes Marx outlined his plan for a view of the world embodying both his early humanism and the theory of surplus value, the final and paradoxical outcome of classical economics. Furthermore, as early as the 1920s, before the discovery of the 1844 manuscripts, the great Hungarian Marxist Georg Lukacs uncovered the concept of alienation in the very body of what had often been regarded as an economic text book by vulgar interpreters, namely *Capital* itself. Lukacs demonstrated that it was no accident that this work had been given the subtitle of a *Critique of Political Economy* by Marx; for what the master was attempting to show was that the abstract units of bourgeois economics embodied human relationships. The telling phrase which expressed this criticism of classical political economy and the very real fact that under capitalism workers were reduced to commodities was 'Commodity fetishism'. We arrive again at a world in which economic imperatives obscur humanity's real potential for self-realisation.

It should also be pointed out that the concept of alienation which informs the *Economic and Philosophical Manuscripts* relates closely to the subsequent central concerns of Marx. The theme relates firstly to a specific set of relations under capitalism and rests upon an extensive acquaintance with classical economics. Furthermore, it clearly connects with the subsequent theory of exploitation, although it certainly does not spell out its detailed economic validation, in so far as the starting point is the separation of the producer from his product, i.e. a world in which the worker is forced to sell his labour and in which its purchaser expropriates the product. There are also connections between the idea of alienation from other men and the investigation of social class and theories of ideology: for Marx is implying that the role men perform in the market determines the relationships between them and their perspectives of the world. Again, however, the origins of Marx's theory of class and ideology clearly relate to empirical investigation and the earlier work of English economists and French historians, as he was fond of pointing out. It is fair to say, therefore, that although Marx never abandoned his early humanism, it was enriched by ideas with a distinct provenance, in particular the theory of surplus value and the materialist conception of history.

To give an adequate account of Marxian economics in this short space is obviously impossible; but there are several salient areas of investigation. Firstly and perhaps most importantly Marx demonstrated that the capitalist system could not survive without exploiting its workers; and this not because of any necessary moral failings on the part of grasping employers but rather for reasons inherent in the structure of capitalist production. In a system in which production was for profit not use, argued Marx, the source of that profit can be located in the extraction of surplus value. This accrues because the worker has only his labour power to sell to his employer in exchange for wages. But this exchange is not a fair one; for labour power is the only commodity which creates value. Hence the strength of capital over labour is reinforced even in this initial exchange. In fact the worker works for a certain length of time to achieve his pay; but this is longer than he would have to work at the same level of technological advance to produce goods to the value of those wages if he owned the product of his labour and did not have to produce his employer's profit. From that surplus labour accrues surplus value. Hence capitalism necessarily entails this form of exploitation: the worker does not receive the full value of his labour.

It is important to note that this theory of exploitation is different from others, for example Lassalle's 'iron law of wages' so vigorously criticised by Marx, which maintain quite simply that the worker is doomed to the lowest possible wages under capitalism. Marx is not saying that the worker is badly paid but rather that he does not receive the full value of his labour; and although these may come to the same thing in many circumstances, they are not necessarily synonymous. Indeed, Marx admitted that state intervention and trade union action could actually force up wage rates in the later volumes of *Capital*. With increases in productivity through the employment of advanced technology it was even possible for the length of the working day to be reduced and for wages to rise; but as long as the worker was forced to sell his labour power he remained subject to longer hours of work than were necessary to produce goods to the value of his wages and thus remained exploited.

These remarks apply equally to Marx's much misunderstood theory of 'impoverishment', according to which the worker becomes increasingly impoverished as capitalism develops. We have already seen that there were circumstances under which Marx could envisage improvements in wages. This suggests, as most commentators would now agree, that the concept of impoverishment is relative: what Marx is saying is not that wages will always hit an absolute minimum, although that is quite likely to be the case in a society in which the laws of capitalist production operate unfettered by various kinds of human action; but rather that the share of total production which accrues to the proletariat steadily diminishes. To put it another way, the wealth of capital advances faster than that of labour. Hence a concept of relative impoverishment which allows even for an absolute improvement in working class living standards.

Two other major aspects of Marx's economic theory which closely interlock

203

are the predictions of cyclical crisis and capital concentration. Production for profit and the competition that ensues therefrom result in the 'anarchy of production' which makes it impossible to measure the needs of the market. Furthermore, the falling rate of profit puts pressure on capital to invest in increasingly expensive technology and increase production; yet this ever expanding production is not matched by developments in the realm of consumption, for here there are limits to the wages that employers can afford to pay to their workforce if they are to remain profitable and survive against their competitiors. The result of this contradiction is recurrent economic crisis. On occasion Marx seems to suggest that capitalism is heading for one final crisis, although the later volumes of *Capital* would seem to contradict this conclusion. What is certainly true, however, is that this analysis saw economic depression and the ensuing unemployment not as a surface scar of the capitalist mode of production, but as an inescapable function of a mechanism in which production was for profit and entailed competition.

One final point about the theory of crisis. Even if Marx did believe that economic laws would lead to the collapse of capitalism as a necessary consequence of structural weaknesses, this is not the same as saying that economic laws will inevitably lead to socialism, as some latter-day Marxists seemed to imagine. The collapse of capitalism and the *creation* of socialism are analytically distinct. As Marx put it on one occasion: should capitalism collapse, then there would be an historical alternative, either a reversion to barbarism or social revolution. The transition to socialism would come from the active intervention of the proletariat in the historical process and not from the mere operation of impersonal economic laws.

Closely related to the theory of cyclical crisis was Marx's belief that capital would concentrate increasingly in a few hands. Small and relatively unprofitable units of production would be unable to resist the superior competition of large-scale, efficient producers, especially at times of depression when the market contracted and prices fell. This process of concentration was crucial for the Marxian prognosis in two respects. Firstly, capitalism had produced an increasingly large-scale and efficient economy; it had unleashed giant productive forces upon which the egalitarian society of the future would be constructed. For Marx, equality could not be built in conditions of poverty: that would simply be to spread misery evenly. Hence his thinking lacked the suspicion of modern enterprise and the hankering for the past which characterised much of French utopian socialism. The second consequence of the concentration of capital was the creation of the industrial proletariat in increasingly large numbers, the creation of the 'grave-diggers' of the capitalist order. This was important because it meant that the achievement of socialism was no longer just a pipe-dream: here was an alienated and exploited class with 'nothing to lose but its chains', a class with no property, a class with an interest in the destruction of the whole class system.

This raises the vexed question of what Marx meant by the term 'class'. His statement to the effect that capitalist society is increasingly characterised by a conflict between two dominant classes, the bourgeoisie and the proletariat, has left him open to criticisms which state that such a dichotomous model of social structure is simplistic and inaccurate. This misses the point. Marx was not saying that only two identifiable groups existed under capitalism. He criticised Ricardo for failing to recognise the emergence of intermediate professional strata (lawyers, doctors and the like) and admitted in *Capital* that his abstract characterisation of class in capitalist society did not apply to any existing historical society, not even to England. Furthermore, his own investigations of concrete historical developments, such as the famous *Eighteenth Brumaire of Louis Napoleon*, identify a host of social divisions, for example, between the lower and upper middle class, between landed and commercial interests etc. Why this apparent contradiction, therefore? Firstly, the problem is a question of definition. Marx reserved the term 'class' not for all observable social groups but only for those who both found themselves in a similar situation in the world of economic production and possessed a consciousness of their communal interests, i.e. there is a subjective as well as an objective dimension to the term. Secondly, Marx was not interested in providing a model of social stratification, but rather in the dynamics of social change. What he was interested in were those social groups whose struggles would result in the emergence of a qualitatively different social order. In fact those groups which he identified as classes were the bearers of specific modes of production. They were also groups which translated their class consciousness into political action; for, as Marx wrote in the *Communist Manifesto*, 'every class struggle is a political struggle'.

It was quite clear to Marx that the working class could not liberate itself through the activities of trade unions, although he did see the achievement of short-term concessions as beneficial to the proletariat in so far as they strengthened the proletariat for future struggles. The point was that economic concessions within the capitalist system could not remove the structural problems of capitalist production, namely unemployment and exploitation, which, as we have seen, follow logically from the private ownership of the means of production in the Marxian schema. Hence a revolution was always necessary to transform social relations. Furthermore, that revolution would be an international revolution; workers of the world in all countries had a similar interest in fighting against their capitalist oppressors, who had in any case created a world market in which individual nations became increasingly irrelevant. This interlocking of the international economy was also why Marx on occasion suggested that revolutions in the colonial countries, for example Ireland and China, might be the spark which would ignite a world revolution. The social revolution would also be a political revolution, according to the author of *Capital*. For the state in capitalist society and its various instruments – the laws, police, army – were the expression of the class interests of capital, and their conquest was therefore necessary both to defeat the historical enemy and to bring into being a new socialist society. When that society had been created, when classes had disappeared, then the state would disappear. The 'administration of people' would be replaced by the 'administration of things'. But in the transition from one society to another its apparatus would be exercised by the 'dictatorship of the proletariat'; although Marx never suggested that this was necessarily synonymous with violent, autocratic rule.

How was this revolution to be brought about? In the first place, we have already seen that Marx did not think that the simple operation of economic laws would bring about qualitative social change. That required the active intervention in the historical process of the proletariat. He criticised the 'crude materialist doctrine that men are the product of circumstance and upbringing and that changed men are the product of changed circumstances and changed upbringing' because it forgot that 'it is men who change circumstances and that the educator himself needs educating'. The materialist conception of history did not negate the role of human praxis; quite the opposite. In the *German Ideology* Marx stressed again and again that 'it is men who make history'. The purpose of that materialist conception of history was simply to counter the idealism and utopianism of some of the early socialists, who thought that the new society could be created virtually out of nothing by all right-thinking men. Marx was pointing out that socialism could only be created on the basis of a particular economic order and by an identifiable group of people with an objective interest in its creation.

Any attempt to discover *a* model of revolution in the work of Marx is doomed to failure. He had several. Not because he was confused or because he contradicted himself; but rather because he believed that different historical situations required different forms of action. Indeed, he specifically criticised a Russian reviewer of *Capital* for seeing in his work a kind of cosmic historical model applicable to all societies and situations. Thus in non-democratic France, still undergoing the early phase of industrialisation in the late 1840s, Marx seems to have thought in terms of a violent revolution. Later, in industrial and democratic England, and where the proletariat had already achieved a high level of organisation, he admitted the possibility of a peaceful transition to socialism. As he made clear in a famous speech in Amsterdam in 1872, it all depended upon the nature of the state and the maturity of the proletariat. This sensitivity to historical differences is equally evident in Marx's discussion of the possibilities of revolution in Tsarist Russia in his correspondence with the populist Vera Zasulich. Here Marx is even prepared to admit the possibility of a transition in Russia to socialism based upon the peasant commune, although this possibility is predicated upon social revolution elsewhere in Europe and the fact that so far capitalism had not made any great impact on the structure of Russian society.

Exactly how Marx saw the society of the future is difficult to say. His own historical sensitivity led him to refuse to 'write recipes for the cookshops of the future'; for the precise nature of socialist society would depend upon the circumstances under which it was brought into existence. In his *Critique of the Gotha*

Programme, however, Marx makes it clear that the transition to a new social order would be a lengthy one in which wages will only gradually be equalised. The earlier stages of this process will constitute 'socialism'. The fully-fledged liberation of mankind which sees the realisation of the dictum 'from each according to his capacity, to each according to his needs' will come later and will finally constitute 'communism'.

This complex doctrine was to be transformed by Marx's successors, as we will see. But it is of course true that his theory was not the only one which attracted the attention of both thinkers and workers in the second half of the nineteenth century. In fact in France, Proudhonism remained the ideology of a significant section of the French working class (see ANARCHISM; SYNDICALISM). In England, Marxism never really gained a hold at all. The practice and the theory of English socialism remained, indeed became increasingly, reformist, eschewing ideas of revolution and replacing them with gradual, piecemeal change. John Stuart Mill, for example, came to reject liberal economics but never broke utterly with liberalism (see LIBERALISM). He advocated a kind of welfare state which looks remarkably like what certain social-democratic governments have erected in parts of Western Europe in this century: a state with progressive taxes which would make some attempt to satisfy the needs of all the different sections of society. This gradualist and reformist approach found its apotheosis in the English Fabians, so-called because they claimed to base their strategy upon that of the Roman general Fabius Cunctator, who defeated Hannibal in a lengthy campaign which avoided head-on collision with the enemy. Edward Pease, Frank Podmore, Hubert Bland, Sidney Webb, George Bernard Shaw, Graham Wallace and Sydney Olivier all believed that the problem of poverty in modern society required urgent solution. Not surprisingly, however, for a group of professional middle class men and women living in the relative calm of Victorian Britain, the Fabians were committed to peaceful change through democratic methods. Indeed their basic strategy appears to have been 'permeation', the infiltration of their enlightened members into the existing institutions of government and the existing political parties. Socialism would come about not through class conflict and revolution, but through welfare legislation, which would finally lead to a more egalitarian society. The 'unearned increment' which the capitalist received at present would disappear, as would the capitalist class. Managerial tasks would now be performed by the community, or rather, by an enlightened state.

Another stream of reformist socialism could be found in Britain in the 1840s and subsequently in the beliefs of Charles Kingsley and Frederick Denison Maurice in the Mid-Victorian era: Christian Socialism. This embraced a concern for the plight of the poor with a vague notion that as all men were equal in the eyes of God, so man-made inequalities should be rectified. Christian Socialism also found an adherent in Saint-Simon, who believed that the new industrial order should be enthused by a new faith and whose *Le Nouveau Christianisme* is perhaps the first Christian Socialist tract. However, a socialism inspired by

Christianity need not necessarily be reformist, as is demonstrated in the case of the utopian communist Wilhelm Weitling in Germany in the 1840s. Weitling received his inspiration from the gospels and believed that a former God-given golden age had been destroyed by private property and the evils of money. All was to be saved, however, by the coming of the second golden age of communism, an age which would be inaugurated by an immediate uprising of forty thousand outlaws.

The reformist version of socialism did, however, also find roots in German soil. Johann Karl Rodbertus (1805-75), for example, remained a political conservative to the end of his days, with a firm belief in the values of autocratic monarchy. He did, however, recognise the existence of a social problem spawned by capitalism and liberalism. In the misery of the 'hungry forties' he identified the problems of economic depression and pauperism, and therefore demanded that the state intervene to control the operations of the free market and give the worker a fairer share of the product of his own labour, thus increasing purchasing power and reducing the possibility of crises of underconsumption.

It was from Rodbertus that the extraordinary Ferdinand Lassalle, subsequently to emerge as one of the founders of an independent labour movement in the Germany of the 1860s, acquired his theory of the 'iron law of wages'. According to Lassalle, the worker was doomed to receive ever-diminishing wages in the system of capitalist production. The only solution to this problem was for the workers to take over the means of production in the shape of producers' co-operatives. For these co-operatives to be viable, however, they would require a considerable injection of capital; and that could only come from the state: but only a state sympathetic to the working class and its problems could be guaranteed to help in this way. And according to Lassalle the only way in which this could in turn be guaranted was by the implementation of universal suffrage.

These theories took a strong hold on some sections of organised labour in Germany in the 1860s and early 1870s. Then, however, a combination of state repression and economic depression seemed to discredit 'state socialism' and validate Marx's predictions of economic crisis and his view of the state as an instrument of class rule to such an extent that by 1891 the German Social Democratic Party came to accept Marxism as its official ideology. This Marxism was essentially the Marxism of Karl Kautsky (1854-1938), the most influential populariser of scientific socialism after the death of Friedrich Engels, in 1895. Kautsky's Marxism seemed to follow Marx in its radical critique of existing society. It reiterated the theory of surplus value, cyclical crisis and class conflict. It was always revolutionary in the sense that it always rejected the possibility that piecemeal reform within the capitalism system could solve the problems of exploitation and unemployment. It also developed an economic theory of imperialism, variously explaining colonial expansion in terms of the needs of financial and industrial capital which could not be satisfied within the domestic market. However, this 'orthodox' Marxism, as it has come to be known, a Marxism propagated not only by Kautsky but also by Georgi Plekhanov in Russia and Jules Guèsde in France from the 1880s and which became the dominant intellectual stream in the Second International in the three decades before the First World War, did not combine its incisive critique of capitalism with any real tactical imperatives apart from the general injunction to 'organise and educate'. In part this may have reflected the impotence of German Social Democracy before the war. It was also the consequence of an almost fatalistic reading of Marx. Kautsky and many of his contemporaries came to Marx via Darwin, or rather a vulgarised rendering of the natural sciences; and they thought they saw in Marx a scientistic version of human development. They believed that Marx had discovered a set of laws which virtually *governed* human behaviour, about which human intervention could do little and which would more or less automatically usher in the socialist order. All they had to do was to sit and wait. Thus the moment of praxis so central to Marx's view of the world simply disappeared. This strange misreading of Marx was a consequence of a particular historical situation, in which the parties of labour seemed to be growing inexorably and yet remained as far away as ever from political power in continental Europe. It was also a product of a positivistic atmosphere of social Darwinism in intellectual life. But it was finally a misreading apparent in the work of Marx's great friend and collaborator, Friedrich Engels. Engels had suggested that the electoral strategy of the German socialist movement might be sufficient to bring it to power, although he remained much more sceptical of this than some of his successors in the ranks of the SPD. He had also attempted to unite general theories of natural and social science and, in the process, had given to the developments identified by Marx the status of natural laws. This was most obviously the case in his *Dialectics of Nature*, but equally true of his most popular propagandistic work, *Anti-Dühring*. This was the legacy inherited by Kautsky and his contemporaries.

The silence of 'orthodox Marxism' on tactical questions, which resulted from its optimistic fatalism, ran foul of both left and right wing socialists. On the left, Rosa Luxemburg, Anton Pannekoek, Israel Helphand (Parvus) and others began to attack Kautsky's position from about 1905 onwards, identifying it as 'passive radicalism' and advocating the adoption of a general strike to break out of the straight-jacket of inaction. On the right, the revisionists around Eduard Bernstein began to attack not only the absence of tactical conclusions in Kautskyite theory but also the premises it had borrowed from Marx. In the mid-1890s, at a point in time when the European economy was beginning to recover from depression, Bernstein denied the theories of capital concentration, cyclical crisis and inevitable revolution. Given this there was no point in sitting back in splendid isolation, relying exclusively on the proletariat and waiting for the great day that might never come. Instead, socialists should ally with progressive elements of the bourgeoisie, convinced of the moral rectitude of socialism or at least democratic values, stop talking about some distant revolution and concentrate on immediate, short-term reforms to better the lot of the working class. It is perhaps not surprising that the German who produced this ethical and gradualist version of the socialist message should have lived in exile in England for some of his life and have been influenced by the Fabian tradition.

The revisionist controversy was not without its echoes in Russia, where Kautsky could rely upon the support of Plekhanov, Lenin and Trotsky in his defence of revolutionary orthodoxy against reformist tendencies (see COMMUNISM). Given the repressive and autocratic nature of the Tsarist state, Russian socialism was more or less bound to adopt a revolutionary formulation. However, that formulation existed in a variety of shapes. In an agrarian society such as Russia, ideas of socialism in the mid-nineteeth century could scarcely relate to industry or an industrial proletariat. As in the case of Alexander Herzen (1812-70), socialism in Russia looked to the peasant commune, the 'mir', with its egalitarian tradition of periodic land redistribution, to form the basis of a regenerated Russian society; although on the question of how this would come about Herzen said little but seems to have subscribed to some kind of gradualist approach. Not so Michael Bakunin, most famous as violent anarchist and hater of all states and institutions with any kind of central direction. For Bakunin, salvation would again come from the peasants; but this time it would come in the shape of a violent revolution (see ANARCHISM).

Thus the idea of an ideal society based upon peasant socialism found two different expressions. There were those who looked to violent action, even conspiratorial deeds like Sergei Nechaev (1847-82) and Peter Tkachev (1844-86), whilst some of the later populists advocated peaceful propaganda in the countryside.

By the 1890s populism (see POPULISM) was far from dead; but it had joined by Russian Marxism. The peasants had failed to respond to the message of student agitators. Individual terrorism had changed little. Russia was beginning to industrialise and an emergent factory proletariat engaged in strike activity in Moscow and St Petersburg. Here was fertile soil for Plekhanov, the 'father of Russian Marxism' to spread his ideas. In many ways these ideas reflected those of Kautsky and other 'orthodox' Marxists; but soon Russian Social Democracy experienced a set of debates that were unique and which were to have lasting consequences. In 1902 Lenin published a pamphlet entitled *What is to be Done?* in which he argued that the working class could not achieve a genuinely revolutionary consciousness if left to its own devices. It would remain at what he called 'trade union consciousness' or 'economism', i.e. the pursuit of immediate, short-term ends within the capitalist system. Scientific socialism could only be imported into the ranks of the proletariat by renegade members of the bourgeois intellegentsia. This theory of 'consciousness from without' was far from novel. Indeed, Lenin was explicitly following Kautsky on this particular point. Moreover, it seemed to make sense of the insight of Engels in Victorian Britain which saw that industrial militancy in terms of strikes and trade union organisation were not necessarily synonymous with political radicalism. However, Lenin took the argument a stage further by advocating the formation of a tightly-knit party of professional revolutionaries and by implying that the ideologically impure should be expelled from the movement. This resulted in 1903 in the famous split between the Bolshevik and Meshevik wings of Russian Social Democracy, with the Mensheviks arguing for a broadly-based party with relatively open membership. Herein lay the germs of the subsequent division of the socialist movement into social democratic and communist ranks (see COMMUNISM).

It soon became clear, however, that the divisions between Bolsheviks and Mensheviks were not solely about the exclusivity of party membership. In the course of the 1905 Revolution in Russia, Lenin distanced himself increasingly from Plekhanov, who had been in agreement on the question of party organisation, and even further from the Mensheviks by seeing the forthcoming revolution in his homeland not as a bourgeois revolution made by the proletariat in alliance with the progressive bourgeoisie – Lenin argued that the latter did not exist in Russia – but as a bourgeois revolution made by the proletariat and a revolutionary peasantry. In the course of the First World War and in unacknowledged imitation of Trotsky, he even took the argument a stage further and argued that a telescoping of the revolutionary process was possible in Russia and that the forthcoming upheavals could mark a direct transition to socialism, although this latter possibility was predicated upon revolution in the advanced industrial countries of Western Europe as well.

These various theories of socialism have had a direct impact upon the world as we know it. The reformist variant has seen application in Scandinavia and much of Europe in the last few years in the form of the welfare state. On the other hand, revolutionary Marxism in its Leninist variant has offered to the Third World the possibility of a direct transition from pre-capitalist modes of production to the new socialist order. It also informs the activity and ideology of a significant section of the European labour movement, even in the advanced capitalist states. It is perhaps the case that as long as capitalism survives, so too do the criticisms of its structural weaknesses.

Further reading

George Lichtheim, *Short History of Socialism*
  The Origins of Socialism
  Marxism: A Historical and Critical Study
G. D. H. Cole, *History of Socialist Thought*
Carl Landauer, *European Socialism* (2 vols)
Claude Willard, *Socialisme et Communisme Français*
George Lichtheim, *Origins*
Frank Manuel, *The Prophets of Paris*
David McLellan, *The Thought of Karl Marx*
Leszek Kolakowski, *Main Currents of Marxism* (Vols 2 & 3)
F. Venturi, *Roots of Revolution*
A. Walicki, *The Controversy over Capitalism*
M. Beer, *A History of British Socialism*
M. Cole, *The Story of Fabian Socialism*

Syndicalism

Syndicalism is the name given to a particular form of trade unionism which developed in France under the name of *Syndicalisme Révolutionnaire* after 1895. Similar groups flourished in Western Europe and America.

In France in the late 1890s, Syndicalism grew out of the workers' disillusionment and bitterness over what they regarded as the inability of political parties to understand and tackle effectively the social problem. The libertarian and violent tradition inspired by Proudhon and Blanqui, which had permeated the French labour movement in the nineteenth century, was considerably strengthened when leading anarchists chose deliberately to appeal to the trade unions in the early 1890s. At Nantes in 1894, the national federation of trade unions rejected Guede's attempt to subordinate the trade union movement to his Marxist party. From then on, Syndicalism developed within two workers' organisations: the *Confédération Générale du Travail*, set up in 1895, and the *Fédération des Bourses du Travail*. The former was a loose confederation of trade unions, whether or not organised in industrial federations. The *Bourses*, which were gradually established in most major industrial cities, allowed workers of various trades to meet and discuss common problems, to educate themselves, and obtain information about employment and social aid. The Secretary of the *Fédération de Bourses*, Pelloutier, did much to develop the basic ideas of Syndicalism and to spread them among workers throughout France. When the two organisations merged in 1902, Syndicalism was given fresh impetus and remained the basic philosophy of the majority of the French labour movement until the outbreak of the First Wrold War. The Syndicalists, like the Marxists (see SOCIALISM), denounced the injustice of the wage system. The existing state of war between the emplyers' class and the exploited proletariat would end in a revolution and the establishment of a classless, collectivist society of producers. Unlike the Marxists and other socialists, however, the Syndicalists believed that political action did not serve the best interests of the working class since political parties were prone to compromise with the bourgeoisie in order to obtain or retain power. They adhered to the anarchist's view, that, the state being coercive by nature, its destruction should be the main objective of the revolutionary struggle. The trade unions would be the spearhead of the irresistible workers' mass movement. Pending the overthrow of capitalism they would lead the daily fight for higher wages, better working conditions and shorter hours and thus develop the worker's consciousness to prepare them for the final revolution. Having rejected the help and guidance of political parties, the Syndicalists urged the workers to make use of purely 'economic' methods in their fight against the employers and the state. The ultimate weapon is the general strike, which will paralyse the industrial society, dissolve the state apparatus, and pave the way for a free society. The Syndicalist conception of this free, ideal society, notably in France, owes much to the anarchist ideology. Pouget, in his book *Comment nous ferons la révolution*, forsees a 'society of producers' in which trade unions would provide the nuclei of a loose federation of industries managed by the workers at local, regional and national levels.

For a time, Syndicalism appeared to draw much of its inspiration from leading anarchist thinkers such as Proudhon and Kropotkin (see ANARCHISM), and the term *Anarcho-Syndicalism* is often used to describe the early phase of the movement. After 1906, however, when the CGT in its celebrated *Charter of Amiens* stressed the paramount role of the trade union movement in the class stuggle, leading anarchists like Malatesta criticised the organisational aspects of Syndicalism which, they feared, would lead to excessive centralism and exclusiveness.

In Italy and Spain, where the labour movement had been deeply influenced by anarchist doctrines, Syndicalism also developed into powerful groups. In 1912 the Italian Syndicalists under Labriola broke away from the Socialist *Confederazione Generale del Lavoro* (CGL) and, two years later, they set up the *Unione Sindicale Italiana*. In Spain the *Confederación Nacional de Trabajo* (CNT) was founded in 1911 on the model of the French CGT. It soon became a powerful force, not only amongst industrial workers of Catalonia but also in the rural South where Anarchism had been kept alive.

Syndicalism in the United States developed as a minority movement which reached the height of its power between 1908 and 1914. Its history is complex. In the 1890s the propaganda of Most, Goldman and other anarchists had influenced the newly-arrived immigrant workers in the mines and textiles factories. These workers expected little of the *American Federation of Labour* whose main objective was the protection of the relatively privilged skilled workers. Anarcho-Syndicalism thus grew as a crude and violent movement among poor immigrants who fought in isolation for survival. The foundation of the *Industrial Workers of the World* (IWW) in 1905 gave shape and organisation to the considerable industrial and political potential represented by the mass of unorganised labour. From its very foundation, however, the IWW was sharply divided on the question of political action. By 1908, the 'Bummery Group' led by 'Big Bill' Haywood – who like the French Syndicalists utterly rejected any alliance with political parties – had triumphed over De Leon's group, who favoured close ties with the Marxist-inspired Socialist Labour Party. Despite De Leon's opposition, which led him to set up his own politically-oriented version of the IWW, known as the 'Detroit IWW', from then on the movement as a whole took a distinct syndicalist turn. Between 1909 and 1914 the IWW led a number of successful strikes, but after 1917 the Syndicalist movement suffered from the repression which befell most radical groups in the United States, and it was all but extinct by the end of the war.

English Syndicalism shared many characteristics with its American counterpart. In both countries massive industrialisation had led to the formation of powerful and somewhat conservative craft unions, which Syndicalists strove to re-activate or supplant. The idea that powerful and well-organised industrial trade union federations were essential if capitalism was to be effectively challenged dominated the development of Syndicalism in England. The movement grew swiftly on the return of Mann from Australia, where he had witnessed the corruption and resulting ineffectiveness of the traditional trade union organisations. Mann was familiar with Syndicalist developments in both France and the United States. Rather than setting up new syndicalist unions having close links with a radical party, as advocated by the British *Socialist Labour Party*, English Syndicalists favoured penetrating the existing industrial trade unions. During the 'Great Unrest' of the years 1911 and 1912, the Syndicalist movement grew rapidly, especially in South Wales where its influence had a decisive effect on radicalising the strikes.

In the years immediately preceding the First World War, Syndicalism had become a force to be reckoned with. The mass strikes of 1911-13, the threat of war and the workers' disillusionment with traditional trade unionism had encouraged many unskilled and semi-skilled workers to espouse the Syndicalists' approach to the class struggle. In 1913 an international syndicalist conference was held in London, but agreement could not be reached on the formation of an international syndicalist organisation. The war cut short the development of Syndicalism in most countries. Many of its leaders were called up or jailed. After the Bolshevik revolution, communism (see COMMUNISM) attracted some of its most prominent activists like Romer and Monatte in France, Mann in England, Nin in Spain and Haywood in the United States. In France the CGT, after co-operating with the government in the war effort, now abandoned its revolutionary goals and methods and sought to secure a gradual reform of the capitalist system for the benefit of its members. In other countries Syndicalism was either crushed by fascist dictatorships, absorbed by communist-inspired trade unions or rendered ineffective by a gradual improvement of living standards which led most trade union organisations to adopt a moderate reformist policy. Only in Spain did Syndicalism regain its strength, after the revolution of 1931. Until the eve of the Second World War the CNT remained the best example of an anarcho-syndicalist de-centralised working-class movement with a membership approaching two million in 1937. Towards the end of the Civil War, however, the influence of the CNT waned as Spanish anarchists became demoralised by political compromises and military ineffectiveness.

Despite its far-reaching, almost messianic, revolutionary claims, Syndicalism was clearly associated with the specific stage of development reached by the labour movemnt at the turn of the century. For this reason it was unlikely to survive the spread of communism in the 1920s, the rise of dictatorships in the 1930s and, above all, the change in the economic and social environment brought about by two world wars. Nevertheless the influence of Syndicalism on modern attitudes is far from negligeable.

In the late 1960s, it coalesced with libertarian and other radical philosophies in search of a more humane and equalitarian society. Today, as in the 1900s, in the countries where it was once powerful it continues to instil in the labour movement a distaste of centralism, bureaucracy and mass organisation, to deprecate state authority and, in time of acute crisis, to welcome the use of violence in furtherance of its economic aims.

Selected Further Reading

J. Joll, *The Anarchists*
R. Rocker, *Anarcho-Syndicalism*
B. Russell, *Roads to Freedom: Socialism, Anarchism, and Syndicalism*
IN ENGLAND
  E. Burdick, *Syndicalism and Industrial Unionism in England until 1918*, unpublished Ph.D. thesis, Oxford, 1952.
  B. Holton, *British Syndicalism 1900-1914*
IN FRANCE
  H. Dubief, *Le Syndicalisme Révolutionnaire*
  F. F. Ridley, *Revolutionary Syndicalism in France*
  F. Pelloutier, *Histoire des Bourses du Travail*
IN SPAIN
  G. Brennan, *The Spanish Labyrinth: An Account of the Social and Political Background of the Civil War*
IN THE USA
  P. E. Brissenden, *The IWW: A Study of American Syndicalism*

Ultramontanism

This is the name given to a doctrine of spiritual jurisdiction in the Catholic Church which has had political and social effects of the first importance. Ultramontanism postulates the absolute authority of the Pope in all questions of faith and morals, inclusive of political morality. The first Vatican Council (1869-70) marked the substantial victory of ultramontane teaching within the Church by its definition of Papal infallibility. The doctrinal restatement and institutional reforms of the second Vatican Council nearly a century later, apparently liberalising in their character, were implemented by a determined exercise of Papal sovereignty to overcome the resistance of ecclesiastical and political conservatives. This may well prove to have been the most significant feature of a reforming period in the Church's history. In lay politics, ultramontanes generally upheld the restoration of the pre-1789 order in Europe, so far as that was possible, after the fall of Napoleon I. The association of liberalism (see LIBERALISM) and democracy with anti-clericalism made this alliance natural for a while: extremely influential theorists like Comte Joseph de Maistre (d. 1821) (see CONSERVATISM) and the Vicomte de Bonald (d. 1840) wrote as if it were a dogmatic truth. But the traditional pragmatism of the Church and Papacy

215

soon reasserted itself in two regions far apart, the Low Countries and South America. When Catholic Belgium successfully rebelled against her union, decided at the Congress of Vienna, with the Protestant-dominated Dutch state under the authoritarian rule of King William I, the revolt and the liberal constitution of independent Belgium received Papal approval as a special case. Similarly, Rome came to terms with South American republics that had thrown off Spanish colonial rule. At the same time, the Abbé de Lamennais (d. 1854) was condemned by Gregory XVI in 1832 for identifying the future of the Church with democracy. The Church, as Pope Leo XIII reiterated in his encyclical *Immortale Dei* (1885), was not committed to any particular form of government.

To this day, there are ultramontane conservatives who adhere to the conviction that the Papacy, if true to itself, must side with the political Right. Rome and the Right have always had in common their emphasis on an ordered society which is organic in nature. Hence the understanding that existed between the Vatican and right-wing régimes during the long period after the 1914–18 war when democratic institutions and liberal economics fell into discredit in one European country after another. In its first year, Hitler's Germany signed a Concordat which guaranteed the internal independence of the Church, but exacted an oath of allegiance to the Third Reich from bishops on appointment and declared the priesthood to be on the same footing as civil servants. Hitler had just suppressed the Catholic Centre party along with all other political parties except the National Socialists, despite the Centre's instrumentality in his capture of supreme power by constitutional methods. To the Church, in Germany as in Italy (see FASCISM) (where the Vatican discarded a stronger Catholic mass party to pave the way for agreement with Mussolini) Christian democracy (see CHRISTIAN DEMOCRACY) was only a means, without absolute value, to unchanging ends. Those ends were the greatest possible freedom and security for the Church's religious and ecclesiastical activities, together with some social legislation in the spirit of Papal pronouncements since Leo XIII's encyclical *Rerum Novarum* (1891). Forms of government differed too much, according to the historical development of individual states, for the Church to express a definitive preference among them. Circumstances dictated Vatican policy. The Christian democratic parties which it allowed to die without protest in Italy and Germany continued to receive positive encouragement from Rome in other places such as Belgium. In advance of European peace after the 1939–45 war, the Roman Curia prepared for new political and social conditions by actively fostering the re-emergence and extension of Christian democracy. The curial functionary specially concerned with this shift of policy under Pius XII was Monsignor G. B. Montini, the future Paul VI (d. 1978). Such variations on a basic principle could not have been made with tangible results unless the Papacy exercised, through its spiritual authority, a profound influence over Catholics in different countries. The doctrine called ultramontane contributed powerfully to that influence. Nothing, perhaps, demonstrates the reality and flexibility of Papal authority more strikingly than the uneasy but viable relationships recently worked out by its agency between Church and government in those officially atheistic Marxist states of Eastern Europe with Catholic or partly Catholic populations.

From the Church's experience in the United States, and Daniel O'Connell's achievement in Ireland, the Papacy realised the potential of democracy for safeguarding and promoting the interests of Catholicism. The famous Syllabus of Errors (1864), issued by Pius IX in seemingly obscurantist defiance of modernity found 'progress, liberalism and recent civilisation' irreconcilable with Catholic truth: but, as with other such statements, ends, not means, were in question. The Church could never accept the ultimate validity of rival principles to her own: but there was no reason why she should not continue to turn the weapons of antagonistic liberals and democrats against them. By deploying their concentrated voting power, urged on by priests instructed by the success of O'Connellite nationalism in Ireland, poor Irish immigrants improved their position in the aggressively Protestant United States of the mid-nineteenth century. Daniel O'Connell (d. 1847) fought British liberalism, especially the aristocratic Whigs, and disliked much about American democracy. An admirer and correspondent of Jeremy Bentham, (see UTILITARIANISM) he had close links with British middle-class radicals: but his deepest beliefs were quite alien to them, as they came to see. His economic liberalism did not extend to sacrificing the Irish peasantry to efficient agriculture. He was a demagogue of genius, something disturbing to British associates, whose intellectual commitment to a popular franchise lacked a strong emotional basis. Above all, he was a devout and ultramontane Catholic who sought and obtained the clerical support and participation characteristic of the Irish national movement then and afterwards. Yet he insisted on lay leadership, and opposed Roman interference with its conduct: the Papacy should provide inspiration, not direction. The attachment to the peasantry, the populism and the ultramontanism were all reproduced in the Catholic mass parties that arose in Europe within thirty years of his death. Ludwig Windthorst (d. 1891), leader of the German Centre party in Bismarck's day, tried to imitate O'Connell's stance towards the Papacy, less effectively. No one, arguably, did more than O'Connell to convince the Catholic Church, by the religious and political victories he won over the British government and Parliament, that, where the conditions were suitable, she had a great deal to gain from bringing the people into politics.

Further reading

M. P. Fogarty, *Christian Democracy in Western Europe, 1820-1953*
E. E. Y. Hales, *Pio Nono*
A. C. Jemolo, *Church and State in Italy, 1815-1950*
M. Oakeshott, *The Social and Political Doctrines of Contemporary Europe*
A. Rhodes, *The Vatican in the Age of the Dictators, 1922-1945*
A. R. Vidler, *Prophecy & Papacy: a Study of Lamennais, the Church and the Revolution*

Utilitarianism

Utilitarianism emerged as a political ideology in Britain at the end of the eighteenth century and beginning of the nineteenth. It was associated particularly with the work of Jeremy Bentham (1748-1832) and his followers, known variously as the 'Utilitarians' 'Benthamites' or 'philosophic Radicals'. Its growth coincided with the early industrial revolution and, despite (or perhaps because of) its radical and reformist character, it provided the most coherent blueprint and self-justification for the developing bourgeois society.

The roots of this new system of ideas were firmly embedded in the scientific aspirations and ethical dilemmas of the eighteenth century 'Enlightenment' (see THE ENLIGHTENMENT). One major hope of Enlightenment thinkers was to construct a science of society, emulating in the social sphere what Newton achieved in the physical. But Newton's method was ambiguous and the search for a social science took two different directions. Some sought scientific knowledge in generalisations from observed phenomena. Others looked for a single, universal principle which would explain social behaviour as gravity had explained the behaviour of physical bodies. This they found in the axiom that human psychology can be explained, in terms of the pursuit of pleasure and the avoidance of pain. The ethical dilemmas of the Enlightenment arose from the weakening of the ethical certainties of Christianity by the insistence that all knowledge, including the knowledge of good and evil, is derived not from revelation or ideas inherent in the mind, but from human experience. In this ethical vacuum, there emerged a new source of moral values in which pleasure and pain are the sole standards of right and wrong. It was from the confluence of these two intellectual movements, the one psychological and the other ethical, that eighteeenth-century Utilitarianism, above all that of Bentham, evolved.

What were the articles of this Utilitarian creed? The first was that men act to maximise their own interests: on the Benthamite definition, their own happiness. Secondly, moral codes should be based on the principle of general utility: the greatest happiness of the greatest number. Thirdly, this principle of utility ought also to be the standard governing legislative rules and political policies.

One difficulty in this theory is an apparent contradiction between its psychological premises and its ethical injunctions. If men are necessarily dedicated to the pursuit of their own happiness, what is the point of urging them to follow a moral principle, the general utility, which might well militate against their own interests? The Utilitarians suggested two answers to this dilemma, with very different political implications. One was that men's natural pursuit of their own interests would automatically further the general utility or, to put this another way, that there is a sphere in which a natural harmony of interest

218

prevails. This was a familiar theme in British social thinking, best summed up in Mandeville's famous dictum, 'Private vices, public benefits', but most fully developed in classical economic theory, whose basic elements were accepted and expanded by Utilitarians such as Ricardo and James Mill. Self-interested men will naturally generate a productive and commercial system maximising general utility. Seeking the means to their own happiness, they produce goods and services which can be exchanged for goods and services they desire. The market mechanism itself will promote the efficient investment of resources and labour. So, at least in the sphere of commercial relations, governmental intervention is not necessary to achieve a reconciliation between individual aspirations and general utility. The Utilitarians could therefore urge a non-interventionist 'night-watchman' rôle for the state.

However, the other response to the Utilitarian dilemma was less critical of governmental intervention. The egoistic drives of individuals can be brought into line with the requirements of general utility by law operating through sanctions. By penalizing actions undesirable on utility grounds, legislators can ensure that rational egoists, seeking to avoid punishment, will contribute to the greatest happiness of the greatest number. Since the infliction of pain is always an evil, legislators should be niggardly with punishment; and, since those subject to law are rational and self-interested the threatened punishments need be only just sufficient to outweigh the possible benefits of the crime. This was the basis of Benthan's advocacy of legal reform, and particularly his demand for the limiting of penal sanctions to what was required by deterrence.

There were then a number of different and divergent strands in Utilitarian ideology: support for laisser-faire policies in the economic sphere; a justification for government interference where social harmony could not be achieved through market mechanisms; and a defence of the classic liberal position that non-restriction of liberty needs no defence, but intrusions on it always require justifications (see LIBERALISM). It thus provided ideological backing for the liberal concern with individual freedom, most particularly in the economic sphere, whilst at the same time supporting a reformist thrust in public administration.

One difficulty Bentham did not face in his early writings was how disinterested legislators, laying down rules to maximize the general utility, could be found amongst men acknowledged as psychologically committed to the pursuit of self-interest. Only after the turn of the eighteenth century did Utilitarians address this constitutional problem. They found the solution in political democracy, and became leading advocates of a radical reform of Parliament. Self-interested MPs could be transformed into disinterested legislators only if they were made responsible to and removeable by a democratic electorate. The theoretical difficulty remained, for the problem was now how egoistic electors, using their votes to further their own interests, could be induced to support policies required by general utility. More specifically, how could the propertyless, who would form the majority of any democratic electorate, be induced to respect the existing distribution of property, whose preservation all Utilitarians agreed was essential on utility grounds. It became one of the most delicate and difficult tasks of Utilitarian theory to argue that democracy would pose no threat to the stability of property.

In one form or another, Utilitarian thought continued to dominate British social thinking until the emergence of neo-Idealist thinking and 'new Liberalism' at the end of the nineteenth century. John Stuart Mill attempted to broaden the Utilitarian ethic by distinguishing between qualities of pleasures and by identifying as a central part of self-interest the individual's development as a social being. Herbert Spencer attemted to give a new base to *laisser-faire* positions and the hedonistic ethic by an appeal to evolutionary thought. But, despite these attempts at adaptation, the Utilitarian position was to weaken before the growing demand that the state should undertake a more positive role in social regulation. Nevertheless, the practical effects of Utilitarian ideas and the political activities of Utilitarians were important and sometimes decisive in the areas of judicial, colonial, electoral, administrative and economic reforms. In all of these areas, the thrust of the creed was towards different and not altogether compatible ends – lessening government intervention and making government intervention more efficient, encouraging *laisser-faire* and reforming the structures of public administration.

Further reading

L. Stephen, *The English Utilitarians*
E. Halevy, *The Growth of Philosophic Radicalism*
J. Plamenatz, *The English Utilitarians*
J. Skintrager, *Bentham*
B. Parekh (ed.), *Jeremy Bentham*
J. Lively & J. Rees, *Utilitarian Logic and Politics*

Whiggism

Whiggism features in both British and American political history. Whigs ruled Britain under limited and constitutional monarchy for the greater part of two centuries following the Glorious Revolution of 1688. The name was originally a seventeenth-century term of abuse, from the Scots dialect word for the uncouth inhabitants of the Western Lowlands, a region strongly against dynastic right in the Exclusion crisis of 1679–81. The genealogy of the modern Tory party goes back to a split among the Whigs in 1783–4; William Pitt the Younger (d. 1806), the first in the succession of Tory leaders since then, never called himself anything other than a Whig. The essence of Whiggism was oligarchy from the great Revolution families like the Russells downwards through a society based on property, clientage and deference in the eighteenth century, and much less changed than used to be thought by the spectacular growth of modern industry, towns and population that commenced after 1750. The old Tory party that expired by 1760 and the new one of the Pittites were similarly oligarchical but at no time were they dominated to the same extent by a few families at the top. Anti-monarchism among the Whigs lapsed soon after the 1688 Revolution, to be revived under George III (1760-1820), and only to become irrelevant when royal powers passed very largely into ministerial hands, Whig or Tory, in the early nineteenth century. The Whigs' division into supporters and opponents of George III had the effect of making the latter sympathise, up to a point, with the American and French revolutions. The Whigs who did not enlist under Pitt thus became liberals abroad and, to a lesser extent, at home. Although Anglicans, their traditional championship of Protestant Nonconformity's interests helped to move them in a liberal direction as the numbers and influence of Nonconformists increased. They were moderate reformers, bent on preserving aristocratic primacy by calculated concessions, as in the famous Reform Act of 1832. When Palmerston and Gladstone called themselves Liberals instead of Whigs, this was done to relieve the party from the imputation of being too exclusively aristocratic in its leadership. Every Liberal cabinet until 1886 continued to be heavily aristocratic and landed, while the social composition of the party's MPs altered in favour of the business and professional classes. In that year came the disruption of the party over the question of Irish Home Rule. A large majority of its peers and big landowners seceded, accompanied by some middle-class MPs, to form the Liberal Unionist alliance with the Tories. This political upheaval really marked the end of the Whigs as a distinct body, if the brand of conservative liberalism with which they had imbued the party long survive their departure (see LIBERALISM)

American Whiggism was a shortlived phenomenon, having an organised existence for some twenty years from the mid-1830s. A reaction against Jacksonian democracy, the Whig party drew together men of substantial property in the North and South of the United States. They took the appellation of Whig in a bid to assert that they stood firmly in the tradition of the historic American Whigs, the rebels against Britain, and so to glean needed popularity. Forming the third main element in the Whig coalition of interests, the egalitarian but expanding communities of the Mid-West were attracted to the Whigs by the prospect of partnership with North-Eastern capitalists. Professional men – lawyers, clergy and most university teachers – very widely turned to the Whigs from the excesses of Jacksonian democracy. The Whigs also successfully exploited racial feeling, Southern fears of negro revolt, and Northern alarm at the massive immigration of Irish paupers, which did not prevent Whig cotton manufacturers in New England from eagerly employing cheap Irish labour and thriving on it. In the nature of things, the party was too disparate in its make-up to endure. Slavery was the solvent. The 'conscience Whigs', opposed to the 'peculiar institution', and the 'cotton Whigs' fell out. The Whigs had won two presidential elections with General Harrison in 1840 and Zachary Taylor in

1848; but their decline was rapid. The Republican party which succeeded them was no substitute, for the disintegration of the Whigs removed an important obstacle to the violent collision of North and South.

Further reading

W. E. Binkley, *American Political Parties: their Natural History*
A. Mitchell, *The Whigs in Opposition, 1815-1830*
D. Southgate, *The Passing of the Whigs, 1832-1886*
F. Thistlethwaite, *The Great Experiment*

Zionism

Like many other ideologies, modern Zionism emerged as the transmutation of a religious impulse into secular politics. In certain respects a revolt against Jewish tradition and a radical attempt to break out of the parochial mould of Jewish history Zionism as an ideology has never altogether discarded the past. It has been able to draw on an age-old belief, sanctified through ceremony, ritual and prayer, in the restoration of the Jews to Zion (synonymous with Jerusalem) while politicising this tradition and giving it new meaning and content. In place of an almost dried-up tradition looking for the advent of a Jewish Messiah at the end of time, Zionism substituted a secular, historical messianism strongly influenced by the nineteenth century cult of progress and science.

In origin the Zionist movement derives from the disintegration of the Jewish religious tradition and community life and from the crisis of Jewish identity brought about by emancipation. However, its first theoreticians, Rabbi Yehuda Alkalai (1798-1878), Rabbi Zvi Hirsch Kalischer (1795-1874) and the German socialist Moses Hess (1812-1875) exercised little influence because European Jewry in the mid-nineteeth century was still preoccupied with the possibility of full social integration and with religious reform. But growing disenchantment with the ideology of assimilation led to the birth of Zionism as a political movement in the 1880s and 90s. The idea of a Jewish national renaissance, which would achieve the emancipation that the modern world had offered the Jews but failed to deliver, became the inspiration for the diverse schools of Zionist thought which emerged.

The Pograms in Tsarist Russia in 1881, which led to a mass migration of Russian Jewry, suggested to Leo Pinsker (1821-1891) a reinterpretation of the whole of post-exilic Jewish history as an insoluble confrontation with anti-semitism (see ANTI-SEMITISM). In his *Auto-emancipation* (1882) Pinsker diagnosed hatred of Jews as a hereditary, psychopathological phenomenon rooted in the permanent minority status of Jews as homeless wanderers in the *Galut* (exile). Only a policy of territorial concentration and planned colonisation of a land where Jews would form the majority, would enable them to be accepted as equals in the modern world. Pinsker's theories inspired the *Hibbat Zion* (Lovers of Zion) movement in Russia and Eastern Europe to settle Jewish farmers and artisans in Palestine (then under Turkish sovereignty). This policy of the gradual consolidation of Jewish settlements was also advocated by the Russian Zionist philosopher Ahad Ha'am (1856-1927), the foremost theoretician of the Hebrew cultural renaissance. Ahad Ha'am was a dedicated Jewish nationalist whose 'spiritual' Zionism was primarily an attempt to preserve the moral values of Judaism through the establishment of a cultural centre in Palestine, rather than to solve the material plight of the Jews. He warned against excessive reliance on power and diplomacy, against attempts to 'normalise' the condition of the Jews through the creation of a Jewish State and against ignoring the Arab problem in Palestine.

The emergence of Zionism as a fully-fledged political ideology was the work of the Austro-Hungarian journalist, Theodor Herzl (1860-1904) whose pamphlet *Der Judenstaat* (1896) became the classic text of the movement. Herzl's philosophy was a reaction to the collapse of political liberalism and the rise of racist and *völkisch* nationalism in Central Europe. The political successes of Anti-Semitism in Vienna and the experience of the Dreyfus Affair in France (see ANTI-SEMITISM) convinced Herzl of the ubiquity and inevitability of Jew-hatred. Anti-Semitism had made the Jews into 'one people' and the 'Jewish question' into an international political issue whose only solution lay in the creation of a Jewish State, guaranteed by the great powers. Herzl established the First Zionist Congress and the official organ of the movement, *Die Welt* ('The World') and negotiated with European statesmen and diplomats to win a charter for the colonisation of Palestine. Though unsuccessful in these endeavours, Herzl's charismatic personality and flair for political organisation gave a new impetus to Zionism, especially among the impoverished and oppressed Jews of Russia and Eastern Europe.

Herzl's diplomatic objectives were achieved by Chaim Weizmann (1874-1952), the Russian Jewish leader who obtained the Balfour Declaration from the British Government in 1917. Weizmann's 'synthetic' Zionism combined Herzl's diplomacy with the moral philosophy of Ahad Ha-am, the empirical rigour of Western science with traditional Jewish values. As leader of the world Zionist movement between the wars, Weizmann's liberal, humanist outlook, his pragmatic approach to colonisation, his policy of collaborating with the British authorities under the League of Nations mandate and his attempts at accommodation with the Palestinian Arabs, came under frequent attack. Added to this, the intensification of the Jewish-Arab conflict and the shift in British policy away from the support of a Jewish National Home eventually undermined Weizmann's leadership. Hegemony in the *Yishuv* (the Jewish community of Palestine) passed over to the Zionist 'activism' espoused by David Ben-Gurion (1886-1973), the leader of the Palestinian Jewish labour movement.

The rise of socialist (see SOCIALISM) Zionism as the dominant ideology among

Palestinian Jews had its roots in the wave of immigration known as the Second *Aliyah* (literally ascent) which came to Palestine from Russia in the years before 1914. These settlers were motivated less by Jewish nationalism than by the mystique of pioneering labour, which would redeem the land of Israel and harness the productive power of the Jewish masses. They interpreted Zionism as a movement of liberation from the *Galut* with its moral, cultural and political dependence on alien values and traditions; as a revolt against Jewish orthodoxy and clericalism; and as a rejection of the petit-bourgeois ethos and parasitic economic existence in the Russian and Polish ghettoes. By reviving the Hebrew language as a living tongue and establishing the Jews as a working people on their own land, they hoped to creat the basis of a new model society which would revolutionise the traditional Jewish way of life. The founding-fathers of this strain of Zionism, Nachman Syrkin (1867-1924) Aharon David Gordon (1856-1922) and Ber Borochov (1881-1917), all of them Russian Jews, insisted on the interdependence of social and national regeneration in Palestine, and the need to involve Jews in the primary processes of production. Socialist Zionism aimed at correcting the anomaly of a nation without territory which had been cut off, in the course of its dispersion, from nature, from the soil and productive work. It sought to invert the Jewish occupational pyramid and transform a nation of shopkeepers, pedlars, petty traders and capitalists into workers and peasants.

The mainstream of the labour movement under Ben-Gurion achieved dominance in the 1930s through its control of the *Histadrut* (a highly centralised trade-union and employers organisation) and the kibbutz movement. Although committed to the establishment of a self-sufficient workers' commonwealth based on pioneering ideals and collectivist values, its leadership was pragmatic and 'constructivist' in its political methods. It had to take account of the pre-dominantly middle-class immigration from Poland and Germany between the wars, of its financial dependence on the World Zionist Organisation and of the priorities of immigration and building a Jewish majority in Palestine. These pressures pushed the labour movement in a reformist direction and led it to stress the co-operation of all classes in the task of achieving an independent Jewish nation. The Marxist wing of the movement regarded Zionism essentially as a means to a broader goal – that of placing the class struggle of the Jewish proletariat into the context of international socialism as a whole. For many years it looked to the Soviet Union as its second fatherland (see COMMUNISM) and as the model of a socialist society.

At the opposite end of the ideological spectrum stood the 'Revisionist' move-ment founded by the Russian Jewish publicist Vladimir Jabotinsky, which con-tinued the tradition of Herzl and interpreted Zionism as a purely political con-cept. The Revisionists rejected the socialist ideology of class struggle and vigorously defended the Jewish *Mittelstand* (artisans, shopkeepers, small businessmen and property-owners) against the threat of collectivism. In his social policy, Jabotinsky was a classical nineteenth-century liberal but in his emphasis on the military virtues and the 'realism' of toughness, he mirrored the social climate of twentieth-century Central and Eastern Europe. Revisionist Zionism called for the militarisation of Jewish youth, the formation of a Jewish army and the extension of Jewish settlement to both sides of the Jordan. Its nationalist ideology (see NATIONALISM) emphasised the secular symbols of State and territory and looked forward to establishing political sovereignty over all of Palestine by armed struggle. Jabotinsky was convinced that these goals could only be achieved by mass immigration and, eventually by military conquest. The Revisionists not only rejected humanist Zionism but initially opposed the religious values of Jewish orthodoxy. However, after their secession from the World Zionist Organisation in 1935, they included a religious clause in their platform, reflecting the beliefs of mar. of their rank and file supporters. Jabotinsky's successors, the leaders of the _Irgun_ (National Military Organisation), David Raziel and Menahem Begin were themselves religiously observant Jews as was Avraham Stern, the founder of an underground, militantly anti-British terrorist group which split off from the Revisionists.

Within the Revisionist ranks a split eventually developed between the secular and the religious ultra-nationalist elements. The secularists were as adamant in their rejection of the Diaspora, of clericalism and Jewish tradition as the Labour Zionists. One offshoot of this tendency was the _Canaanite_ ideology of Hebrew nationalism which was developed in the 1940s and 50s by a small group of literary intellectuals. They argued that a new Hebrew nation had been born in Erez Israel which had nothing in common with historical Judaism and should sever all links with Diaspora Jewry.

Other revisionists, including the Hebrew poet Uri Zvi Greenberg, were more sympathetic to the individualist values of Judaism and its struggle to preserve the national consciousness, historical continuity and uniqueness of the Jewish people. Except for the _Land of Israel_ movement (which also contained former labour Zionists in its ranks) Zionist nationalism since 1967 has tended to shed its secularist elements in favour of an ideology of Biblical fundamentalism. This finds its most characteristic expression in the _Gush Emunim_ (Block of the Faithful) movement whose spiritual leader is Rabbi Zvi Yehuda Kook and which is predominantly supported by religiously observant Jews. The messianic ideology of this movement is focused on the mystical bond between the Jewish people and the Biblical land of Israel, a bond which derives directly from God's election of the Jews. The nationalist current within religious Zionism holds that the return of the Jews to Zion is the beginning of a messianic, redemptive process. Abandoning the moderate posture on foreign affairs which previously characterised the mainstream of religious Zionism, the _Gush Emunim_ believe that the expansion of Jewish control over the whole Land of Israel is a divine commandment. Eretz Israel in its Biblical boundaries (including Judea, Samaria and other occupied territories) is its rallying symbol and settlement of these territories its primary goal. This trend towards legitimising Israel's territorial claims in Biblical promises is a comparatively recent development in Zionist ideology and one that increasingly divides the nationalist Right from the liberal and socialist currents in Israeli politics.

Zionism in the course of its history has always been a pluralist movement containing diverse ideological trends. Its most important single achievement – the establishment of the State of Israel in 1948 – has not, however, resolved all its ambiguities or led to the fulfilment of all its aspirations. The messianic goal of an 'ingathering of the exiles' has not been achieved, since four-fifths of world Jewry still live outside the Jewish State. Nor has it succeeded in halting the processes of assimilation in the Diaspora, though the State of Israel has acted as a new geo-political and spiritual focal point for Jewish feelings of solidarity.

This contemporary role of Zionism as a specific expression of Jewish identity has tended to increase as its own credentials as an authentic movement of national liberation have come under attack. The impact of the holocaust of European Jewry, the unresolved conflict with the Arab world and the rise of anti-Zionist sentiment in the international community has solidified the existing ties between Israel and the diaspora. Thus a movement and ideology which originally began as a revolt against the *Galut* has increasingly returned to its Jewish roots while continuing to play a central role in the life of the diaspora.

Further reading

Ben Halpern, *The Idea of a Jewish State*
Arthur Hertzberg, *The Zionist Idea. A Historical Analysis and Reader*
Walter Laqueur, *A History of Zionism*
Eliezer Livneh, *Israel and the Crises of Western Civilisation*
Joseph Schechtman, *Fighter and Prophet: The Vladimir Jabotinsky Story*
Michael Selzer (ed.), *Zionism Reconsidered*
David Vital, *The Origins of Zionism*
Chaim Weizmann, *Trial and Error*